KNOWING BODY, MOVING MIND

OXFORD RITUAL STUDIES SERIES

Series Editors
Ronald Grimes, Radboud University Nijmegen
Ute Hüsken, University of Oslo
Eric Venbrux, Radboud University Nijmegen

THE PROBLEM OF RITUAL EFFICACY
Edited by William S. Sax, Johannes Quack, and Jan Weinhold

PERFORMING THE REFORMATION
Public Ritual in the City of Luther
Barry Stephenson

RITUAL, MEDIA, AND CONFLICT
Edited by Edited by Ronald L. Grimes, Ute Hüsken, Udo Simon, and Eric Venbrux

KNOWING BODY, KNOWING MIND
Ritualizing and Learning at Two Buddhist Centers
Patricia Q. Campbell

Knowing Body, Moving Mind

RITUALIZING AND LEARNING AT TWO
BUDDHIST CENTERS

Patricia Q. Campbell

OXFORD
UNIVERSITY PRESS

OXFORD
UNIVERSITY PRESS

Oxford University Press, Inc., publishes works that further
Oxford University's objective of excellence
in research, scholarship, and education.

Oxford   New York
Auckland   Cape Town   Dar es Salaam   Hong Kong   Karachi
Kuala Lumpur   Madrid   Melbourne   Mexico City   Nairobi
New Delhi   Shanghai   Taipei   Toronto

With offices in
Argentina   Austria   Brazil   Chile   Czech Republic   France   Greece
Guatemala   Hungary   Italy   Japan   Poland   Portugal   Singapore
South Korea   Switzerland   Thailand   Turkey   Ukraine   Vietnam

Published by Oxford University Press, Inc.
198 Madison Avenue, New York, New York 10016

www.oup.com

Oxford is a registered trademark of Oxford University Press

Library of Congress Cataloging-in-Publication Data
Campbell, Patricia Q.
Knowing Body, Moving Mind : Ritualizing and Learning at Two Buddhist Centers / Patricia Q. Campbell.
    pages cm.—(Oxford ritual studies)
Based on the author's thesis (Ph.D.)—Wilfrid Laurier University, 2009.
Includes bibliographical references.
ISBN 978-0-19-979382-2 (hardcover)—ISBN 978-0-19-979381-5 (pbk.)
1. Learning, Psychology of.   2. Ritualization.   3. Learning strategies—Ontario—Toronto.
4. Meditation—Buddhism.   I. Title.   II. Series.
BF318.C36 2011
294.3'4435—dc22   2010042935

1 3 5 7 9 8 6 4 2

Printed in the United States of America
on acid-free paper

For my parents, for everything.

Acknowledgments

A NUMBER OF people have made important contributions to the development of this book. First and foremost are the members and teachers at Friends of the Heart and Chandrakirti Centre, especially those who generously gave their time and took the risk of participating in interviews for this study. Sharing one's experiences one on one with a researcher is a very different thing than seeing one's words appear in print several years down the road. I have made every attempt to ensure that interview participants' voices are heard and that the contexts of their responses have been preserved. Despite the strangeness of ethnographic research that some participants may experience, I believe that it is important to record Buddhist practitioners' personal experiences and reflections, so that we may begin to better understand the different ways that Buddhism is developing in our world. To all of my interview participants, therefore, I offer my sincere thanks. I am also very grateful to Lama Catherine, Gen Thekchen, Gen Zopa, Joyce, Richard, Meg, Gwen, Marlene, David, Priscilla, Marlon, Carol, and Chenma for their generous guidance and assistance at Friends of the Heart and Chandrakirti Centre as I conducted my research.

I would also like to thank Mavis Fenn and Faydra Shapiro for their encouragement and assistance as they read the manuscript drafts and provided very helpful comments and questions. Special thanks to Ronald Grimes, without whose patience, understanding, and wisdom this project would never have seen completion. And, as always, to my husband Robert, whose enduring confidence, encouragement, and humor support me in all things.

Contents

Note on Buddhist Terms and Diacritical Marks

THERE ARE SEVERAL Sanskrit, Pali, and Tibetan terms appearing in this text that have become so familiar among English-speaking Buddhist practitioners that they have been, for all intents and purposes, appropriated into English (e.g., Mahayana, sangha, Pali, etc.). Where such is the case, the terms appear without diacritics. Some terms which would not be pluralized in their original languages appear in the plural here because that is the way they are commonly used among participants at the centers involved in this study. The title of the historical Buddha is always written in both centers' literature without diacritics: Shakyamuni. Buddhist terms that are less familiar to English speakers appear with the appropriate diacritics. Unless otherwise noted, such terms appear in Sanskrit. Finally, because "Chandrakirti Centre" is the name of the organization in question; I maintain its Anglicized (Chandrakirti) and Canadian (Centre) spelling.

KNOWING BODY, MOVING MIND

Ritual activity may serve as a mode of inquiry and discovery.

—THEODORE W. JENNINGS

Introduction

A SOLITARY LAY practitioner enters his local Buddhist temple one afternoon every week to change the offerings on the shrine. Alone in the darkened temple, he retrieves a bucket from the basement kitchen and carries it upstairs to the empty shrine room. Carefully pouring the old water from the offering bowls into the bucket, he cleans the bowls, placing each upside-down on its altar before refilling each in its turn. He drips a bit of scented oil into one of the water bowls on each of the three shrines, and replaces the chocolates in another. He then takes a fine china cup from one of the shrines and refreshes the tea offering for the guru. Finally, he changes the food offerings that are placed before the images of the deities. As he performs this rite, his demeanor is formal, respectful, and calm. As he has been taught, he tries to maintain pure thoughts while making the offerings.

What is most intriguing about this scenario is that this man is not, in his own mind, a Buddhist—at least not yet. Born and raised in Canada, his religious background is Catholic. He became involved at this particular temple, Chandrakirti Centre, at a time in his life when he was looking for something different, as he said: a new way of living. While he admits to being uncomfortable with the ritual aspects of the center, he feels honored to have been asked to perform this weekly duty of refreshing the offerings on the shrines. He says that changing the water offerings is helping him learn something, not only about the deities, the shrines, and the center, but about himself. After a few weeks of performing the water offerings, he begins to think of himself as a Buddhist.

Changing the water offerings is just one type of ritual activity that Gerald engages in as he participates at Chandrakirti Centre. He also attends regular Tuesday evening meditation classes at which he and others sing a prayer to honor Shakyamuni Buddha, and where they learn to practice different meditation techniques.

Across town, a group of practitioners stands silently in the hallway outside a small Buddhist center called Friends of the Heart. Some are members of this center, others are visitors. None was raised Buddhist. They await the beginning of a *pūjā* or prayer service to Chenrezig, the Tibetan Bodhisattva of Compassion. One by one, a senior member pours saffron water into the cupped hands of each of the participants, who then rinse their mouths with the water. Following this, they place their dampened hands on the crowns of their heads, then over their eyes, ears, and mouths, a symbolic gesture which they have been taught will seal these openings following the purifying mouth-rinsing rite.

One by one, participants enter the colorful shrine room. A golden statue of Chenrezig occupies the central position of the small shrine. The lama asks the first participant to enter to perform three prostrations facing the shrine, and those entering afterward follow suit. But the instructions are not repeated, and those who enter when no one else is prostrating do not perform prostrations. Participants seat themselves facing the shrine. Most are seated on cushions on the floor; two sit in chairs.

The lama instructs the participants in the ritual that will follow. She tells them that this initiation service, or "empowerment" as it is called, is to be viewed as a beginning, the start of a practice that they can make part of their daily lives and can turn to in times of stress or emergency. The lama says that if participants complete this practice, then higher level practices will come with ease. Despite the formality of the event, some participants are taking notes during the teaching, perhaps out of habit, since this Monday morning ritual is taking place during the usual Tibetan Meditation class. The lama does not ask anyone to put notebooks away. She then takes some time to draw the energy of Chenrezig into herself, softly chanting to herself as her students quietly wait. The saffron water, prostrations, and the lama's chanting are only the preparatory rites for the hour-long prayer service that is about to begin. Most of the participants in this rite attend Monday morning sessions at Friends of the Heart in order to learn about Tibetan Buddhist teachings and meditation practices, but today they will honor the Bodhisattva of Compassion and receive initiation into his rites.

How do people like Gerald and the participants at the Chenrezig pūjā, Buddhist practitioners from non-Buddhist backgrounds, begin to learn such practices? What do they learn from performing them? This book explores the role that formal rituals and ritualized practices play in the learning experiences of meditation students at these two Toronto-based Buddhist centers, Chandrakirti and Friends of the Heart.

"WESTERN" BUDDHISM

In the greater Toronto area, there are literally dozens of meditation groups, dharma centers, and Buddhist temples that offer teachings and meditation sessions to the general public. Some of these centers structure many of their regular public events not as services or meditation sessions, but as meditation classes offered to people from non-Buddhist religious and cultural backgrounds. Friends of the Heart and Chandrakirti Centre are two such organizations. Friends of the Heart is an independently run group founded and led by Lama Catherine Rathbun. Chandrakirti Centre is part of a large, international organization called the New Kadampa Tradition (NKT, also known as the International Kadampa Buddhist Union), which was founded by Geshe Kelsang Gyatso. Both based in Tibetan Vajrayana Buddhism, the unique expression of Buddhism that developed in Tibet, the centers' teachers as well as most of their members hail from non-Buddhist backgrounds. Newcomers participate in the introductory classes at Friends of the Heart and Chandrakirti Centre, where they are introduced to a tradition and a set of ritual activities with which most are unfamiliar. Because of this, they have much to learn. Each center's introductory course has a particular focus: At Friends of the Heart, students are primarily taught how to meditate; at Chandrakirti, the emphasis is on Buddhist teachings and ethics as well as meditation practice. Students participating in either course are exposed to new ritual activities, which include the formal postures, gestures, and techniques of meditation.

Each of these centers represents a new expression of an ancient Buddhist tradition, each tracing a lineage back through its teachers' teachers to lamas trained in Tibet. The centers owe their existence to several significant events that profoundly shaped Tibetan Buddhism in the twentieth century. The Chinese invasion of Tibet in 1950 and the consequent exodus of Tibetan refugees, particularly that of the Dalai Lama in 1959, have brought the plight of Tibet and the religion of the Tibetan people to the world's attention. Displaced from its homeland, Tibetan Buddhism has been seeded by Tibetan teachers and their students in nations around the globe. Kelsang Gyatso, founder of the NKT, is one such teacher, as are the Tibetan lamas under whom Catherine Rathbun trained and was ordained.

Buddhism has been present in Canada since the middle of the nineteenth century, when Chinese and Japanese Buddhists settled in its western provinces and territories. But it was not until changes in immigration laws in the mid-1960s opened up immigration from previously restricted regions in Asia that the tradition came to the full attention of the broader public. Janet McLellan notes that the first Tibetan Buddhists to come to Canada began arriving in the 1970s when the Canadian government agreed to accept 228 individuals and families. They were settled in four provinces. Some, like the group that settled in Lindsay, Ontario, were accompanied by a Tibetan monk. Monastics are necessary for maintaining a viable religious practice and community among Tibetan Buddhists, and the Dalai Lama himself requested that each of the Tibetan groups that settled in Canada be accompanied by a monastic.[1] In 1999, there were approximately 133 Tibetans in Toronto, about thirty families. McLellan discovered that Tibetan communities in Canada maintain a strong sense of ethnic and religious identity that continues with the second and third generations.[2] The Lindsay and Belleville communities are still strong, and there is also a significant community in Barrie, just north of Toronto. In 2000 and 2001, some three thousand Tibetan refugees came to Canada via the United States and settled in the Toronto area. Their presence has augmented the small Tibetan community already present, and expanded cultural celebrations and political activism in the city.[3]

Some Tibetan Buddhist temples in the city maintain parallel congregations,[4] serving Tibetan Buddhists in the community while catering to practitioners from non-Buddhist backgrounds as well. Other Tibetan-based centers, like Friends of the Heart and Chandrakirti, are strictly "westernized," having memberships comprised of practitioners from non-Buddhist backgrounds. According to McLellan, Tibetan and westernized Tibetan-based Buddhist communities sometimes connect through political advocacy for Tibetan independence.[5] Friends of the Heart has a connection to a Toronto-based Tibetan monk named Karma Thinley Rinpoche, but neither it nor Chandrakirti Centre have ties to other Tibetan Buddhist groups in the city. It is also the case that many independent westernized centers have little or no contact with each other, let alone with organizations whose members are from different linguistic, religious, and cultural backgrounds. Individual members of westernized groups are themselves somewhat nomadic, in that they often read publications by a wide range of organizations and visit a number of different dharma or retreat centers. Even so, there is little if any official rapport between leaders or teachers of different organizations, a fact that creates considerable factionalism among Buddhist groups in Canada.[6] While there is substantial interaction between Canadian NKT centers, the organization is itself insular, and few NKT centers have any contact at all with non-NKT organizations.

All of this brings us to the problem of terminology. How do we identify the various groups, communities, and expressions of Buddhism present in the West? For some time now, scholars have spent much ink (and some vitriol) over appropriate means of classifying Buddhist communities in pluralistic societies like Canada. In some sense it is a rather fruitless task because there are no defining, long-lasting features by which we can clearly identify any of these groups. In a study such as this, however, it is necessary to choose appropriate, well-understood terms to distinguish among different expressions of Buddhism. Recent developments in the argument over terminology in contemporary Buddhism—contributions from Victor S. Hori, Natalie E. Quili, David L. McMahan, and Wakoh Shannon Hickey, for example[7]—have highlighted problems of ethnocentricity, racism, and privilege. While it is not my intent to reproduce those arguments here, I do want to take a moment to set out the terms I use in this book, for better or worse, and the reasons why I use them.

This study explores the experiences of a number of practitioners who fall into a loosely knit, numerically small expression of Buddhism in Canada whose members, for the most part, share a common cultural background. It is an expression that has equivalents in many other western, pluralistic nations around the world. It is comprised of people whose religious, cultural, or familial backgrounds are non-Buddhist. Sometimes these practitioners are called "converts." I avoid this term because many have not fully accepted a Buddhist identity, an issue I will address in chapter 2. Sometimes these practitioners are called "nonethnic" Buddhists, a term intended to contrast them with practitioners born and raised in Buddhist cultures, families, or both. But, as several of the scholars noted above have rightly pointed out, the term "nonethnic" is not only an unfortunate means of "othering" some Canadian Buddhists, it is simply incorrect.[8] The expression of Buddhism that this book explores *is* ethnic, in that its practitioners and practices are shaped by a shared culture and set of worldviews, namely those broadly associated with "the West." These worldviews tend to attract such practitioners to a particular, modernized form of Buddhism that has been developing around the world since it emerged in Asia in the late nineteenth century.[9]

These practitioners have another shared experience: As people who are interested in Buddhism, or have even taken up a committed Buddhist practice, they have turned to a new spiritual tradition that is not dominant in the culture in which they were raised. Based on this important element of their experience, I sometimes use the term "adoptive" Buddhists to describe practitioners and sympathizers[10] from non-Buddhist backgrounds. Readers no doubt will point out that this term, like the term "convert," does not account for children and grandchildren of such practitioners. But in my research I have found that it is quite rare for children of adoptive Buddhists to take up the tradition of their parents. Very few of the adoptive Buddhists I have spoken to have raised their children in the tradition or had parents who were Buddhist. Until there are numerically significant second or later generations of adoptive practitioners, I propose the term "adoptive Buddhist" as a means of highlighting the experience of turning to Buddhism in a non-Buddhist cultural environment.

Even so, the term is strongly etic, not one with which practitioners themselves identify. The term that is most commonly used and understood by practitioners and scholars alike is "western" Buddhism. It is, in fact, the term used by all of my interview respondents. One problem with this term is that this usage excludes Canadian Buddhists with cultural or familial ties to Buddhists in Asia, people who are also westerners. Also, the term "western Buddhism" is sometimes mistakenly identified with the modernist stream of Buddhism which is now found all over the world. In his text, *The Making of Buddhist Modernism*, McMahan shows that this particular stream of Buddhism is influenced by discourses in Christian mono-theism, scientific rationalism, and western Romanticism.[11] Even so, "modernist" Buddhism is a stream which started with revival movements initiated by and for Buddhists in Asia[12] and should not be mistaken as a strictly "western" movement. While most of the people I interviewed implicitly accepted the modernist ideas that McMahan describes—that Buddhism is compatible with science and west-ern rationalism, that it is nontheistic, nonritualistic, demythologized, and even nonreligious—westernized Buddhism in Canada is only part of the broader mod-ernist movement driven by Buddhists all around the world. For this reason, the term "modernist Buddhism" cannot be limited to discussions of adoptive Buddhists in Canada.

Despite its problems, I frequently return to the term with which my respon-dents most readily identify: "western" Buddhism. As it is used in this text, it describes a disparate group of Buddhist communities based in a variety of differ-ent Buddhist schools, ranging from Theravada to Zen to Vajrayana. Western Buddhism also includes many secularized or nonsectarian organizations. Scholars often point out that members of westernized centers are predominantly of European ancestry, but in my experience such groups in Toronto are starting to become more diverse. Because of this, the line I draw to distinguish western or adoptive Buddhists and sympathizers is based not on racial heritage but on their western cultural influences and their experience of turning to Buddhist practices and teachings. This means, for example, that individuals with an Asian heritage who were raised in Canada may also fit into this category. Two such individuals were interviewed for this study: of Asian but non-Buddhist heritage, they partici-pated at westernized centers. Another interview participant, Catherine H., was from a Chinese Buddhist family and moved with them to Canada as a young woman. I interviewed her to learn about the differences between Chandrakirti practices and those of her family. Interestingly, she insisted that she saw little difference other than language. Catherine really straddles the line between the broad categories of Buddhists that scholars struggle to name: She has a Buddhist heritage, but she chooses to participate at a westernized center where she can hear dharma talks in English. She is very interested in the intellectual side of the talks she attends, she rarely meditates, and sometimes she asks her mother to perform prayers and offerings for her. Were I forced to categorize practitioners like Catherine, I might be tempted to call them western heritage Buddhists. But then, so are her parents. It is important to remember that the lines are never very distinct, terms used are not fully satisfactory, and setting firm categories is always a risky business.

As we begin to listen to the voices of the interview respondents, we will see that, in many ways, the principles and practices taught at Friends of the Heart and Chandrakirti Centre are influenced by the "tradition" of contemporary North America.[13] Meditation students at both centers learned adapted or westernized forms of Buddhist teachings and practices. Teachers did not often draw attention to the original Buddhist sources of the teachings they gave. Occasionally, they reinterpreted the more strongly religious or metaphysical teachings. At Friends of the Heart, for example, the concept of karma was sometimes discussed in terms of cause and effect without reference to the cycle of rebirth. This approach made classes attractive to introductory students, who were usually less interested in learning about Buddhist doctrine or cosmology.

Adapting teachings to suit a particular audience is frequently justified through references to *upāya* or skillful means: The Buddha himself is said to have adapted his teachings according to the capacity of his audience to understand. The discourse of upāya is a strong current in westernized and modernist expressions of Buddhism. It is a means of legitimating change through reference to a long-standing, revered tradition.[14] Throughout its history, as Buddhism has spread to new cultural environments, its teachers have struggled to find a balance between preserving the heart of the tradition and the adaptations necessary to attract new followers. This text presents many concrete examples of the ways in which this balance is being sought among new Buddhist practitioners and sympathizers in Toronto. Comparing different practices across cultures helps us understand the significant underlying influences that account for those differences. But it is a mistake to try to judge newer expressions of Buddhism by a monolithic notion of what went before—that is, by a vision of what "traditionalist" Buddhism is or may have been. Natalie E. Quili argues this point: Western scholars, she writes, express a kind of nostalgia for Buddhist tradition, something that never really existed as a homogeneous, long-standing entity in the first place.[15] Buddhism has always been embedded in one culture or another.

Modernist and adoptive expressions of Buddhism can be informatively discussed on their own terms, without constant evaluation (positive or negative) against ideas of what Buddhism has been or "should" be.

This book covers some under-explored territories in contemporary Buddhist studies. To date, only a few studies have presented detailed ethnographic data on adoptive or western practitioners in North America.[16] Drawing upon the personal reflections of individual participants, this study explores some of the reasons they became interested in Buddhist teachings and practices and sought out a meditation center. It explores their reflections on their experiences participating at the centers, their responses to the variety of formal practices they encountered, and their experiences practicing meditation. The focus of this project is on ritual, another area that has received little attention in the study of westernized Buddhism. Later chapters describe in detail the meditation classes and the formal rites and rituals that took place at the centers. I also investigate the less formal, but still ritualized, activities that students learned in the meditation classes and at other events they attended.

THE R WORDS

It may appear to be a contradiction, studying ritual among practitioners who very often deny the ritualized aspects of the tradition altogether, but the rituals are there nonetheless. As the vignettes above indicate, even some newcomers at Friends of the Heart and Chandrakirti Centre participated in chanted prayers, making offerings, performing prostrations, and so forth. And, despite the fact that most adoptive practitioners do not think of it this way, meditation is itself a ritual.

Now we have arrived at another thorny question concerning terminology: What do we mean by "ritual"? Once again, it is necessary to pay attention to emic and etic meanings: Scholars of ritual at times use the word differently than almost everyone else. Popular usage of the word usually evokes images of empty, repetitive performance, fossilized by long-standing tradition, often specifically religious tradition. But sometimes people use the term to refer to something special, set aside from the everyday. For example, a friend recently told me that he and his friend used to go to a bookstore in Toronto's Greek town every Sunday night at midnight. He said: "It became our ritual." I asked him: Why do you call it a ritual? He said that it was something they did every week that became special to them. I understood his description to mean that the bookstore visits, which were probably not considered a ritual until they had happened more than once or twice, were meaningful to the two friends. It was not simple repetition that defined the events as ritual. The visits took place at a special time: midnight. They also created a greater bond in the friendship between the two men. In that sense, they were transformative or efficacious in some manner. And yet, there are several elements common to "ritual" that are missing: The friends' excursions were not religious or even spiritual; they did not have a set script, for there would have been considerable informality and variability each time the friends visited the store; and so forth. This is the case with most of the events we identify as rituals: Like Buddhist practitioners, they do not fall into easy categories.

As a scholarly concept, "ritual" is meta-category covering a wide range of events and behaviors that are ritualized to one degree or another. In a useful analogy, Ronald L. Grimes points out that ritual is not digital. "It does not operate with a simple off/on, yes/no logic in relation to ordinary activity. Rather, ordinary activities become more or less ritualized; ritualization takes place by degrees and in many forms."[17] Similarly, Jan M. Snoek argues that ritual is best understood in terms of fuzzy sets or polythetic classes. A fuzzy set is "a class of objects with a continuum of grades of membership."[18] Some rituals are highly formalized, for instance, some less so. Polythetic classes allow for characteristics commonly associated with ritual but not present in all rituals. Rituals may be religious, communal, repetitive, efficacious, or magical, but any one ritual may have none of these features. The advantage of keeping our definitional boundaries open in this way is that it enables us to explore and compare different kinds of events and to analyze the ritualized facets of each without the need to first determine whether or not they constitute rituals as such.[19] This approach is particularly useful for this study because it is open to different participants' interpretations of what constitutes ritual.

Snoek argues that clarifying our uses of the word "ritual" necessitates a comprehensive listing of all of the fuzzy or polythetic characteristics that we associate with ritual. This would be a very long listing indeed, and other scholars have produced lists that are more comprehensive than needed here.[20] For this study, ritual may be understood as typically repetitive, formal, embodied, special, set aside from ordinary time and space, elevated, and sometimes spiritual or religious. The rituals and ritualized behaviors discussed in this book are also sometimes described as stylized, communal, deliberate, received, traditional, symbolic, or reflexive. Sequences of behavior that are associated with an increasing number of these qualities, or are more strongly characterized by them, are more ritualized. Behaviors are less ritualized if few of these characteristics are present or when their opposites dominate: when they are informal, one-time, diffuse, secular, invented, solitary, and so on. These opposites do not necessarily disqualify an event as ritual. From time to time, we do encounter rituals that are one-time, informal, secular, or invented.

While none of these characteristics of ritual is itself definitive, there is one that is consistent. Ritual is something that is *done*: Grimes describes it as "performed" when the action is either observed or fictional and as "enacted" when the action puts something into force.[21] A ritual is thus an event, something that transpires in a specific time and place. In addition to the scholarly meta-category, then, the word "ritual" also refers to an individual event such as a religious or secular ceremony. While Snoek suggests that "ceremony" can reasonably substitute for this use of the term "ritual,"[22] there are times when other words are more appropriate. We tend to talk about a wedding ceremony, but a funeral service, for instance. The weekly meditation sessions at the Zen temple I attend are called "members' services," not ceremonies; Friends of the Heart and Chandrakirti members called pūjās, prayer rituals, or services. The terms "ritual," "ceremony," and "service" are somewhat interchangeable, but they do have nuances that are appropriate in some situations and not others. In this book, all three are used to denote individual performances of ritualized events.

The other "R" words that appear in this book are "rite," "ritualization," and "ritualizing." "Rite" is sometimes used to refer to a full ritual, service, or ceremony. I find it more useful as a referent for smaller units of behavior. "Rites" are the different activities that take place over the course of a ritual: prayer, lighting incense, chanting a mantra (sacred syllables or verse), performing one or more prostrations, and so on. Gerald empties a water-offering bowl and refills it: this constitutes a rite. The whole activity of changing all of the water offerings, from beginning to end, is a ritual. Setting out water offerings is a rite when it is preliminary to a full pūjā, and so on. A ritual, ceremony, or service, therefore, is a collection of rites.[23] Participants in this study have learned to call many of their rites "practices," a term that appears frequently in this book: It refers to individual ritualized activities such as meditation, chanting, and so on, whether they occur within the context of a full service or not.

Because this study investigates events and practices that are not full rituals but have several ritual qualities, I also use the terms "ritualization" and "ritualizing." Ritualization refers to human (or animal) behavior that is stylized, symbolic, and therefore interpreted on a nondiscursive level among performers and audience. Much of our everyday behavior amounts to ritualization. From handshakes to general body language, ritualization is meaningful and communicative, while at the same time taking place on a less-than-conscious level.[24] I describe "ritualizing" as a conscious experimentation with ritualization. Ritualizing can be formative or creative. While ritualization does take place within the context of a ceremony, the majority of behaviors in such a context are much more intentional, their stylization more conscious—the uniquely formalized style of walking up the aisle during a wedding ceremony, for example, or the reverent way in which one lights a candle or incense on an altar. These constitute ritualizing.

This book bridges disciplines. To inform my analysis of ritualizing and learning, I draw together a few different theoretical frameworks, from ritual studies to embodiment and learning theory. The inspiration for the project began with an idea from Theodore W. Jennings, who argues that an important function of ritual is the generation of new knowledge. In this view, ritual is a means by which its participants make discoveries about themselves and about their world.[25] Interested, I decided to investigate the idea that ritualizing, the behaviors through which rituals are formed, adapted, and preserved, may lead to new learning. Introductory meditation classes, where students were learning rituals and practices that were new to them, seemed appropriate sites to explore this idea. The question with which this study began was this: How or to what degree does ritualizing contribute to learning about a new spiritual tradition?

From this starting point, I began exploring classes and other events at the two centers, drawing on insights from performance theory. An approach that originated in the late 1970s with collaborations between anthropologist Victor Turner, sociologist Erving Goffman, and theater director Richard Schechner, and developed in much of Grimes's work,[26] performance theory is a relatively recent movement within the larger history of ritual studies. It highlights connections between ritual and other kinds of cultural performance such as theater, play, games, sports, dance, and music.[27] It is an approach that illuminates ritual by focusing on its enactment, comparing and contrasting it to other types of performance. What do people actually *do*? Where do they put their hands and feet, what gestures do they enact, what songs do they sing? What ritual spaces are involved? Who are the primary performers and what roles do they assume? Performance theory is an approach that emphasizes action that is witnessed, that calls attention to itself by nature of its performativity. It expands on earlier methods in ritual studies that were strictly textual or liturgical. Studying ritual *as* performance makes us sensitive to the reception of actions by audiences and to the presence and significance of the body that performs ritualized activities. Performance theory also highlights the fact that rituals are enactments that disappear in the doing, as opposed to being fixed, or preserved as text or myth.[28] I use the performance framework to push against conceptions of ritual as invariant, conservative, unchanging. Ritual can be fluid, innovative, and changeable, even in the face of its repetition and formality. I believe, with Jennings, that ritual's capacity for novelty and change is what enables new learning or a different kind of knowing.[29]

In Jennings's view, ritual transmits "ritual knowledge," an understanding of the ways of being and acting in the world gained through the ritual actions themselves.[30] Taking the chalice during communion, he says, one's hand "discovers the fitting gesture," which only later does one "cerebrally" determine as being right. Jennings notes that this type of embodied knowing is developed through less ritualized activities as well. He uses the analogy of cutting wood. "The axe 'teaches me' through my hands, arms, and shoulders how it is to be used."[31] Through the activity, I learn the best way to hold and swing the axe, as well as "how it is" with the axe, with my body, and with the world. Through trial and error, repetition, and refinement, I learn what to do and how it should be done. This knowledge is gained by the whole body, and is located in muscle and blood and bone rather than just the brain. Jennings also notes that this type of knowing, gained in the ritual context, is then carried out of the ritual space. We thus learn not only how to conduct ourselves during the ritual itself, but how to behave in the world as well.

Jennings's description of ritual knowledge—the hand that comes to know the chalice, the arm that knows the axe—is reflected in the works of Nick Crossley, Michael L. Raposa, and Kevin Schilbrack, who take a philosophical approach to the study of ritual.[32] According to Schilbrack, the usual view of what constitutes knowledge is based in a persistent sense of mind-body dualism, which limits knowledge to the mind or brain. In this dualistic perspective, movements cannot constitute thinking.[33] But Schilbrack argues that the body itself is a means of thinking and that knowledge is necessarily embodied. Crossley regards ritual as "embodied practical reason."[34] Building on the work of Maurice Merleau-Ponty, Crossly discusses patterns of movement called "body techniques," which are means of learning about ourselves and the uses to which we put our bodies.[35] Though preconscious, they are significant, active learning experiences. Raposa, like Crossley, observes that ritual can be regarded as a kind of thoughtful action, arguing that ritual is a means of "thinking through and with the body."[36] Raposa, Crossley, and Schilbrack offer the notion of the thinking body; the idea, similar to Jennings's, that ritual activities act as inquiries or means of learning. The "knowing body" of this book's title refers to this type of ritually generated, embodied learning.

Ritual, of course, is not the only means by which the body learns. Body techniques, or "embodied cultural competencies,"[37] are performed, transmitted, and interpreted through all of our social interactions. This notion of a type of knowing that is located in and accessed by the body is described in a number of sociological and anthropological studies. Pierre Bourdieu calls it *habitus*, which he describes as gestures and postures that are second nature, a kind of tacit, habitual knowledge that becomes distorted when subject to conscious reflection.[38] Some of my respondents described this type of knowing as muscle memory or dancer memory. The actions and movements informed by this embodied, inarticulate knowledge are equivalent to ritualization as described above. When this type of knowledge develops in the more deliberate and reflexive context of a ritual (or through ritualizing), it is what Jennings calls ritual knowledge. The term I use in place of Crossley's embodied practical reason, Bourdieu's habitus, or Merleau-Ponty's body techniques is "embodied knowing." It is embodied because it is gained through practice and repetition, but not, as I will explain in a moment, because it does not involve the mind. I call it "knowing" to distinguish it from intellectual or cognitive knowledge. I do not mean to suggest that cognitive learning is not embodied, only that it is qualitatively different from embodied knowing, which develops in part through physical movement.

These tacit schemes that the body learns and draws upon through social and ritual action inform what Thomas J. Csordas calls "the socially informed body."[39] Another concept developed by Bourdieu, the socially informed body is regarded as the unifying principle through which we embody our culture and create it anew. In this view, our social interactions are means of re-inscribing, interpreting, and transmitting the meanings and symbols of our culture. Csordas takes the socially informed body as the starting point to develop a "paradigm of embodiment," the aim of which is to provide a "fully phenomenological account" of human experience[40] which breaks down subject-object and body-mind dualisms. In this paradigm, the socially informed body is taken as the ground of culture and experience. Embodiment, Csordas argues, is pre-objective, in that it begins on the level of perception where there are no external objects, just a sense of being in the world.[41] "Our bodies are not objects to us," Csordas writes. "Quite the contrary, they are an integral part of the perceiving subject."[42] Crossley, drawing on Merleau-Ponty, points this out as well: The body is not a tool we use to experience the world; it is the ground of that experience.[43] Even so, it is important to recognize that the socially informed body is not prior to culture: It is already socially and culturally inscribed. So, even before we begin to regard our body as an object to ourselves, we are culturally conditioned in the ways in which we do so.

Csordas's resolve to start with the socially informed body stresses the importance of what and how the body learns through its actions. What I am calling "embodied knowing," however, is not intended as a conclusion in and of itself. It remains to be seen whether or in what ways it develops through the practices that meditation students learned. In a sense, the knowing body is a metaphor: I am not arguing that somewhere in the cells of our muscles or bones there is a mechanism of storing knowledge that science has not yet uncovered. But the knowing body is in some sense literal as well. In our experience, it *feels* like the body knows what to do, how to move and perform. Embodied knowing is thus a phenomenological concept, in that it depends upon human perception and subjective experience. Discussing the way ritual inscribes new knowledge on the body, Grimes writes:

> Effective ritual knowledge lodges in the bone, in its very marrow. This metaphor first struck me with force while in a discussion with an archaeologist. He was explaining how certain values and social practices can be inferred from ancient bone matter. An archaeologist can deduce from bone composition that the men of a particular society consumed more protein than women....Certain social practices are literally inscribed in the bones. Even though we imagine bone as private, and deeply interior to the individual body, it is also socially formed.[44]

Grimes's description of the socially informed body is both metaphorical and literal. We feel that our body is inscribed with knowledge and, in a very real sense, our social and ritual activities change us.

Now, it is vital that we understand that the socially informed body and embodied knowing do not exclude the mind. Csordas's conception of embodiment is non-dualistic. The body is neither distinct from nor in opposition to the mind.[45] Unfortunately, in English there is no easy way to speak about a unified entity consisting of both body and mind. Occasionally I use the term body-mind to refer to such an entity, a term I borrow from Buddhist sources. I deliberately use the term "embodied knowing" as a reminder that the mind *is* embodied. It is this body-mind, the existential ground of culture, through which we experience our world and which learns and is inscribed with cultural and social norms. I do not mean to say that body and mind are identical. My mind is not my body in the same sense that my hand is not my body: It is part of the body, but not coextensive with it. Nor are mind and brain identical. Subjectively, the brain is the physical foundation of the mind. Meditation techniques discussed in this book have the meditator directing his or her attention to various areas in the body or focusing the mind on an object of meditation. In these practices, the mind acts as a gestural entity that is the center of our awareness. We will see that, through meditation practice, the mind learns through these kinds of movement in much the same tacit, noncognitive way that the rest of the body learns. This, then, is the "moving mind."

This study therefore takes a bit of a departure from performance theory, in that it expands its view of ritualizing beyond physical, performative postures and gestures. Learning through ritualizing takes place in all aspects of body-mind: Physical *and* mental aspects change through the development of knowledge *and* skills.

Buddhist perspectives on body and mind are much less dualistic than those originating in western traditions. In an article on Indian perspectives on the body, John M. Koller writes:

> Buddhists resist the tendency to see persons as two different kinds of being—either self and body-mind, or mind and body—in some inexplicable relationship. Instead of being forced to see the body as somehow foreign to oneself, as an object-like being appended to or imprisoning the self, the Buddhist perspective facilitates seeing oneself as a creative, unified, and continuous process of becoming—as a lived-conscious-body capable of actualizing the potential represented by the so-called objective factors of existence.[46]

This summary of Buddhist views on self-body-mind corresponds remarkably closely to Csordas's paradigm of embodiment.

LEARNING THEORY

The concept of embodied knowing suggests that there are different ways that we gain new knowledge or understanding. Similarly, learning theorists point out that there are distinctive categories of learning, and a number of different learning objectives or tasks involved in each. In order to fully explore all of the ways in which meditation students learned, it will be useful to become familiar with these different learning categories.

I recently attended a conference on teaching and learning in higher education. A number of presenters at this conference paid a nod to Bloom's taxonomy, an influential learning model that breaks learning down into a hierarchy of different tasks under three broad domains: the cognitive, affective, and psychomotor.[47] Many educators are familiar with this model. What I found intriguing was that the majority of presenters who referred to "progressing through Bloom's taxonomy" were not talking about the three larger domains, but only about the tasks listed under the first: cognitive learning. In effect, the most common understanding of learning consists of gaining factual knowledge, followed by comprehension, organization, and analysis of that knowledge—all of which are cognitive learning tasks. Certainly, most university and college courses are designed to emphasize cognitive learning. But a number of educators at this conference were advocating the significance of the affective domain—that of feelings, emotions, and values. Most intriguing to me, however, were two workshops on movement that stressed the psychomotor domain as an important means of teaching and learning. Participants at these workshops tossed a ball around, followed or chased one another around the room, performed various movement techniques and exercises, and created and performed scenes. The premise of both of these workshops was that, for many students, teaching and learning can be more effective when (more of) the body is involved in the learning process.

Psychomotor learning emphasizes movement and motor skills. As Jennings's argument suggests, ritualizing can be one way of developing psychomotor learning. I find that perspectives drawn from ritual studies can fruitfully expand on Bloom's third domain. Ritual certainly involves movement, and the physical side of meditation was a significant part of my respondents' learning experiences. In fact, several respondents suggested that the mental aspects of meditation practice were akin to a physical type of learning. This is an important premise of this study and will be explored in some detail in later chapters. But meditation students' experiences also demonstrate that learning through ritualizing involves all three of Bloom's domains. Through meditation, chanting, and other ritualized practices, participants' learning experiences formed a pattern that flowed through cognitive, affective, and psychomotor learning. The chapters that follow will demonstrate how that pattern developed.

RELIGION AND SPIRITUALITY

Throughout this text, I often use the terms "spirituality" and "religion," which, like "ritual," are also difficult to define. For my purposes here, spirituality refers to a person's ultimate concerns,[48] those which relate to the whole experience of the person. Spirituality refers to a felt connection to something beyond one's immediate experience. It may be a connection to others, consisting of compassion or empathy concerning the human condition. For some individuals, spirituality refers to a connection to the transcendent, to deities, spiritual beings, or an afterlife. It is not possible to separate spirituality completely from other aspects of one's experience. It encompasses all the particulars of everyday, ordinary living, and relates such particulars to the wholeness of our experience. Spirituality involves a quest for answers to life's big questions such as: Who am I? How should I lead my life?

Religion refers to spirituality that has been organized or institutionalized into a formal tradition.[49] Each religion has its own, characteristic responses to the question of how we experience a connection to the human condition or to the transcendent. In this sense, then, spirituality is an orientation; religion is an affiliation. This use of the term "religion" differs in some respects from that of my respondents. Where respondents also make a distinction between religion and spirituality, they more often associate religion with certain Christian expressions.

Most felt that Buddhism was not a religion because they believed it to be nontheistic, not necessitating faith or belief, and not based on the concept of sin. By contrast, I refer to Buddhism as a religion because it is a long-standing, organized, and institutionalized spiritual tradition.

SETTINGS AND CHARACTERS

In 2006 and 2007, I conducted participant-observation fieldwork at Friends of the Heart and Chandrakirti Centre and interviewed twenty-four of the centers' members, students, and teachers. Friends of the Heart was the primary research site, partly because it was the first of the two centers at which I conducted any systematic fieldwork for this project. Furthermore, the closure of Chandrakirti Centre for renovations in June of 2007 resulted in less fieldwork data and fewer interview participants from that center. Despite the disparity, I felt it was important to include both centers in the project, so that one not bear alone the brunt of this kind of academic scrutiny. I also felt it was informative to offer a comparison between two centers with different approaches to Tibetan-based Vajrayana Buddhism. I have made every effort not to make value-laden comparisons between the style, teachings, practices, memberships, or management of the two centers. Comparisons are intended only to illustrate different ways in which two different centers, both based in the same historical tradition, approach meditation classes and other services offered to westerners. I want to make it clear to readers at the outset that Friends of the Heart and Chandrakirti Centre are distinct from one another, having separate memberships, teachers, and deriving from different Tibetan teaching lineages.

The paradox of this kind of study is that it attempts to analyze personal, non-cognitive experience, but must necessarily do so through second-hand, cognitive methods. Listening to what people have to say about learning and ritualizing, then writing about for others to read and evaluate, places readers several steps away from the original, immediate experience I attempt to record. Internal, subjective states are notoriously complicated phenomena to study. Nevertheless, I strongly believe that the best way to obtain information of this sort is to consult the people who know about it. In my interviews, I asked some of the same questions in several different ways in order to draw out detailed information about students' learning and to encourage them to reflect on their learning in new ways. What do you learn at the classes? How do you learn it? What do you learn through the practices and rituals? Are meditation postures important for what you are learning? Can you teach me something you were taught? In the chapters that follow, we will hear from the various interview participants—introductory students, more experienced members, and some of their teachers—as they helped me answer these questions and more.

In addition to the interview participants, there is another character in this story. As a participant-observer at the meditation classes and other Friends of the Heart and Chandrakirti events, I shared many of the same experiences as other students and participants. Like the majority of my interview respondents, I am an adoptive or western Buddhist sympathizer. Unlike many of them, I am not a newcomer to Buddhist teachings and practices, and I do self-identify as a Buddhist. My meditation training, however, is based in a westernized expression of Zen, and I have been a member of the Korean-based Zen Buddhist Temple in Toronto for over fifteen years. In 2005, I conducted an ethnographic study of a prayer service at Chandrakirti Centre, called the "Offering to the Spiritual Guide." Apart from that earlier study, I had had no previous relationship with either Friends of the Heart or Chandrakirti Centre before taking on this project. I enrolled in their introductory classes and participated at other events as other visiting members did. Being personally unfamiliar with Tibetan-style teachings and practices, my learning experiences at the two centers was similar to those of the students and members I interviewed. As a scholar of Buddhism, however, I had the advantage of knowing more about the origins of those teachings and practices and the history of their development in western, North American, and Canadian cultural contexts. Academic studies sometimes obscure the voice of the researcher, but this practice assumes a degree of distance and objectivity that is not possible with this kind of ethnographic study. As researcher, I am the narrator of this story; as a participant at Friends of the Heart and Chandrakirti classes, I was also a student. When I refer to groups of students at the meditation classes, therefore, I frequently include myself.

We have already had a brief introduction to the two centers involved in this study. Chapter 1 introduces them more fully, providing some detail on the backgrounds of their teachers and the classes and other events each was offering at the time I conducted my research. Concentrating on the stories of six of the interview respondents, chapter 2 explores the reasons they became interested in Buddhism and their earliest experiences learning about Buddhist principles and practices. Chapter 3 consists of a detailed description of the classes, including a survey of their educational and ritual elements. This is followed in chapter 4 by a discussion of learning in which Bloom's taxonomy is applied, and expanded, in order to illuminate interview participants' reflections on their learning experiences. In chapter 5, the formal practices such as prostrations, offerings, and prayers are explored as means of learning, but the primary focus is on what and how students learned through meditation. It is this chapter that establishes the link between mental and physical forms of ritualizing, arguing that meditation's formal, repetitive, and mental techniques train the mind in the same way its postures and gestures train the body. Chapter 6 assesses respondents' learning by tracking change: What had changed between introductory students' first and second interviews, and how did newcomers' reflections differ from those of experienced members? The concluding chapter looks at the ways the ritualized nature of the practices linked physical learning to changes in attitudes, emotions, and values. More importantly, it stresses once again that ritualizing includes physical as well as mental practices, and that the learning that takes place through both is akin to physical training. Embodied learning is gained by the knowing body and the moving mind.

Finally, unlike the lives and experiences of the people it describes, a text, once published, does not change. By the time this story was written, its characters and settings had already moved on. Friends of the Heart had changed its class structure and two of the teachers I interviewed had resigned. Chandrakirti Centre had closed for renovations and has since reopened as a fully renovated temple, the NKT headquarters for Canada. What is written here is a snapshot of a particular time and place in the histories of Friends of the Heart and Chandrakirti Centre and the history of Buddhism in Toronto. I believe that that snapshot provides important and illuminating information for understanding the state of Buddhism and Buddhist-style practice in Canada. But it is still important to keep in mind, as Buddhist teachings remind us, that everything changes.

1

Friends of the Heart and Chandrakirti Centre

MEDITATION IN TORONTO

AT A SMALL Buddhist center on Yonge Street in Toronto, a dozen or so people gather every Wednesday evening for ten weeks to participate in an introductory meditation class. In the small third-floor unit that houses the center, a shrine room has been set up. The shrine is adorned with candles, offering bowls, and three gold-colored *rūpas* or Buddha statues. The walls are decorated with several Tibetan-style devotional paintings (*thangka*). On arrival, students take off their shoes and enter the shrine room. They pull out *zafus* (round, firm meditation cushions) and a variety of other cushions from a pile beneath the windows and lay them out in a semicircle facing the shrine. A few of the students choose to sit in chairs. The teacher sits on a cushion with her back to the shrine, and begins the class by reciting the Refuge Prayer, a short reading in English written by the center's founder. Following the prayer, the teacher leads the students in guided meditation using one or more of the concentration techniques taught at this center; some are based on Tibetan Buddhist practices, some on Theravada meditation techniques. Some are newer practices adapted to the needs and preferences of western Buddhist sympathizers.

Over the course of the ten-week class, students learn several different meditation practices. They perform movement exercises based on *qi gong* and yoga. They listen to talks given by the teacher on topics ranging from stress reduction to developing loving-kindness, and they discuss their experiences practicing meditation. Two guided meditation sessions take place each Wednesday evening, and students are strongly encouraged to keep up a daily meditation practice at home. Teachers hope that, by the end of the course, students will have experienced some benefits from meditation, developed a commitment to continue the practice on their own and, perhaps, taken out a long-term membership at the center.[1]

Some distance farther west, on Crawford Street, not far from Bloor Street, one of Toronto's main thoroughfares, another introductory meditation class is offered, this one on Tuesday nights. This center, also based in Tibetan-style Buddhism, is situated in an old Protestant church and, until major renovations began in the summer of 2007, much of the feel of that church remained. Shrines adorned with several different statues and three sets of eight offering bowls occupy the former chancel. More than half of the pews have been removed at the front of the nave and replaced by one row of meditation mats and cushions and three long rows of chairs. From twenty to thirty people attend the Tuesday night class at this center. Students are welcome to come as frequently or infrequently and for as long as they like.

On entering, students take off their shoes and take a seat in the meditation hall. Some will sit on cushions, but most sit in the chairs or pews. They await the arrival of the teacher, who assumes a seat on a mat and cushion resting on a platform before the shrines. The class begins with the chanting of a prayer in English honoring Shakyamuni, the historical Buddha. The teacher, often a monastic wearing the red and yellow robes of the Tibetan tradition, then guides students in meditation focused on the breath. Following this meditation, he or she will give a talk, usually over an hour in length, on topics dealing with happiness, compassion, letting go of self-cherishing, and other related subjects drawn from Buddhist teachings. A second session of meditation follows, during which students reflect on the topic of the talk. Questions and discussion often follow the second meditation. After the class, some students gather in the basement for tea and cookies and some informal discussion. Teachers express the hope that those who attend the class find better, more positive ways of dealing with difficulties in their everyday lives, and begin to develop concentration and compassion through meditation and reflection on the lectures. Some newcomers to this class will, over time, participate in numerous other events offered at the center, and some may move on to its more intensive training programs.

Despite the differences in their settings and the organization of their classes, these two centers have several aspects in common. Both base their teachings in the broader tradition of Tibetan Buddhism, although the first also adds some meditative techniques from Theravada Buddhism in addition to teaching movement techniques derived from yoga, t'ai chi, and *qi gong*. Further, both centers draw on both Theravada and Mahayana teachings and practices from time to time. Their classes are designed to appeal to people from non-Buddhist familial and cultural backgrounds—people referred to by just about everyone at these centers as "westerners." At both centers, the teachers are also westerners from non-Buddhist backgrounds. The Crawford Street center is associated with a large international organization founded by a Tibetan monk and based in England. The Yonge Street center is founded by a woman who was born and raised in Canada and who studied in India with Tibetan teachers.

Both centers teach newcomers how to meditate as well as some basic ethical values rooted in Buddhist teachings. At both centers, there are numerous ways or means by which newcomers learn: lectures, question-and-answer sessions, group discussions, observation of others, reading books, informal questions of teachers and other members, and so forth.

Students also learn through the practices that they perform. Such practices include formal activities such as spoken or chanted prayers, prostrations, bowing, special hand postures called *mudras*, and the chanting of mantras. Formal practices also include meditation, its postures and gestures, and its concentration techniques.

This book examines all of these different ways that newcomers at both centers learned about and through Buddhist practices and teachings. Over a period of several months, I participated in meditation courses and other events at Friends of the Heart on Yonge Street and Chandrakirti Centre on Crawford and interviewed members and teachers from both. What follows is the story of these two centers and the experiences of some of their practitioners. The story begins with the centers themselves, their histories, settings, and teachings.

FRIENDS OF THE HEART

Friends of the Heart had its official beginning in October of 1980 when its founder and spiritual leader, Catherine Rathbun, began teaching in Toronto. Born in Canada, Catherine had lived and taught for a time in New Zealand, where she still has students who keep in touch via the internet. Catherine began her training in Tibetan Buddhism in 1969 with Canadian teacher Namgyal Rinpoche. Born Leslie George Dawson, Namgyal was recognized as a *tulku* (an incarnate lama) by the sixteenth Karmapa Lama, head of the Kagyu school of Tibetan Buddhism. Dawson was one of the first westerners to be recognized as such.

Catherine also studied in Sikkim with the sixteenth Karmapa Lama. Other teachers included Kalu Rinpoche, Karma Thinley Rinpoche, and John Coleman.[2] Karma Thinley is a teacher in the Sakya and Kagyu schools of Tibetan Buddhism who is based in Toronto. In 2002, he ordained Catherine as a lay teacher and gave her the teaching name Lama Jetsun Yeshe. She is known by her students as Jetsun-ma. According to other teachers at Friends of the Heart, this lay designation is one that is present in traditional Tibetan Buddhism and is much more practical than the full ordination, especially for a wife and mother, as Catherine is.[3]

The Toronto group originally met in Catherine's home. Some students had met her through a course she taught from 1989 to 1997 at York University, called Meditation and Movement.[4] In the early 1990s, several of the group's students rented a house and offered its living-room area as a permanent shrine room and teaching space. Around that time, the group was given the charitable corporation for Namgyal House, which they re-registered under the new name, Friends of the Heart. According to its official registration, the group has an educational objective as part of its mission statement.[5] As a reflection of this mandate, all of its regular weekly meetings are structured as classes.

Friends of the Heart's membership had grown to more than fifty students by the late 1990s. In April 1998, the group moved into its current quarters on Yonge Street. Several of its earlier members trained under Catherine as teachers and started offering meditation classes at the center. Joyce Allen and Richard Johnson, for example, are a married couple who became Catherine's students in 1990 and who were both senior members and teachers at Friends of the Heart at the time this study was conducted.

Richard noted that Friends of the Heart, through most of its history, has been centered on Catherine. There were changes taking place beginning in the spring of 2007 as Richard and Joyce began to take on a greater leadership role and Catherine pulled back a little, but Catherine was still viewed as the center's primary teacher and spiritual leader. In the fall of 2007, Joyce and another teacher, Meg Salter, resigned from teaching the introductory classes at Friends of the Heart. Senior member David Liang took over their classes.

The Friends of the Heart website provided the following description of the center:

> We offer meditation instruction and classes in Toronto. By emphasizing individual attention, discussion, and dialogue in small classes, you will learn how to live in the world with a compassionate heart and a clear mind. Find peace, calm, and joy in your life. Friends of the Heart is a group of lay people who actively pursue the deep philosophic and ethical teachings of East and West while maintaining an active, ordinary life within the community. From the Buddhist path, we take teachings and meditation practice from the Theravada, Mahayana, and Vajrayana streams.[6]

The description of the center emphasized lay practice led by lay teachers and the significance of practicing in the world, traits that have become definitive of modern forms of Buddhism around the world. While the model of the enlightened layperson appears in Mahayana scriptures, revered teachers, primarily monastic ones, have historically been the heart of Vajrayana, or Tibetan tantric Buddhism. In many western cultures, monastic lifestyle is not as revered and is perhaps less feasible than in traditional Buddhist countries.[7] Many Buddhist teachers in the West have therefore de-emphasized the monastic role, as Friends of the Heart has done. As this description suggests, Friends of the Heart has an eclectic approach to its teachings. Early on, Catherine taught not only from the Tibetan and a more general Buddhist background, she also periodically introduced students to a western mystery tradition based in Rosicrucianism. Due primarily to time constraints, these teachings were no longer offered.[8] Adding to its eclectic nature is the fact that some of the Friends of the Heart teachers teach Theravada insight meditation (*vipaśyanā* or *vipassanā* in Pali). This kind of eclecticism is another common feature of western Buddhist organizations. While contact between different Buddhist communities in Canada is rare, borrowing from a variety of different traditions is not.

Located on Yonge Street north of Eglinton in Toronto's North York district, Friends of the Heart is in a third-floor suite consisting of a long, rectangular unit separated into three rooms. The first is a small area at the entrance, which serves as a lobby and office space. Passing between two tall wooden pillars and beneath rows of Tibetan prayer flags, we enter the main space, the meditation hall or shrine room. In the center of the left-hand wall is a shrine with three golden rūpas or statues, each about a meter in height, draped with white silk scarves called *katas*. There are two smaller images, one of Shakyamuni Buddha, sitting below and to the left of the central, raised icon. The other is a small Tara, draped like the others in a white scarf. A small, framed photograph of the Dalai Lama sits near the Buddha figure. Two vases of flowers also adorn the shrine. Depending on the practices being performed, the three main rūpas, Tara, Chenrezig, and Vajrasattva, will change positions.

In a row along the front edge of the shrine, seven small offering bowls are laid out in front of the icons. The bowls contain water, rice, flowers, and cookies or crackers. Incense is in one of the bowls, but it is not often lit. I was told that the smell of the incense was too strong for the small shrine room. At each end and in the middle of the line of offering bowls are glass candle-holders with lit white tapers or sometimes tea lights. Catherine taught students at the Tibetan Meditation class that the offerings in the bowls symbolize a step-by-step path in Buddhist practice. Describing each offering in turn, she explained that the two bowls on the left are filled with plain water, which represent water for washing and water for drinking. These offerings symbolize a desire to purify oneself externally and internally. The next bowl contains flowers, symbolizing the recognition of beauty in the world, or in the Buddhist path. The incense in the next bowl, Catherine said, indicates a desire to dedicate oneself to spiritual purification. It is followed by a candle, whose light represents enlightenment. Next is a bowl of scented water, signifying the deeper realization of spiritual cleansing. The next bowl contains food, usually cookies or crackers placed in a handful of uncooked rice. Catherine said that the food represents the nourishment of the path. The last bowl contains a seashell, which is a symbol of music, the divine sounds that are heard at the culmination of the path. These offerings have a long history in Tibetan Buddhism. The two candles on either end of the row of offering bowls are an addition to the traditional format.

On the wall to the right of the shrine are two large bookcases containing the center's lending library, which contains numerous books on a wide variety of topics, mostly religion or spirituality. Several different traditions are represented, including Christianity, Judaism, Islam (and its Sufi variant), as well as all of the main streams of Buddhism. Pictures of the Dalai Lama, the Karmapa Lama (sixteenth and seventeenth), and of Catherine also adorn the bookcases. There is a small frame containing a photo of a stained-glass depiction of Jesus.

The main hall has a large, Persian-style carpet in the center placed over a layer of grey berber. There are windows along the right side of the room revealing a brown brick wall across a narrow alley. A shelf or wide windowsill that runs beneath the windows bears a large tape deck, flyers and brochures about the center, a water jug, and cups. Piled beneath this shelf are numerous zafus in forest green, along with other cushions in various sizes, shapes, and colors. Yoga mats are rolled and stored in a corner nearby. The *zabuton*, or traditional meditation mat, is not used at Friends of the Heart. Around the walls are hung various Tibetan-style thankghas. At an open house, Meg Salter identified White Tara for me, in the thangka hanging above and to the left of the shrine. Another framed picture is of an eleven-headed, thousand-armed statue of Chenrezig.[9] Despite the center's nondenominational, east-west syncretic approach, the shrine room has a strongly Tibetan-influenced décor.

The center's third room is a general meeting room. A door set into a glass wall at the far end of the meditation hall opens in to this space. There are some comfortable chairs, a television, and equipment for making tea or coffee. This room is used as a storage area as well as a meeting room. The low wooden tables used for Tibetan Meditation classes are stacked under the windows here. The windows along the far wall of this room look out over the public parking lot behind the building.

Nearby, there is a small theater that was running a show called "Menopause Out Loud" in the winter of 2006–2007. The show's music could be heard in the meditation center after 8 PM each evening. Friends of the Heart teachers noted the music with some humor, acknowledging that it was an intrusion on meditation practice. Some pointed out that the disturbance could help practitioners improve their concentration. In the winter months, the heating system contributes to the soundscape in the meditation hall: Intermittent sounds of rushing air and high-pitched squeaks and pops from the ceiling vents fill the room, loud enough that teachers must raise their voices.

In the evenings, the main door to the building at street level is locked. On the door is mounted a clear plastic panel which holds a radio-operated doorbell, a sign for the center, and a slot for its brochures. People arriving at the center after 6 PM must ring the bell, which produces a quiet squeak from its receiver in the center's office area. Someone must then run down the stairs to the landing on the second floor and press a button to unlock the main door. Late comers often interrupted meditation classes as a result.

From fall 2006 through to spring 2007, Wednesday nights were dedicated to the introductory meditation classes. Every ten weeks, these classes switched back and forth between Calm and Clear taught by Meg Salter, and Introduction to Insight taught by Joyce Allen. Joyce also led the Healing Body, Healing Mind class on Thursday nights, which included an hour of yoga and an hour of meditation, and was open to practitioners of all levels. Most of those who participated in interviews for this project had attended the Wednesday introductory class, but one had enrolled in the Thursday evening one. Other meditation classes included Richard's Intermediate Meditation class every Tuesday night, preceded by an hour of hatha yoga. On Monday mornings from ten to noon, Catherine conducted the more advanced Tibetan Meditation course. When I attended this class from December 2006 to April 2007, its teachings were on Vajrasattva and Guru Yoga, two of the traditional Tibetan preliminary practices (Tibetan: *ngöndrö*[10]). Twice during fieldwork, this class offered initiation ceremonies, called "empowerments," first into the deity and practice of Chenrezig and later into White Tara.

Every ten weeks or so throughout the year, Friends of the Heart also holds a Saturday afternoon open house, where newcomers interested in the center and its courses can visit in an informal atmosphere, ask questions, and participate in a guided meditation with one of the teachers. Friends of the Heart also holds several yearly retreats at the Harmony Dawn retreat center near Cobourg, Ontario, and teachers also offer various workshops or lectures throughout the year. They occasionally give lectures at Snow Lion, a Buddhist bookstore and meditation supply shop in Toronto's Danforth Village.

The schedule of teachings and classes has changed somewhat over the years, primarily for practical reasons. For some time, Joyce had taught the Healing Body, Healing Mind class on Saturday mornings. She later decided that she needed to have her weekends free, and around this time, Gwen Robart joined the center. With twenty years' experience studying and teaching t'ai chi, Gwen agreed to take over the Saturday morning time slot, turning it into a t'ai chi class.

Some interview participants attended the Friday evening Energy Training class taught by Myra Willis. Myra had also studied under Namgyal Rinpoche around the same time that Catherine had. Because Namgyal was often away traveling, many of his earlier students came to Catherine after she had been given authority to teach. Myra's interests were along the lines of healing and energy work such as reiki and *qi gong*. Her Energy Training class, which focused on developing healing energies in the body, was less of a meditation course and less Buddhist than other courses offered at Friends of the Heart. It was also an introductory-level class, but was cancelled in spring of 2007 due to lack of attendance.

In recent years, Catherine has reduced the number of public classes she personally offers in order to focus on one-on-one instruction with dedicated students. A survivor of breast cancer, she also needed to cut back some of her responsibilities in order to care for her health. At the start of my fieldwork in November of 2006, she was offering the two-hour Tibetan Meditation course, but relinquished that course in May of 2007. At that time, she was writing a book that would serve as a meditation and practice manual for Friends of the Heart members in her absence. In the summer of 2007, she conducted a *Mahāmudrā* meditation retreat[11] at Harmony Dawn and gave a few guest teachings in the fall of 2007, but has, for the most part, stepped back from regular teaching. In her absence, other members and teachers have taken over her classes.

Friends of the Heart students generally begin with one of the two ten-week introductory meditation courses. Some may attend both. If they choose to stay on, they can then begin regularly attending the Intermediate Meditation class or the more advanced Tibetan Meditation class. That said, all of the classes are open to newcomers, and teachers adapt the classes, giving instructions where needed. Members interested in becoming more involved and in following a more rigorous Buddhist path can undertake the Friends of the Heart foundation practice, which is based on Tibetan ngöndrö or preliminary path in which practitioners perform one hundred thousand prostrations, mantras, and chanted prayers. Finally, there is the IMP or Intensive Meditation Program, in which individual students enter into mentoring relationships with teachers or senior members and receive more in-depth tantric teachings and practices. This is an advanced program whose content is restricted to committed and initiated practitioners, a reflection of the esotericism of tantric tradition.

In an interview, Catherine told me that her teaching goals at Friends of the Heart are to engage students' curiosity, show them the beauty of the dharma, and teach them ways to overcome negativity in their lives. In her view, such goals as completing foundation practice are only there "to help us humans have a sense of linear accomplishment." She said that the true objective of her teaching is to effect long-lasting changes wherein practitioners find practical applications of the dharma and meditation in their lives.

CHANDRAKIRTI CENTRE

Chandrakirti is one of numerous centers around the world associated with the New Kadampa Tradition, also known as the International Kadampa Buddhist Union, which is headquartered at Manjushri Kadampa Meditation Centre in Ulverston, England. Kelsang Gyatso, its founder, is a Tibetan monk who fled his homeland in 1959. He trained for a time in India and then traveled to England in 1976, where he developed a following of western students. According to Chandrakirti members, his objective was to preserve in exile the lineage of the Kadam school (Kadam-pa), and to introduce it to western students. He began training and eventually ordaining westerners in the practices of his lineage. In 1979, Kelsang Gyatso assumed spiritual directorship of an existing Buddhist center in England, and the organization was officially consolidated under the title New Kadampa Tradition (NKT) in 1991. Since that time, it has established numerous temples, dharma centers, and smaller groups in western nations around the globe. Of primary importance to Chandrakirti Centre is its NKT education program, which consists of three levels, the General Program (GP), Foundation Program (FP) and Teacher Training Program (TTP). According to the NKT website, it has 1,100 centers in forty countries around the world,[12] although this number may include sites where classes take place in public libraries and other rented spaces.

Chandrakirti's parent organization has been the subject of controversy over the worship of Dorje Shugden, a spiritual being whose worship has been present in Gélukpa practice since the seventeenth century. Several Tibetan leaders have discouraged the practice, including the thirteenth Dalai Lama (d. 1933). The current Dalai Lama, who had spoken out against the practice since 1976, finally issued a formal ban against Shugden worship in 1996. The NKT, whose practices include Shugden worship, organized public protests during the Dalai Lama's trip to England in 1996. Protesting against the popular figure of the Dalai Lama, however, drew a great deal of negative attention to the NKT in the media. The controversy over the general ban of Shugden worship escalated in 1997 in the Tibetan community in exile when a senior monk who had supported the ban was murdered along with two younger monks in Dharamsala, India. The controversy over Shugden practice continues to this day, with considerable vitriol from several of the parties involved. The NKT has officially taken an arms-length position, continuing to espouse Shugden practice[13] but making no reference to the Dalai Lama or to the controversy on its website.[14]

While it is necessary to locate Chandrakirti Centre within the NKT and to situatethe NKT within the broader context of Tibetan Buddhism, it is not the object of this study to enter into a detailed discussion of disputes arising within Tibetan Buddhist traditions. The focus here is on the participants at Chandrakirti Centre and the means by which they learned at Chandrakirti classes. In fact, many participants to whom I spoke were unaware of the controversy and, for the most part, unaware of Dorje Shugden or the worship of such a figure at the center. General Program classes, which are the focus of this study, did not involve mention of the figure during my fieldwork, nor did they include devotional practices concerning any spiritual beings, with the exception, perhaps, of Shakyamuni Buddha.

Over time, NKT texts and practices have been adapted to a more western style. Prayers were originally performed in Tibetan, but are now translated into the native languages of the countries in which they are used. Practitioners now chant the prayers along with recordings produced at the organization's headquarters and distributed on CD to its numerous centers around the world. Gradually, the use of Tibetan terms is being replaced by local vernacular. For example, the *gompa* (Tibetan: *dgon pa*) is now more often called a shrine room or meditation hall.

Chandrakirti Centre started off in 1993 in a rented venue called Friends House, a Quaker facility in central Toronto. From the mid- to late nineties, the center occupied various small sites in different areas of the city. Over this time, its membership grew, and it eventually settled into a large Victorian house on Parkside Drive in the city's High Park district, where it remained for several years. The shrine room was in the spacious main floor living room, and upstairs rooms were used as residential spaces and secondary meditation halls. By the turn of the new millennium, the membership had grown and the house on Parkside was no longer sufficient. An NKT temple established in nearby Mississauga had also begun attracting a fair-sized membership, and the two centers often participated in shared events. Clearly, more space was needed. In 2006, the organization bought an old brick church on Crawford Street, in the west end of the city, and transformed it into a dharma center. The group now had a large shrine room and meditation hall and a basement common room in which to conduct its weekly services and classes, along with retreats and numerous other special events. The move to Crawford Street was evidently a success.

In January 2007, a series of rapid changes began, changes that were still in progress at the time of writing. From January to August, four different monastics consecutively served as head teacher at the center. The long-time head teacher had left in January to start up a center in Winnipeg, and two subsequent teachers took charge for approximately three months each. In August, Gen Thekchen (pronounced TEHchen), a monk who had been head teacher at the Kingston, Ontario, NKT center for nine years, was assigned to lead the Toronto center. Thekchen is a Canadian from a non-Buddhist background who originally hails from Toronto. He developed an interest in Buddhism while traveling in India after graduating from university. He studied with Tibetan teachers in Dharamsala, India and in Nepal. On his return to Toronto, he discovered Chandrakirti Centre and enrolled in several of its courses. He later took NKT teacher training in England and ordained there in 1998. Half a year later, he was assigned to the Kingston dharma center as resident teacher and taught there for nine years until being assigned as resident teacher in Toronto in August 2007.

Substantial structural changes began taking place at Chandrakirti Centre as well. In May of 2007, officials from England visited the center to announce that it was to become the main NKT temple for Canada. The temple in Mississauga, just west of Toronto, was to be sold and renovations on the Crawford Street church to turn it into a proper temple would begin as early as June. Within two weeks of this announcement, the Crawford Street site was closed. The organization bought two houses nearby and began renovating them into residential and teaching facilities. At this time, it was expected that the new Toronto temple, replete with three nine-foot-tall Buddha statues, would open its doors in the spring of 2008. In the end, however, final renovations were not completed until 2009. Since the Crawford Street site closed in the middle of fieldwork for this project, and remained closed at the time of writing, my description of the center is out of date. As is the case with all fieldwork studies, the following description is of a particular time and place. It is now a record of part of the history of Buddhism in Toronto. I include the description in order to give the reader a sense of the ritual space at the time my fieldwork was conducted, regardless of the changes that have since taken place.

On the front of the square brick church that houses Chandrakirti Centre there is a large, backlit sign. Below a photo of a pair of hands holding a string of prayer beads and a flower, it advertises meditation classes on Tuesdays and Wednesdays, 7–9 PM and Sundays 11–12 PM. Steep concrete steps lead up to the large, central doors of the church. These steps open into a small lobby. To the right, a staircase leads down to the basement common room, offices, washrooms, and kitchen. To the left is a small room that was once used as the teacher's office. In late 2006, it was converted into a shop for the center, selling various ritual objects and Kelsang Gyatso's numerous books in paperback.

The large shrine room is in the main hall of the church. Prior to Chandrakirti's purchase of the church, its central aisle, steps, and chancel had been carpeted in a fine burgundy-colored broadloom, a perfect color for this Tibetan-based center. Many of the original church pews remain, but a few rows were removed at the front, where a row of dark red mats and cushions and three rows of pink uphol-stered chairs are set up. In the summer, air conditioners hum in the windows of the main hall. In the winter, the radiators of the old steam-powered heating system rattle and ping loudly. This cacophony frequently elicits comments and laughter from teachers and students alike. Some point out that the replacement of the old, noisy heating system will be a welcome part of the center's renovation.

On the raised section of the former chancel stand three shrines in a long row, each set on a wide wooden cabinet. The small gold statues on each of the shrine cabinets are raised, sitting on long, narrow platforms that are covered in gold damask fabric. Below and before the statues on each shrine are seven large, blue glass offering bowls. The offerings are similar to those on the Friends of the Heart shrine, beginning on the left with water for drinking and water for washing, fol-lowed by a flower and then incense. Light, present in the form of a candle on the Friends of the Heart shrine, is at Chandrakirti Centre represented by a bowl filled with colored glass pebbles. The next two bowls contain scented water and a food offering, usually chocolate. There is no bowl symbolizing music on the Chandrakirti shrines; one member told me that music is present in the chanting of the prayers. As at Friends of the Heart, the incense here is rarely if ever lit, out of respect for people with allergies.

Each shrine bears three statues, averaging around forty centimeters tall. On the leftmost shrine the largest statue, in the center, is of Je Tsongkhapa or Tsong Khapa, founder of the Géluk school of Tibetan Buddhism and the main spiritual guide of the NKT. Sitting on the same level on either side of this figure are two smaller similar figures, two of Je Tsongkhapa's disciples. All three statues are adorned in colorfully fringed robes and yellow pandit's hats. Beside them sits a collection of Kelsang Gyatso's texts, bound in red and gold. On this leftmost shrine, on the right end of the line of offering bowls, sits a mandala, a gold-colored structure composed of several layers of rings, each smaller than the one below. The mandala is crowned with an ornament resembling a gold finial. The rings contain colorful beads, pebbles, and rice. At some of the services performed at Chandrakirti Centre, the assembly of the mandala is performed as an offering. All three shrines hold small, artfully arranged collections of bottles and packages of food offerings.

The central shrine has the largest and highest of all of the figures, that of Shakyamuni Buddha, draped in a golden yellow cloth. The Buddha sits on a square platform raised above the statues on either side of him. He is flanked by Green

Tara, draped in a green silk cloth, and Avalokiteśvara, with a large, decorous crown. On the third shrine, the central figure is Mañjuśrī, bearing a flaming sword. The smaller, colorful image to his left is Dorje Shugden, depicted as a fierce-looking figure riding a Tibetan snow lion. On the right stands a brass-colored cylindrical icon resembling a *stūpa*. On a smaller ledge, below the statues but above the main offering bowls, sit five very small colorless glass bowls below the image of Dorje Shugden. These bowls contain offerings of alcohol, tea, cookies, milk, and yogurt, offerings listed in some of the chanted prayers. Between the shrines are two large glass vases supported on black metal stands and bearing large silk flowers and leaves in red and brown tones.

Behind the shrines, closing off the remainder of the chancel, hangs a wide gold-colored curtain, which provides a backdrop for the shrines. Just before the shrines, several carpeted steps lead down to the main level of the meditation hall. In the very middle of these steps, part of the original church architecture, is a raised square platform carpeted in the same burgundy color as the steps and aisle. This platform is used as the teacher's seat. On it is a thick meditation mat upholstered in deep red and gold. A deep red zafu sits atop the mat. Beside the teacher's seat are several ritual objects, including a vase of flowers and a framed portrait of Kelsang Gyatso. There is also a small, cylindrical metal bell sitting on a wooden rest. When struck, it rings with a high, pure sound. Carol, a long-time Chandrakirti member, told me that some teachers ring this bell to start and end meditation. Other teachers dispense with this practice. The bowl-shaped brass bell often associated with Tibetan Buddhism is not present at Chandrakirti Centre.

Since its reformation as the national center for Canada, Chandrakirti has been renamed the Chandrakirti Kadampa Meditation Centre of Canada (CKMCC). In late 2007, the center's website offered the following description:

Chandrakirti Kadampa Meditation Centre Canada's (CKMCC) purpose is to act as the principal, mother center of Kadampa Buddhism within Canada and to function as an international spiritual community dedicated to achieving world peace through following the Kadampa Buddhist Path. Ongoing Buddhist meditation classes, study programs, and meditation retreats taught by CKMCC offer us the opportunity to discover our innate capacities for happiness, wisdom, and compassion. These classes are open to everyone regardless of background. Kadampa teachings offer us special advice that touches our hearts, so that we can learn to become happy and to lead meaningful lives that have the power to greatly benefit others. This Centre has arisen from the pure intention and vision of Venerable Geshe Kelsang Gyatso, Spiritual Director of the New Kadampa Tradition–International Buddhist Union (NKT–IKBU), and is dedicated so that everyone may be happy and free from suffering.[15]

The focus on world peace sounds like social activism, but Chandrakirti Centre is not an overtly socially or politically engaged organization. The intention is to teach individual students ways of finding peace in their own lives, through meditation practices and teachings on such topics as compassion and letting go of anger.

The website's description of the center also highlights the international nature of the organization. The NKT is one among many Buddhist groups that operate as highly globalized organizations employing the latest modern communications technologies. As part of such an organization, Chandrakirti Centre is subject to top-down governance. Some decisions about the center, such as the assignment of resident teachers and the structural changes that took place in 2007 and 2008, come from the leadership in England. The NKT has also developed a highly structured teaching system that is standard at its centers around the world, a system based on Kelsang Gyatso's teachings and written commentaries on historical Buddhist texts. Class subjects and structures, as well as the timing and content of many NKT devotional services, are also standardized throughout the organization. I noticed during my fieldwork that different NKT teachers tended to give very similar teachings, right down to similar phrases and syntax. Individual teachers do have their own styles, however, and Chandrakirti's schedule has shifted from time to time according to the specific needs of its membership.

Up until its closure in June of 2007, Chandrakirti Centre offered regular introductory meditation classes on Tuesday evenings. The Wednesday and Sunday classes advertised on the sign on the front of the building were not regularly being offered in 2006 and 2007 due to lack of attendance and the availability of teachers. During the renovations, introductory classes continued at several libraries and coffee shops on different weekday evenings throughout the Toronto area. Such venues had been in use for additional classes around the city even before the closure of the main center. These are the General Program classes, and many of those attending are newcomers to Buddhist teachings and practices. More long-term Chandrakirti members often move on to the Foundation Program, which usually takes place on weekends, although its scheduling changed several times during my fieldwork. Those who wish to take on a leadership role and teach NKT classes enroll in the Teacher Training Program, which usually meets early in the morning several times a week. A nun at Chandrakirti Centre told me that some very dedicated practitioners will take on the ngöndrö or preliminary practices, performing thousands of mantras and prostrations, as is the case at Friends of the Heart.

Chandrakirti Centre also holds regular devotional services or pūjās. These services involve the chanting of prayers, making offerings, and sometimes performing meditation and visualizations. The main pūjā is Heart Jewel which is performed every weekday at five in the afternoon. The Offering to the Spiritual Guide is performed on the tenth and twenty-fifth of each month, as it is in all NKT centers around the world. Other regular pūjās include the Wishfulfilling Jewel and the four-hour Melodious Drum. In addition to these pūjās, the center offers several retreats of various lengths throughout the year as well as numerous social events. Initiation ceremonies or empowerments take place from time to time, wherein participants receive the blessings of the guru Je Tsongkhapa or a deity such as Green Tara or Medicine Buddha.

In an interview in late 2007, Thekchen expressed his objectives for teaching at Chandrakirti Centre. He said he hoped the classes would provide a place where people can develop inner peace through meditation and a place where they can question and discuss the teachings that they hear at the classes or, possibly, read in Kelsang Gyatso's books. I asked Thekchen if one of his goals was to encourage people to move on, from the General Program to the Foundation Program, for example, or to encourage them to become more involved at the center. He said that the numbers were not important. He admitted to going through periods when he assessed his teaching ability by the numbers of students who moved on to Foundation Program, but that this was not an appropriate measure. For him, teaching is a practice. "I love teaching, because I have to practice what I teach. It keeps reminding me of the path and it allows me to create enough merit to gain the actual realizations. So I think it is quite a brilliant process." In this way, he feels he becomes a role model: He is not teaching only through his words but through his own commitment to the practices and ethics of his tradition. "As long as I keep opening my heart, practicing patience, improving my study and keeping my vows and commitments, [I will be] proving year by year and creating the right causes."

OUTREACH

Many of the regular events at Chandrakirti Centre and almost all of them at Friends of the Heart are structured as classes. Newcomers are invited to come and participate for a time and learn something new. While some become regular members, others move on after attending a few classes. One of the key goals of these centers, then, is to continually attract new students to their classes. Most events are open to people from all levels of experience, from newcomers to trained meditation teachers. The introductory meditation classes at both centers act as their primary forms of outreach, introducing newcomers to meditation, to some Buddhist teachings and, ideally, to a new way of relating to themselves and their world.

The centers also use other forms of outreach. Both maintain websites that introduce their teachers and the centers' objectives and describe their classes and other events. Friends of the Heart offers its open houses several times a year from September to April. Teachers at both centers give talks at public venues: Many General Program classes take place in public venues in the community. Friends of the Heart teachers have held corporate workshops on meditation in downtown boardrooms and talks at a local Buddhist bookstore. Both centers also publish regular community newsletters, distributing them to interested members and visitors via email. At Chandrakirti classes, pamphlets advertising upcoming events are set out, and there are always several of Kelsang Gyatso's books available for purchase. When I was participating at Friends of the Heart in January of 2007, printed postcards advertising the center were introduced. Members were asked to post them in their neighborhoods or workplaces in an effort to help expand the center's membership. There are many means and opportunities to discover these or, indeed, numerous other meditation centers in Toronto.

Who responds to this outreach, and why? In answer to these questions, we shall hear from several of the people who were participating at Chandrakirti Centre and Friends of the Heart in 2006 and 2007.

2

Discovery Stories

EARLY ON IN my fieldwork, while still deciding which Buddhist centers to include in this study, I attended an event at Chandrakirti Centre called Stop the Week. It was held on a Friday evening in October 2006. With a donation, participants attended a brief lecture or dharma talk, titled "What does the Buddha see?" The talk was given by Gen Zopa, at that time Chandrakirti's resident teacher. What we see is not real, Zopa told his audience. We think that what we see and experience is what makes us happy and we get attached to things. This belief creates desire, desire for more, and desire for it not to end. Pleasure creates desire. But Buddhas, he said, can feel pleasure without desire or attachment. Buddhas know that what we think is reality is only a projection of the mind. On one hand, Zopa said, we can never, ever realize the illusory nature of the world. On the other hand, he said that when we become Buddhas (which, he said, might be this week, next spring), we will see what Buddhas see—pleasure without attachment. We need only be patient and content.

Following the teaching, a fine three-course vegetarian dinner was served in the basement common room. It was prepared by Chogyan, another monk and teacher at the center. At the meal I met Gerald, a newcomer and regular participant at Chandrakirti's General Program classes. We talked about the food and the evening's teaching. I told him about my project, and he agreed to participate in an interview. Gerald was the first interview participant,[1] and over the next year I interviewed twenty-four people involved at either Friends of the Heart or Chandrakirti Centre, including newcomers, experienced members, and teachers.

Since the majority of interview participants were from non-Buddhist backgrounds, I typically started the interviews by asking how respondents became interested in Buddhism and why they chose to enroll in a meditation class. The range of responses to these questions was what first highlighted the relevance of Bloom's Taxonomy for understanding what and how—and, indeed why—participants were learning at the centers. Their different spheres of interest—simple curiosity; attraction to a nonwestern worldview; a search for meaning or change of perspective on life; a desire to improve concentration or achieve stress relief; and so on—correspond in various ways to Bloom's three learning domains. I also discovered that participants' initial motivations for taking meditation classes strongly influenced what they took away from those classes in the end. Participants' discovery stories, the stories of how they discovered and became involved in Buddhist practice, convey a great deal about their initial learning about meditation or Buddhism. Six of those stories will be explored in detail in this chapter, along with reflections from other participants.

But before moving on to those stories, I would like to briefly introduce all of the interview participants. The following chart (table 2.1) lists participants' names

TABLE 2.1 Interview Participants

Friends of the Heart			
Students			*Teachers*
Newcomers		*Experienced Members*	
Tanit	Gwen	David	Joyce and Richard
John	"Anna"	"Marconi"	Meg
Diane	"Margaret"		Catherine R.
	Nicolette		
	"Dennis"		
	Erin		

Chandrakirti Centre			
Students			*Teachers*
Newcomers		*Experienced Members*	
Gerald	Brenda	Marlon	Thekchen
Carol	Bronwen	"Priscilla"	
Alan	Catherine H.		

according to the centers they attended and their roles at the time they were interviewed. Names appearing in quotation marks are pseudonyms, chosen by those
who opted for anonymity. For a more detailed introduction to each of the student
interview participants, see the appendix.

A small group of informants such as this is known as a nonprobability sample.
These people were selected based on their cultural competence and expertise,
rather than their statistical representativeness.[2] In other words, they were sought
out on the basis of their involvement at Friends of the Heart or Chandrakirti
Centre and their experience as participants in those settings. In the chapters that
follow, we will hear from all of these interview respondents as they reflect on their
experiences at these centers. In order to preserve participants' voices as best I
could while quoting from lengthy interview transcripts, I decided to focus on six
individuals—the principal participants—whose stories the following chapters will
trace most closely. Selection of a core group of participants was not a simple task.
Every one of the respondents had an interesting story to tell and informative
insights on their learning experiences. In the end, I settled on two basic criteria for
selecting principal participants: I chose respondents who had taken one of either
center's primary introductory classes and were available for a second round of
interviews. I then selected an equal number of men and women, and an equal
number of principal participants from each center.

The distinction between newcomers and experienced respondents was not as
clear-cut as this table might suggest. For example, Nicolette and Gwen had been participating at Friends of the Heart for less than a year, but both were involved in
advanced rather than introductory-level courses. Furthermore, Nicolette had participated for some time at other Buddhist centers, and Gwen had over twenty years of t'ai
chi training and teaching experience. Gwen was also a teacher at Friends of the Heart,
leading weekly t'ai chi classes. I list Nicolette and Gwen as newcomers because they
were new to Friends of the Heart. The responses they gave in their interviews were
comparable to responses from other newcomers as well as experienced members. By
contrast, Carol, a long-time member of Chandrakirti Centre, had participated only at
the introductory-level classes. I initially interviewed her as an experienced member,
but in the end listed her with newcomers because her reflections on the General
Program classes corresponded well with those of other newcomers.

While this book is, to some extent, a story about Buddhism, it is not necessarily
about Buddhists. Many of the people involved at Friends of the Heart and
Chandrakirti Centre did not identify as Buddhists. Catherine H., whose family was
Buddhist, said she had recently accepted that this was the religious identity into
which she had been born. Brenda, a newcomer at Chandrakirti Centre, did consider herself to be Buddhist because she believed in Buddhist teachings. All of the

other respondents I identified as newcomers said they were not Buddhist at their first interviews. By the second round of interviews, only Gerald had changed his mind. All four experienced members said that they were Buddhist, although Marconi said he was sometimes uncomfortable with the label.

In the scholarship on Buddhism in the West, there is much debate over how to identify who is and who is not a Buddhist. Membership or attendance at Buddhist centers fail as criteria for establishing Buddhist identity since they do not account for a large number of unaffiliated people who view the world in terms of Buddhist teachings or follow Buddhist practices.[3] Thomas Tweed argues that scholars have not paid sufficient attention to those whom he calls sympathizers, people who are interested in Buddhism but do not fully or formally embrace it. In 1979, Charles Prebish suggested that a person should be considered a Buddhist if that is how they self-identify.[4] But self-identification still does not cast a wide enough net. Many practitioners who have been involved at Buddhist centers for some time, even some who have taken initiation or ordination, are sometimes uncomfortable saying that they are Buddhist.[5] Reasons for this vary. Some are affiliated with more than one religion and do not want to limit their identity. Several interview participants said they did not want to affiliate with any kind of religious organization. Still others, like Marconi, were simply uncomfortable with labels and the expectations that tend to come with them. When I asked Nicolette, for instance, if she considered herself to be a Buddhist, she jokingly replied that perhaps if she was asked at gunpoint she would say yes. Then she said: "I really feel uncomfortable with people who cling even the slightest little bit to a particular philosophy, religion, whatever. It makes me uncomfortable, for example, to see people wearing crosses or even OM symbols." Similarly, when I asked Diane if she was a Buddhist, she said that she had an interest in the dharma and she would call herself a practitioner, but: "I wouldn't use the label. . . . I don't label myself generally." Later in her interview, Diane said that she did not believe that the Buddha was a Buddhist. Tanit and Gerald also claimed that they were uncomfortable with the Buddhist label. It is important to note that many of the people I interviewed had discovered Buddhism after breaking with an earlier religious affiliation: Discomfort with religion in general, particularly organized religion, is likely a strong factor in their unwillingness to take on a religious identity.

After asking respondents if they were Buddhist, I then asked them to describe what they considered to be a "proper" Buddhist. Most of them had surprisingly high standards: years of practice, involvement with a knowledgeable guide, celibacy, vegetarianism, faith in Buddhist teachings, acceptance of Buddhist ritual, taking vows or precepts, even ordination. Despite the fact that interview participants were engaged in Buddhist teachings and practices that had been explicitly adapted for westerners, most of them defined Buddhist identity in terms of more monastic, long-standing expressions of Buddhism than the modernist form with which they were themselves engaged. Newcomers especially did not see themselves as being fully engaged with what they regarded as "real" Buddhism. In their view, they were part of a less formal circle of involvement[6] that was not to be mistaken for full affiliation. Respondents clearly identified another, more committed level of affiliation that they regarded as "properly" Buddhist. The high standards that respondents used to define Buddhist identity is another reason that few of them personally identified as Buddhist.

Given my definitions of spirituality and religion (see introduction), I am inclined to classify as Buddhist those participants who are long-term members of a Buddhist organization, or those who identify with Buddhist worldviews for the primary reason that they *are* Buddhist. That is to say, a Buddhist is someone who has a special affiliation either to a Buddhist center or to Buddhist teachings and practices, whether they self-identify or not. As this was not the case for most newcomers who participated in interviews, Tweed's term, "sympathizers," is appropriate. With Tweed, I believe that the stories of people who are even peripherally involved or interested in Buddhist practices and teachings are important indicators of the ways in which Buddhism is developing in North America, no matter how they self-identify. As Tweed points out, it is important to remember that any religious identity is often hybrid, contested, and complex[7] and that the boundaries of Buddhist identity are not clear.

What follows are respondents' discovery stories, descriptions of how and why they became interested in Buddhism and involved in meditation classes. Most participants had had some contact with Buddhist teachings or with other Asian traditions before arriving at the door of a Buddhist center. Their stories thus describe what they had learned prior to their involvement at Friends of the Heart or Chandrakirti Centre. Most importantly, the motives that respondents had for seeking out introductory meditation classes indicate some of their early learning objectives. The reasons respondents gave for their initial interest in either meditation or Buddhist teachings were multilayered: A variety of different needs, opportunities, and expectations were involved in their initial encounters with Buddhist practices or teachings. Reasons for their interests were therefore as individual as the participants themselves.

GERALD

Two weeks after our first meeting at the Stop the Week dinner, Gerald and I met for an interview at a coffee shop in Toronto's east end. Gerald was forty-six at the time and an artist who was busy running his own house-painting business. He said he had been raised as "quite a liberal Catholic" but had fallen away from the church. Prior to participating at Chandrakirti Centre, he had explored some Hindu-based teachings on the internet. He had also read a few books on Buddhism, and said he knew "something of its spirit," but nothing of the doctrine. "And so I didn't really know anything about Buddhism in particular," he said. In Gerald's view, it was at Chandrakirti Centre that the real learning had begun. When I asked him what had first piqued his interest in Buddhism, he replied:

> It was available.[8] A friend of mine was going there [to Chandrakirti] for about a year. He doesn't go too much now. And he was telling me about it. And he was just reminding me about principles that I'm trying to put into practice without having any real education behind them. So, I thought it would be good to get out for the night, because I work and I have kids and I don't do anything—I don't drink or anything so I don't go out. So I thought this was like a night course. It was something intellectually stimulating and I wanted to see if it was related to what I felt should be happening in my life. So I was really kind of thrilled to see that everything corresponded with what I thought happens in life and feels like in life. And, the principles of Buddhism, I feel quite comfortable with their approach and their beliefs. So that was the reason for going: a friend introduced me to it, to the fact that there is a center and it was available....

Gerald had begun attending General Program classes in July 2006, and said he had not missed a Tuesday night in the three months since he had started. He had not been to any other Buddhist centers before Chandrakirti Centre, and when we first met he had not attended any events other than the Tuesday night classes and the Stop the Week dinner. When I asked why he attended the General Program classes, Gerald responded with a list of increasingly important reasons.

> From the bottom: one, it's a social occasion, just to get away from my environment at home, which my wife encourages. I don't have any place to go so it's: one, to get out; two, intellectual stimulation; and then three, curiosity. And then it gets more profound, more profoundly stimulating intellectually, more profoundly stimulating emotionally, and more comfortable socially, as you get to know more people there. And then, once you see the effects of practicing meditation—it took a little while to adhere to. They encourage you to practice; I think it's four times a day or something like that. I don't know how long. Once you try that, you can sense the benefits, so that makes you even more profoundly interested in finding out more about it.

Gerald noted certain results from his experiences at the class which became, in turn, motivations for continuing and objectives for new learning. Later in the interview, Gerald said that his main reason for continuing to attend General Program classes was out of intellectual curiosity: he wanted to learn more about Buddhist teachings on the mind. "I'm interested in how the mind works and how it doesn't. I've been interested in that for quite a while." Initially, the class was, like any other night course, a chance to get out, to socialize, and to learn something new.

Gerald also said that he practiced meditation on his own outside the center. He said that, with attendance at the classes, his personal practice had become more rigorous. He had been very reluctant to try meditation initially. "There was a lot of resistance at first. I felt like an idiot when you sit there. And it was hard." But he believed that attending the General Program classes allowed him to become more comfortable and more familiar with the practice. Thus, the class taught more than just the principles and practices of meditation: learning also included developing a new attitude toward the practice. It also included some physical and emotional changes. Gerald believed that meditation helped him release tension and develop and maintain concentration. Describing the guided meditation sessions, he said: "They'll try to get you to remember a feeling or a situation in your life which makes you feel compassion for something. They ask you to remember when someone was good to you to try to stimulate that feeling." The objective of some of the practices, therefore, was the development of positive or beneficial emotional responses.

Among his experiences at the classes, Gerald identified several different but overlapping spheres: experiences that were intellectual, emotional, social, and physical. Each of these spheres was an important part of his motivation for coming to and continuing at Chandrakirti classes. Additionally, Gerald indicated a progression in his involvement: he described his experiences as becoming increasingly profound. This observation suggests that his experiences at Chandrakirti Centre touched him on a deeper, perhaps a spiritual level. Spirituality was not a word he used in his first interview, but he would later look back on those early experiences and describe them in spiritual terms. Initially, Gerald had spoken about applying principles that he had been testing out in his life, without having much education behind them. On an intellectual level, he wanted to learn about Buddhist teachings on the mind. Reflecting back several months later, Gerald revealed that his relationships with his teenage children were among his initial motivations for coming to Chandrakirti Centre. "It was a chance to keep the boat away from the rocks, so to speak, because with children, especially teenagers, I was getting into a lot of conflicts at home. So, I was really searching for any sort of philosophy that might give me help with being a better parent. And I was always trying to be a better person, but specifically a better parent. So, the focus for me at first was just to find a life raft."

With this hindsight, Gerald noted that he had been looking for practical solutions to certain problems, but also for insights into being a better person and parent. It is possible that he had been less conscious of his spiritual motivations for attending General Program classes when we first spoke, or less comfortable speaking about them. Perhaps longer term exposure to the classes, which frequently highlighted spirituality in Buddhist teachings, had influenced Gerald's later interpretation of his initial motivations. In any case, he had said at his first interview that he hoped Buddhist teachings on the mind would help him interpret his life situation, a motivation he later described as spiritual.

While some of Gerald's motives for participating at Chandrakirti Centre may have been spiritual, he was initially skeptical about some of the center's more religious elements, especially its rites and rituals. At his first interview, when speaking about the practice of bowing or prostrating to the teacher, he said: "I was really wary. I don't prostrate unless I really feel the need, so I went in there being very wary of the whole thing, whether I sensed that it was false; false respect: just to smell that sense of falseness, and I didn't get it from anything. And the brief introduction I've had gives me a sense of respect for the teachings, so I'm more than willing to be respectful."

Although observing prostration practice and bowing had given Gerald a sense of respect for the center and its teaching, he said that he still found some of the center's religious symbols confusing. Referring to the numerous icons on the shrines, he said: "All those little statues—I have no idea what they're for." He also said he was curious about the lifestyle of the monastics, but did not want to ask or to research it on his own. After four months attending the General Program classes, Gerald was aware that there were many things yet to learn about the religious side of Chandrakirti Centre.

The different areas of interest that had motivated Gerald to attend General Program classes—the intellectual, social, emotional, physical, and spiritual—were present to varying degrees in other respondents' reasons for participating at Friends of the Heart or Chandrakirti Centre. Some respondents spoke about wanting to gain new knowledge about Buddhism and its teachings and practices. Others wanted to change their perspectives on living, while some were very interested in Buddhist ethics or in developing concentration or other skills through meditation. We could say, therefore, that respondents were interested in new knowledge, new attitudes, and new skills, or were interested in exploring a new expression of spirituality. There were, naturally, clear overlaps between these different spheres of interest. Tanit, for example, was very interested in the practical and physical aspects of meditation practice, but her interest in meditation was primarily spiritual.

At forty-eight, Tanit was a university professor and a theater production designer. When we met, she was on sabbatical and taking some time to explore her interest in meditation. We met in November 2006 at Joyce's Healing Body, Healing Mind yoga and introductory meditation class at Friends of the Heart. Because I had also studied and worked in theater, Tanit and I shared some common ground. I told her about my research and she expressed an interest in participating in an interview. We met over lunch in December.

When I asked Tanit how she came to be participating at Friends of the Heart, she said that she had, for the past six years, been very interested in Daoism.

> My father had bought a book, *The 365 Dao*, and I thought: this looks really intriguing. And I went out and bought it. It's basically meditations for each day of the year. And I started to read it, not in a very consistent way to begin with, but if I was feeling restless or unhappy or something I'd think, oh yes I should read the Dao. And then, within the last two years I have become much more regular with it, reading it virtually every day....Certain meditations are absolutely intriguing. I became really intrigued with the fact that life is a dream and that many of the sages profess this, and that we aren't really awake. I kept thinking, so what does that mean if I'm not awake? And how come everybody comes to my class on time if we are all in a dream?

As Tanit began reading the book on Daoism more and more frequently, she began to apply its teachings and practices in her life. "One of the things that the Dao continually makes reference to is meditation," she said: "that this is really an essential part of reaching enlightenment. So, I got a book out on it [meditation]...and I found that there were many, many different types." But Tanit soon decided that reading about meditation practice was not enough. "When I was reading about meditation, it didn't have any primacy of the experience. It's words. So what you have to do is actually translate those words into movement and thinking."

On a trip to China in October of 2006, Tanit had visited several Buddhist temples. The trip inspired her. "When I came back, I thought okay: I want to learn how to meditate. It just reinforced the idea that there's a way to reach enlightenment, which is pretty exciting." At the Buddhist temples she visited, Tanit discovered that there were similarities between Buddhism and what she had learned about Daoism. "I don't think they always make a really fine distinction between what is Buddhist and what is Dao [sic]. So, for me, in my mind, they are conflated as well....They suggest very similar items, particularly meditation as being a very important part of it."[9] Before ever seeking out a meditation class, then, Tanit had learned something about meditation and certain Daoist and Buddhist concepts such as the illusory nature of ordinary life. She had also developed a strong interest in the concept of enlightenment and the possibility that she might follow certain practices to achieve that goal.

On her return from China, Tanit searched the internet for Daoist meditation centers in Toronto, and found none. Widening her search to "meditation in Toronto," she found the Friends of the Heart website. She attended the open house held in November 2006. "I liked the approach of the open house: come see if it suits you.... I liked the openness. And I also really appreciate the fact that there's a ten-week period where you can try it, see whether it works in your life." Due to a prior commitment, Tanit could not attend the introductory classes on Wednesday evenings, but someone from the center advised her to try the Thursday evening Healing Body, Healing Mind course instead. The classes began with an hour of yoga exercises, followed by an hour of meditation. The second hour was dedicated to teaching and practicing meditation. Joyce made some adjustments to the usual Thursday night session, repeating the teaching from the Wednesday night so that Tanit and other newcomers had the opportunity to learn more about insight meditation practice.

Tanit spoke primarily about her participation in the class and the different practices and techniques she was learning. She was surprised that there was considerable flexibility in the meditation postures used and that the general guideline for postures was to make oneself comfortable. "I think that was the thing that crossed my mind when we were beginning to do meditation was: am I going to be able to sit still for this long? Because I don't sit still. I move around a lot." One of the first things that Tanit learned, therefore, was that she would be able to meditate: Joyce told the class that if anyone should become uncomfortable during meditation, it was all right to change posture.

For Tanit, the practicalities of posture and technique were important elements of meditation. But meditation itself was the practical means to a primarily spiritual goal. In her first interview, she made several references to enlightenment. She was intrigued by the belief that achieving enlightenment was possible and spoke of meditation, Buddhist precepts, and the Friends of the Heart Refuge Prayer in direct relation to the goal of enlightenment.[10] Tanit was one of few student respondents who mentioned enlightenment as a personal goal. Respondents spoke more often about ethical, emotional, or practical results of meditation: stress release, developing concentration or compassion, a different outlook on the world, or a means of understanding the mind and the self. For Tanit, at least at her first interview, meditation was significant primarily as part of the path to enlightenment. She had learned through her readings on Daoism that meditation was an "essential part of reaching enlightenment." The physical practices, the development of awareness—in Tanit's perspective, all were geared to that goal. Enlightenment, as she described it, was the means of waking up, of emerging from the dream that is ordinary life.

Tanit was undoubtedly interested in the spiritual side of Buddhism and Daoism. Like Gerald, however, she was not looking for what she regarded as religion. "There is something extremely accessible about the Buddhist thinking," she said. "And I like the idea also that, in the handbook that we have, they describe Buddhism as not a religion per se. It is actually about stilling the mind and becoming more aware but it doesn't necessarily have ties to a religious ideology."[11] Like the majority of respondents, Tanit preferred to regard Buddhism as a practice or a way of life rather than a religion. Western Buddhist sympathizers often extend this worldly perspective to the ultimate goal of the tradition as well: Buddhist cosmologies linking enlightenment with the cessation of the cycle of birth and death (samsara) are less appealing to many western Buddhist sympathizers. Many are uncomfortable with concepts such as karma and rebirth, associated as they are with religious ideologies, to use Tanit's phrase.

Despite indicating some discomfort with certain Buddhist religious concepts, respondents made certain references to religion—that is, forms of spirituality institutionalized within Buddhist traditions—when discussing their motives for coming to Friends of the Heart or Chandrakirti Centre. Speaking about her reasons for attending Friends of the Heart, for example, Gwen said:

> I wasn't consciously searching for Buddhism or for spiritual practice per se....And I met Catherine. And I felt a strong pull, like I felt a strong sort of emotional pull. I wouldn't say it was even spiritual, but I don't know sometimes the difference. And then I went to the open house where I met Richard and Joyce and then I just thought I really like this, I really like this place. And I'm drawn to Buddhism over any other religion.

Although she began by saying her motivations were not spiritual or religious, Gwen concluded by saying that the religion that interested her most was Buddhism. She did, therefore, associate the center with Buddhism and Buddhism with religion.

Margaret said that the reason she went to Friends of the Heart was to learn how to meditate. "I think I was primarily looking for a method, a way to change the kind of frantic lifestyle and busyness in my head, to find some way of finding peace in the middle of chaos." She had a busy job and while she said she enjoyed the chaos, she wanted to find a way of balancing the stress that accompanied it. But she also said that she had not had a "religious-spiritual connection" in a long time, and "I feel that's something I would like to have." Margaret was to retire in a few months, and she said that finding a religious or spiritual connection was on her list of things she meant to do. Margaret thus regarded her motives for attending Friends of the Heart, at least in part, as religious or spiritual.

Bronwen, who had been introduced to Chandrakirti Centre by her father, said that she agreed to attend the classes because she wanted to find a way to improve her relationship with her stepmother. "[My father said] you can't change a person, you have to accept. He wanted me to see it from the Buddhist point of view, where you can be more compassionate to the person and still go on with what you want to do, don't stop seeing each other. But you want to try and feel for her pain...." Bronwen thus indicates that among her primary reasons for attending the General Program classes was a desire to learn about specific Buddhist teachings. Hence, among other, more practical concerns, Gwen, Margaret, and Bronwen referred to spirituality and religion as motivations for taking the meditation classes.

Another respondent who referenced the religious, among other, spheres was Marconi, one of the experienced members of Friends of the Heart. He traced his path to Buddhist practice and to Friends of the Heart through several personal crises, including two divorces. Searching for solutions to these crises, which he identified as emotional and spiritual, he became involved with several different spiritually based groups that, for various reasons, did not work out. His partner then introduced him to Friends of the Heart to what he called "the Tibetan stream, the Vajrayana stream." Despite Friends of the Heart's self-description as an eclectic center, Marconi definitely associated it with that specific Buddhist school. At the time of his interview, Marconi and his partner were attending the Monday morning Tibetan Meditation classes, the most strictly Tibetan Buddhist of the regular offerings at Friends of the Heart at that time. Marconi also emphasized the significance of the practices he followed, particularly meditation and yoga. Thus, his path into Buddhist practice also involved the physical, spiritual, emotional, and religious spheres.

Like Tanit, several respondents traced their interest in either Buddhism or meditation back to the discovery of a book or other materials on Asian religion or philosophy. Nearly half of all student respondents indicated that what they had read about Buddhism, meditation, or other eastern religions or philosophies had been an important motivation for seeking out a meditation course. Their readings also constituted an important part of their overall learning. If they learned about Buddhism as a world tradition, about its history and its diverse schools, it was primarily through reading books or conducting internet research. Friends of the Heart and Chandrakirti meditation classes, by design, did not provide much factual data about Buddhism. Chandrakirti classes included considerable detail on

Buddhist teachings, but the emphasis was more on ethics and applying those ethics in contemporary Canadian life rather than factual, historical details about Buddhist traditions. Describing what she learned at General Program classes, Carol said: "Initially I really felt it was Buddhist thought, but they really focus on practical applications of Buddhist thought." Carol, in fact, was another participant who had initially become interested in Buddhism by reading various books.

CAROL

Strictly speaking, Carol was not a newcomer at Chandrakirti Centre. She had been attending classes at the center on and off for seven years. I wanted to interview her primarily because, after all of her years at the center, she was still attending the introductory classes, choosing not to move on to any of the higher level programs. As a volunteer at the center, she was knowledgeable about its operations and kind enough to answer many of my questions, in addition to participating in an interview.

Carol was fifty-six and had a background in nursing. She had been raised in a Baptist church when she was growing up. As a teenager, she took the baptismal classes required prior to making a full commitment to the tradition. When the classes concluded, however, she could not make that commitment. "I couldn't do it. It didn't sit right with me.... Thinking back now, I think it was pretty amazing. Usually, I would have just complied. That's when I really pulled away from my religious upbringing." For several years after that, Carol said, "I just backed off from religion, that type of religion, altogether. It just wasn't an issue."

I asked Carol when she had first taken an interest in Buddhism. She replied:

> I guess I was in my thirties. I had just started having a small family. And I just started reading. I was interested in Asian cultures; I had some kind of affinity to those kinds of things. But I didn't get in to that, except very superficially. That had pleasing aesthetics, pleasing ideas, et cetera. So, I just started reading, initially about cultural things and then that progressed. I can't remember the first Buddhist book.... Suzuki, the Japanese monk that came over first and started the San Francisco Zen Centre.... That might have been the first.

Carol then read several more books on Zen and developed a strong interest in the arts and culture of Japan. She said she found the simplicity of the Zen aesthetic most appealing. She had not been involved with any kind of Buddhist practice at that time, however. "It was just really reading." Her readings did introduce her to Zen concepts, however, and she said that Zen spoke to her more than her previous religious education had. Eventually, she started looking for somewhere to practice.

> I thought, well, I want to find out more about meditation. I went to the Zen Centre here, actually [in Toronto's west end]. It's not far from the old Chandrakirti Centre. And I had young kids at the time, and time constraints prevented me from doing something personally, for myself. Fitting all of that in was challenging. So, I really continued to read and do sporadic meditation.

Years would pass before Carol once again decided to go to a Buddhist center. She eventually came across a flyer for Chandrakirti Centre and, she said, "I liked the idea of classes. At the Zen center, the times I went anyways, it was more just meditation. I kind of wanted some direction: more direction and discussion and that kind of thing. So, that's why the Chandrakirti Centre worked out for me." Hence Carol's primary motive for going to the center was to learn, to take part in a class where she would gain some formal instruction in addition to practicing meditation. Carol's process of turning to and learning about Buddhist practices and teachings had several key turning points. Beginning with an intellectual curiosity and emotional attraction to eastern cultures, she became fascinated by Zen aesthetics and concepts. She then became interested in meditation practice. Eventually she encountered Chandrakirti Centre, where she was attracted by its focus on Buddhist teachings and applied Buddhist ethics. She stressed that hearing the teachings at General Program classes was her main formal practice, although she also practiced meditation on her own. Her path to participation at Chandrakirti thus touched on several broad spheres of interest, from the cognitive through the emotional, physical, and spiritual.

After some time at the center, many Chandrakirti members move on from the introductory classes to the higher level education programs. Carol instead continued to attend the introductory class, primarily due to other commitments. She had some interest in the Foundation Program, but for years it was offered on Sunday, the day Carol set aside for time with her family. While her primary involvement at the center continued to be at the Tuesday evening General Program classes, she did take part in some empowerments (ritual initiations) and retreats, in addition to working at the center as a volunteer. Carol was not overly concerned that she had not moved on to higher level classes. She believed that she continued to benefit from the General Program classes, even when the topics were repeated.

> It's interesting, because, with Zopa, often he would do a series and then that series would get repeated to a certain extent. And I thought: Oh dear, same old, same old. But I realize now, and obviously he improved over time, because he

talks about the first time he talked. But there was always something new, another discussion and other things. And just his presentation [was appealing]. And, I'm a slow learner; I needed it to be repeated over and over. To let it sink in.

Here Carol reveals something interesting about attending the General Program course: each time the same topic came up, new things arose; new discussions took place that became new learning experiences. Repetition also helped Carol learn the topics better as she heard them over and over. Repetition of the class topics itself is comparable to the repetitive performance of a ritual. Ron G. Williams and James W. Boyd, in their study of a Zoroastrian fire ceremony, argue that the very means of learning something new from a ritual is its repetition, the fact that it is performed without variance. They compare this process to appreciating a classic piece of artwork or music: with each new encounter with the same piece, the viewer or listener discovers something new, something that, like a steady but far-off horizon, draws one ever onward to newer and deeper understandings.[12] General Program classes are less rigidly structured and more variable than the kinds of rituals Williams and Boyd discuss, but combined with their insights, Carol's description suggests an almost-ritualistic element to the repetition of topics at the classes. Repetition, she suggested, improved her learning.

Alan, who also attended the Chandrakirti General Program classes, said something similar. He said he was still learning, even after attending the class for over a year and hearing many of the same topics discussed. "It's the same message, really. You evolve each time you're practicing these things. Suddenly I notice I've moved a little bit forward from what they said a year ago. I hear it again and think about it in a different way now."

ALAN

At sixty-five, Alan was a menswear retailer who owned a shop in Toronto's Yorkville district. We first met at a Tuesday evening General Program class and chatted afterward over tea and cookies in the basement common room. Alan often attended the classes with his daughter, Bronwen. Father and daughter both took part in interviews. Alan and I had our interview in a park not far from his shop in May of 2007.

Alan had grown up in England, in an environment in which he said religion did not play a large role. "Coming from a working-class background, church really didn't fit in to your life. It was there, but it was really more for other people than it would be for yourself. I was confused by that," he said. When I asked Alan what had brought him to Chandrakirti Centre, he replied: "Basically, I've always been interested in the idea that there's something else other than just means and ends." His interests, then, leaned toward the spiritual, that which transcends everyday concerns. Alan became interested in Buddhism after his wife had introduced him to *Siddha* Yoga. "A couple of times I took a meditation course. But I didn't like the structure there. There's still a god. I didn't like the god thing.... That's never sat well with me." Like several other respondents, then, certain religious elements—in this case, theism—were of less interest to Alan.

About a year prior to our interview, Alan had seen a sign for a meditation class offered through Chandrakirti Centre at a church in his neighborhood. Intrigued, he began attending that class regularly. Eventually, the class was cancelled due to low attendance, so Alan sought out the main center on Crawford Street. The course appealed to him, he said, because of its focus on happiness. "I've always been fascinated by the Buddhist idea. Typically you hear about Buddhists because things will pass over them, they'll let things go.... [At the class] they seemed to talk about happiness. And I thought: you know, I don't think I'm very happy. It hadn't really occurred to me about not being happy." The teachings on happiness made Alan realize that, for years, he had regarded his business as his only pursuit. "You're tied to that. There's a structure and it's debt or profit." The possibility of pursuing happiness apart from the success of his business had not occurred to him until he took the class. "The idea of being nonmaterialistic has always been counter to my thinking," he said. Alan learned that the Buddhist perspective advocated "not hanging on but letting go of materialism." The General Program lectures introduced him to some new ideas. "You're not going to be happy until you stop thinking about yourself and be unattached. I thought: well, that's a switch. It means going in another direction."

Alan spoke about his motivations for attending General Program classes almost entirely in terms of the ideas and concepts he was learning. Learning meditation techniques was part of the class, but Alan viewed meditation more as a means to achieve the transformations he sought. He said he had been meditating before he attended the General Program classes, in the yoga style he had learned, but Chandrakirti classes gave him a new outlook on the practice. He had thought meditation was about blocking out thoughts, but now regarded it as a means of working on oneself, of "moving forward," as he put it. "It's about working on merit, as they say. I like that idea."

Merit (*punya* in Sanskrit) refers to "karmic fruitfulness,"[13] a kind of storehouse of positive energy that is believed to be generated through meditation, prostrations, prayers, offerings, and adherence to Buddhist ethics. In Mahayana and Tibetan schools, it is common to dedicate the merit one gains through practice to others. Historically, laypersons would gain merit through *dāna*, generosity or almsgiving, or perhaps through reciting or distributing scriptures. At both Friends of the Heart and Chandrakirti Centre, it was understood that participants accrued merit through all practices, including prayers, offerings, prostrations, listening to or participating in talks and discussions, and meditation. I was interested to discover that many of my participants readily accepted the idea of merit as a kind of beneficial energy that accumulated through practice and was then dedicated to the benefit of all beings. Merit was a frequent theme in General Program lectures, and many Chandrakirti students described it as a common element of their practice. Several Friends of the Heart students also accepted this idea. Tanit, for example, appreciated the fact that the merit prayer always concluded with a gesture symbolizing the dedication of merit to others: "I love the fact that it ends opening up the hands for merit, letting the energy flow out, and it's so fantastic." Studies of Buddhism in the contemporary West often characterize adoptive Buddhists and Buddhist sympathizers as being uninterested in the accumulation and dedication of merit found in more long-standing expressions of Buddhism. I found, however, that many of my interview participants had accepted the idea, including a significant number of newcomers. Some newcomers had accommodated merit dedication into their personal practice.

Alan's appreciation for the concept of merit indicates that he regarded the outcome of his involvement as spiritual, something that went beyond what he called "means and ends," the day-to-day, materialistic concerns of his business life. From his earliest experiences at the General Program class, he said, he had discovered a new ethical perspective: new ways of looking at the world and of transforming his life. While Alan's learning objectives and outcomes included gaining new information and meditation skills, they were oriented more toward developing new values and attitudes.

DIANE

Like Alan, Diane was interested in finding ways to change her outlook and her way of life. At fifty-nine, Diane was a semi-retired former civil servant and another respondent who discovered Friends of the Heart via the internet. We met at Joyce's Introduction to Insight course and at the Tibetan Meditation classes conducted by Catherine Rathbun in 2006 and 2007. Diane told me that she had been interested in Buddhist teachings, but the "in," as she put it, was meditation. From her interview, however, it seemed that Buddhist concepts had equally inspired her to become involved at Buddhist centers.

Diane had encountered the work of a woman called Byron Katie, who teaches a method for discovering one's essential nature and a sense of no self. Diane said, "I got a copy of a book of hers and have gone to a couple of workshops that she has done." But Diane did not understand some of Katie's ideas. "She would write ... about having no self and the world being a projection and nothing having inherent reality. And I thought: What the hell is all of this? And then I was interested in meditation and I started hearing some of the same things." Having determined that there was a connection between Byron Katie's writings and certain Buddhist concepts, Diane decided to find out more about Buddhism.

Diane then attended some talks at Snow Lion, the Buddhist bookshop where several Friends of the Heart teachers had made public presentations. She said that the talks helped her understand some of the concepts she had found confusing. Following that, she enrolled in two adult-education courses, one in world religions and the other in philosophy. "I knew what I was interested in had something to do with religions and philosophy, but I didn't know what exactly. But it was more along the lines of: Who am I? What am I doing here? What is the meaning of life?" Throughout her interview, Diane often noted that she had an intellectual or cognitive interest in Buddhist concepts, but that she was also seeking answers to spiritual questions. She found that the academic courses did not offer the answers she sought. "I dropped those two courses," she said, "and just started going to two different Buddhist centers. I go to Friends of the Heart and I go to another place called Atisha in the Beaches." Diane first attended the November 2006 open house at Friends of the Heart and then enrolled in its Introduction to Insight course. At the same time, she began attending General Program classes at Atisha Centre. Atisha is another Toronto-area NKT center and is considered to be Chandrakirti's sister center. Atisha's class structure and content follow NKT guidelines and are similar to Chandrakirti's. Shortly after those classes started, Diane learned about the Friends of the Heart Tibetan Meditation class on Monday mornings and began attending that as well. She said she did not want to divide her time between two different centers, but found she was interested in both the meditation instruction at Friends of the Heart, and the Buddhist teachings at Atisha Centre. Although she was less engaged by the chanted prayer services and empowerments performed at the Friends of the Heart Tibetan Meditation course, she was impressed by teacher Catherine Rathbun and continued attending that class until Catherine left in May of 2007.

I asked Diane why she was interested in Buddhism, and she replied: "Buddhism is the closest philosophy that I feel I can identify with and [I] really want to live my life according to those kinds of principles. ... It feels like there are more answers about meaning in Buddhism than I have had in any other place." Diane had been raised Catholic, and, like Gerald and Carol, had fallen away from her family's church. "I'm not into any kind of dogma," she said. "I was raised Catholic and I was turned off to organized religion." Despite this view, Diane said: "Buddhism really appealed to me." As noted earlier, many western Buddhist sympathizers, including some long-term practitioners, often declare that they do not like organized religion—even some who are involved at a Buddhist center following structured teachings and practices and participating in various rituals. This apparent contradiction is another indication that many westerners do not regard Buddhism as a religion. Diane plainly understood it instead as a philosophy or way of life.

Diane's involvement at Buddhist centers began due to an interest in meditation, but by the time we spoke, she was most intrigued by the teachings she heard, particularly those at Atisha Centre. When I asked which teachings appealed to her, she replied:

> Well, to start with, at the most basic level it's the concept that everyone has a Buddha inside. It's so different from the original sin concept....It's a very different approach. Your job, then, is to uncover the blockages and allow that Buddha to shine forth. I really, really like that. I like the teachings around the noble path: right thinking, right behaviors. And [at Buddhist centers] people seem to live that.

Throughout our conversation, Diane made connections between her understanding of religion and what she learned and experienced at Friends of the Heart and Atisha Centre. Sometimes she contrasted the two, as she did when speaking about Buddhist teachings and the concept of original sin. At the same time, she was intrigued by historical Buddhist doctrines such as the eightfold path and the Buddhist precepts. Because such doctrines were new to her, however, she had no reason to identify them with religion per se. But there were times when she encountered elements she did associate with organized religion at Friends of the Heart and Atisha Centre. When speaking about the possibility of becoming more involved at Atisha Centre, she said: "You know, there's a part of me that wants to hold back, because of my experience in religion, being raised in a very authoritarian Catholic environment. I'm always kind of questioning. At the Atisha Centre, all of the books are written only by the one guy, Geshe-la. And I'm thinking: okay, they only have this one guy; it's too god-like for me. But I have been looking at the books on the shelf and I might open some next time." Where Diane did associate her experiences at the centers with religion, she was clearly uncomfortable. This discomfort extended to the more formal practices at the Friends of the Heart Tibetan Meditation class.

> I'm a little concerned that it's too ritualistic for me. You know, the beads and the chanting. It just evokes in me: Catholic Church, the rosary beads. You know, when I was a kid, it was all in Latin, and this seems to me just a different language.

You know, it's the same...feeling. I'm not sure. It may be that that's a blockage that I have and that may open up. I certainly like Catherine and feel very warm and open towards her and that's why I'm coming. I'm just not sure about some of the practices.

These reflections on religion and ritual once again underscore the "adoptive" or convert experience: a need to find a spiritual affiliation that is familiar enough to be welcoming and yet different enough from earlier experiences that the practitioner now regards as negative. While Diane is uncomfortable with religious symbols and devotional practices because they remind her of her Catholic upbringing, it is interesting that she has chosen to attend two Tibetan-based centers, in a city where numerous more secularized and less overtly ritualized options are available. It is possible that the colorful ritual symbolism at Friends of the Heart and Atisha Centre—the very elements she is consciously wary of—may actually provide an unconscious sense of familiarity.

Before coming to Friends of the Heart and Atisha Centre, Diane had learned about Buddhist teachings and practices from a few different sources. In addition to the Byron Katie material and the talks at Snow Lion, ten years earlier she had taken another meditation course. It was based on the teachings of Jon Kabat-Zinn, a western teacher and author who created a secularized system of teaching meditation called Mindfulness Based Stress Reduction. But while she was working full time, Diane was unable to keep up the practice she learned at that course.

> When I was doing the course I did meditate, but I found my job was very, very stressful and I found that with the job I could be a mother, I could be a daughter (both my parents were ill) and I could have that job, but there was nothing else in my life. There was no room for meditation. It was just caring for my kids, caring for my parents, and doing my job. And I felt my soul was dying. I didn't have time for meditation and so I just felt that my soul was dying in that job.... [Then] there came a point in my life where my kids had left home, off to university, and I was no longer happy in the job that I was doing. I decided to leave it. You know, these questions: Who am I? were coming up. And it just seems like it converged with this Byron Katie and then her observations about not attaching to the goal and being selfless. So, that's really what brought me into the Buddhist part of it. I was trying to understand, conceptually, any sort of a philosophical framework, too, for living.

Diane felt a strong desire to find a spiritual path for transforming her life. This desire combined with an interest in meditation and a strong intellectual curiosity about Buddhist concepts. She was motivated to continue, especially at Atisha Centre, mainly out of an interest in learning more: that is, in gaining new knowledge. Several times in her interview she said that she preferred the intellectual side of what she was learning. She sometimes conceded that her spiritual needs were not satisfied by strictly cognitive learning, but insisted that she was "a head person" and needed more cognitive understanding than what she called experiential learning in the meditation class. Even so, the intellectual, experiential, and spiritual were all factors in Diane's motives for attending introductory classes at Friends of the Heart and Atisha Centre. Beginning with an interest in meditation and a need to find out who she was, she became more interested in gaining new knowledge about Buddhist teachings.

Intellectual curiosity, a spiritual quest, and emotional attractions to Buddhism or to Asian philosophy or cultures: Many respondents, like Diane, indicated an array of different reasons for attending introductory meditation classes. Some respondents, however, were strictly interested in learning how to meditate. John was one.

JOHN

John was taking the same Introduction to Insight class as Diane and I at Friends of the Heart, beginning in November of 2006. When John and I met for an interview in February of 2007, the class was coming to an end. John introduced me to a downtown coffee shop where, he said, the poor quality of the coffee would ensure a quiet environment for our interview. He was right.

At age sixty, John was retired from his former careers as a teacher and a systems analyst. His interest in meditation began when he was in his twenties. At that time, and occasionally over the years since, he had read some books on meditation and relaxation. When he retired in his late fifties his interest rekindled. "This seemed like a good time to get back to it," he said. He first discovered a Toronto-area group called Spring Rain Sangha that met weekly at a Presbyterian church, but found that the group was rather advanced. There was little instruction and the meditation sessions were forty-five minutes long. John said he needed to find something at an introductory level. He heard about Kabat-Zinn's Mindfulness Based Stress Reduction course, which was being offered at the Toronto General Hospital, but that course would not begin for a few months, so John decided to look for another group in the meantime. He found information online about Friends of the Heart and went to the open house in November 2006. He started attending the Introduction to Insight course immediately following that open house. By January 2007, he was also participating in the Kabat-Zinn program at the hospital.

John made it clear that his primary interest was meditation. When I asked if he had any interest in Buddhism, he said only that he was a little curious about the symbolic objects in the Friends of the Heart shrine room. "I suppose it would be interesting just to have someone who sort of knew all the details about the statuary and the symbols on a lot of things," he said. Despite this curiosity, he had not asked about the objects on the shrine, focusing instead on learning meditation techniques and practices. He mentioned that he had once encountered another group, one that he found to be "very, very Buddhist." From his description, it may have been a General Program class conducted through Chandrakirti or Atisha Centre. "There was very little of a sit involved and an awful lot more listening to real Buddhist theology, really. He [the teacher] talked a lot about reincarnation, things like that." These teachings did not appeal to John. He went to Friends of the Heart looking for meditation practice rather than religion or spirituality. I asked John if he came from a religious background, and he replied: "No. Not particularly anti-religious. My parents were churchgoers, United churchgoers. I went to Sunday school as a kid." Unlike others I spoke with, John had no particular discomfort with or objection to the religious elements he encountered at Friends of the Heart, but he was not particularly interested in them, either. "I would not be going to a Buddhist temple to become a Buddhist or to join a congregation," he said.

When I asked John why he attended the Friends of the Heart meditation course, he said, "Well, certainly an anti-stress component, the relaxation component, that sort of thing." John disclosed that he had an arthritic condition called *ankylosing spondylitis* which causes excess growth of bone in the spine. "So, your spine ends up pretty stiff. And the trick is to keep yourself stiff and upright.... So that, I suppose, has been a factor in whatever I do, in terms of physical movement.... This is like a "move it or lose it" type of arthritis, so I do a lot of stretching exercises. Any type of relaxation, anti-stress, is great for that type of arthritis; it really keeps your pain level under control." The Friends of the Heart meditation class included some *qi gong* and yoga exercises, and John said that some exercises were helpful for his condition, but that some yoga postures were difficult. At that point, he mentioned that he had taken some t'ai chi classes for about a year. I asked him how meditation, apart from its stress-reduction component, affected his condition. "It's sort of neutral physically, the actual meditation part," he said. "I seem to be noticing more of a connection between meditation and mood, possibly, but not between meditation and anything physical." With reference to the erect posture used in meditation, John said: "It doesn't hurt. That is a good posture, certainly, to be in. I should be trying to keep [that posture]."

Despite his earlier learning about Buddhist-related topics, John said he had not explored much about Buddhism itself, its history, or its doctrines. Nor was that kind of learning of interest to him, before or during the classes. His learning objectives at Friends of the Heart were focused strictly on developing skills that promoted stress release and possibly pain reduction. Despite some experience with Buddhist and other Asian practices, John had not developed an interest in eastern spirituality or religions.

Two other respondents from Friends of the Heart enrolled in its introductory classes strictly to learn how to meditate. Erin, a thirty-year-old sales representative for a clothing company, was looking for ways to reduce the stress that came with her job. Like John, she was somewhat curious about Buddhism. She had done some research on the internet and had read two books by Vietnamese monk Thich Nhat Hanh, but her main goals at the course were to learn different meditation techniques and to develop the skills to maintain a meditation practice. Erin had initially been attracted to Friends of the Heart because its website did not emphasize the fact that it was a Buddhist center. "For me, it was much more about the meditation than it was about Buddhism." She said: "My main reason for wanting to go to meditation classes and learn how to meditate . . . , I would say the number one reason is stress. I just wanted to reduce my stress. My job is pretty demanding and I feel like I work a lot and I bring that upon myself as well. So, I just wanted to be able to have a way to get away from that." Erin's learning objectives, therefore, were more practical than spiritual or intellectual. She wanted to gain skills that could help her manage her stress, but was not particularly interested in Buddhist values or ethics.

The other respondent interested solely in meditation was Dennis, a financial analyst who was thirty-three years old. He said "I play a lot of poker and a lot of poker players meditate to help their poker game. So that was the very first thing that piqued my interest. And I went through a little while where I had trouble sleeping at night, so I thought I would give it a try." A year prior to coming to Friends of the Heart, Dennis had taken a three-hour meditation class at a Toronto-area yoga center, but was now looking for a more comprehensive course. Dennis said he knew nothing about Buddhism, nor was he particularly interested. For respondents like John, Erin, and Dennis, then, there was a clear distinction between meditation practice and Buddhism.

WHY TAKE A MEDITATION CLASS?

Learning to meditate, therefore, was one among a range of different motivations for taking a meditation class. Six of eleven Friends of the Heart students interviewed, and two of eight from Chandrakirti Centre, said that learning meditation was their initial motivation for participating at the centers. From Friends of the Heart, Tanit, Diane, John, Margaret, Dennis, and Erin claimed that meditation was the main reason they enrolled. Diane, Tanit, and Margaret also expressed certain spiritual objectives among their learning goals. Although she had been originally interested in eastern arts and cultures, Carol was one Chandrakirti respondent who said that she initially went to the center primarily to learn meditation. Brenda was the other. Like John and Diane, Brenda had taken the Kabat-Zinn meditation course, but when she first came to Chandrakirti Centre it was to attend a prayer service. She quickly developed an interest in the teachings and the more spiritual practices taught at the center. At the time of our interview, she said she rarely practiced meditation. She said that her primary practice was to be patient and compassionate and to wish well-being to others, a practice called *metta* or loving-kindness. "One can turn one's whole life into a meditation," Brenda said. "It's about being in the moment and being respectful and about seeing the beauty that lives in the world." Other Chandrakirti respondents, including Gerald, Carol, and Alan said that meditation was part of their practice, but they gave a wider variety of reasons for initially attending Chandrakirti Centre: curiosity about the applicability of Buddhist teachings to every day life, an interest in Buddhist teachings on the mind, an attraction to eastern cultures, a desire to learn about Buddhist practice and principles, or a search for happiness and detachment. Those whose were primarily interested in meditation most often spoke about what they learned at the classes in terms of meditation postures and techniques. Those interested in Buddhism or in spirituality more often spoke about the changes in attitude, values, and behavior that resulted from the classes. There is an indication, therefore, that students' initial motivations for attending corresponded to what they said they took away from the classes.

We can see that a noticeable trend emerged from interview participants' stated reasons for attending the classes, a trend that distinguished Friends of the Heart participants from those at Chandrakirti Centre. Most respondents taking the Friends of the Heart meditation class indicated that their primary reason for participating at the center was to learn and practice meditation. Fewer indicated that an interest in learning about Buddhism or its teachings was foremost among their motivations. While most respondents from Chandrakirti introductory class were interested in meditation, and many meditated at the center and at home, most indicated an interest in Buddhist teachings as their primary motivation for attending General Program classes. This trend, in fact, reflects the different approaches of the two centers. At Friends of the Heart, introductory classes were structured to teach meditation first and foremost. There were some teachings on Buddhist ethics, but direct references to Buddhism were minimal. Students spent much of the time meditating or discussing their meditation experiences. At Chandrakirti Centre, introductory classes usually began and ended with meditation sessions, but much of the class time was dedicated to lectures and discussions on Buddhist ethics and worldviews. One might conclude from this trend that respondents found whatever it was that they were looking for, that their objectives and expectations for coming to Friends of the Heart or Chandrakirti Centre were fulfilled by the course content they encountered. Conversely, one might speculate that respondents, who had been participating at the centers for some time when they were interviewed, assessed their initial motives and interests in light of the learning they had experienced there.

Both centers' introductory-level classes were advertised as meditation classes, even at Chandrakirti Centre with its lecture-style approach. The following description of the General Program course appeared on Chandrakirti Centre's website: "Chandrakirti KMCC offers introductory meditation classes throughout the GTA [Greater Toronto Area]. Each class includes a simple breathing meditation, a short talk on Buddhist thought, and a concluding meditation. There is also time to ask questions and discuss."[14] While this description of the General Program class was accurate, in my experience the main event in the class in terms of time spent was the talk followed by questions and discussion. Meditation sessions were brief and less time was given to teaching, discussing or practicing meditation techniques than at Friends of the Heart. Because the classes were advertised primarily as meditation classes, it is possible that Chandrakirti Centre did, in fact, attract more people initially seeking meditation instruction than indicated in the interview material. Both Alan and Carol, it seemed, first came to Chandrakirti Centre after finding its advertisements for meditation classes, although they indicated other equally important motivations for enrolling. Even so, both indicated that it was only after they participated at the classes that the teachings on Buddhist principles began to interest them more than meditation itself. Diane, who was taking courses at Friends of the Heart and at Chandrakirti's sister center, spoke about both meditation and Buddhist concepts among her interests, although she did say that meditation was her first interest. It is possible, then, that respondents expressed their most recent experiences when reflecting upon their preexisting interests.

Nevertheless, participants at both centers probably would have remained only if they felt that the teachings matched their initial learning goals. Those who found that the introductory classes were unsuited to their initial interests and expectations would not have stayed around long enough to be interviewed. Newcomers were coming and going all the time, especially at Chandrakirti Centre where students could attend weekly or just occasionally, rather than enrolling for several weeks up front. John, as an example, had encountered what might have been a General Program class once, and because of its emphasis on Buddhist religious teachings—what he called theology—he did not go back. Diane became more interested in the teachings at Atisha Centre and left Friends of the Heart at the end of her trial membership. Moreover, both centers offered different options for meditation versus teaching. For a time Chandrakirti Centre offered a class called Stress Factor Zero, which focused on meditation practice, although it also included some teaching. During fieldwork for this study, however, that course was sporadic and had a very small attendance. None of the interview participants had enrolled in that class. At Friends of the Heart, the Monday morning Tibetan Meditation class offered much more on Buddhist teachings and included more formal practices such as chanted prayers. Friends of the Heart respondents who did not indicate meditation among their initial motivations for participating at the center—Anna, Nicolette, David, and Marconi—attended that class. Gwen, who worked on Monday mornings, was the only respondent initially motivated by an interest in Buddhism and spirituality who did not attend that class. While interview responses about their earlier motives may have been influenced to some extent by experiences at the courses, both centers' participants had enough choice that they were able to select organizations and classes that appealed most to their needs and expectations.

From respondents' stories of turning to Buddhism or to meditation practice emerges a picture of several connected spheres of interest: intellectual, emotional, practical, physical, spiritual, and religious. These elements are significant because many of the same descriptors correspond to the different means of teaching and learning at Friends of the Heart and Chandrakirti classes such as lectures, meditation, discussion groups, and so on. That is, respondents' motivations for attending classes and their initial learning goals fell into categories that also corresponded to the different means and types of learning that took place at the two centers. The various means and types of learning are explored in chapters 3 and 4, respectively.

As we can see from the discovery stories above, participants' perspectives on religion in general had some influence on their acceptance of Buddhist teachings and practices. A significant number of respondents had ambiguous or negative views about religion, what many termed "organized religion." One of the very reasons that some people participate at westernized Buddhist centers is because, like Diane, they have moved away from a religious tradition in which they were raised and were seeking something else. Brenda, for example, had a colorful way of describing her involvement at Chandrakirti Centre in contrast to her perspectives on Judeo-Christian doctrine.

You go to this amazing place, you listen to this ancient, two and a half thousand year old teacher who busted his you know what to figure this stuff out, didn't lay on you that it has all to do with some beastly bloody god who's going to judge you and if you're not a really good person you're going to burn in hell. You know, there's none of that. None of that nasty stuff. Mind you, I think that the wheel of life and multiple rebirths is a much a scarier place than being sent into purgatory. I think it's much scarier. That you have to keep doing this?

Although she felt it was "scarier" than Christian conceptions of hell and purgatory, Brenda at least provisionally accepted Buddhist rebirth cosmology. In that, she differed from most respondents. The interesting thing is that some early Buddhist teachings, as well as some contemporary Buddhist schools, actually do reference hell-realms and ghost-states into which beings with negative karmic conditions are believed to be born. Adoptive Buddhists and sympathizers, however, usually receive a selective version of such teachings. When they do learn about hell-realms and hungry ghosts, the concepts are often taken metaphorically or psychologically. The founder of the westernized Shambhala Buddhist organization, Chögyam Trungpa, for instance, was famous for offering such interpretations of the different realms of rebirth, comparing them to emotions or psychological states.[15] By contrast, sometimes western teachers and students simply dismiss rebirth and hell-realms as Asian cultural accretions that are not essential to the heart of Buddhism.

Previous experiences with religious traditions may influence a person's overall conceptions of what constitutes spirituality. Diane told me that when she attended the Friends of the Heart Tibetan Meditation class, she always asked herself why we were performing certain practices and, as she put it, "How is this different from Jesus?" I asked her: "Is it important that it's different from Jesus?" She replied, "No, and it's kind of interesting because I feel I'm a little bit reconnecting with Jesus. Because I always like him, but I kind of let everything go when I was letting religion go, it all went, because it all seem to me to be a package." Similarly, Tanit said, "I had my experience with Catholicism, and it had not been of the most joyful order. So, I had not had a lot of interest in that kind of spiritual experience. And, you're right; I tend to attach it to: spiritual, Catholicism, not good, not interesting." Preconceptions about ritual and religion, therefore, have a strong influence on what Buddhist sympathizers are attracted to, and what they find surprising or disconcerting when they begin to learn more about the tradition. People like Diane and Tanit are evidently looking for spirituality, but have a strong desire to separate it from their earlier conceptions of religion. Such attitudes account for the desire to regard Buddhism as nontheistic, demythologized, and nonritualistic.

The prevalence of such attitudes among adoptive Buddhists and sympathizers thus tells us something about what they expect to find when they go to a Buddhist center. Many are looking for something different from their previous religious experience, something they can regard as nonreligious and nonritualistic. These attitudes indicate the necessity for Buddhist centers' organizers to adapt to meet the needs and expectations of their anticipated audiences. The fact that many potential meditation students would rather participate at a center that has no Buddhist or religious elements puts some teachers of western sympathizers in an awkward position. As suggested above, some people may find ceremony and symbolism familiar and welcoming, while others may be put off. Organizers must therefore decide on how much Buddhist symbolism, rites, and religious teachings they will reveal or conceal in order to attract new participants. While teachers at both Friends of the Heart and Chandrakirti Centre have adapted to some of the expectations of their western students, both centers retain a primarily Buddhist orientation. For many participants, this is not a problem. Others choose not to stay.

A key motivation for participating at the meditation centers is yet to be discussed: the desire to be part of a community. I asked respondents whether they thought it was important to practice with a group or to meditate in the company of others. Significantly, many of them replied using the same language, referring to the impact of participating with "like-minded individuals." Gwen, for example, said, "I just like to come together with like-minded, like-hearted people who are close enough on the same path that I feel nourished by it." Diane agreed: "I need a place to be where there are other like-minded people." Brenda, Alan, Anna, and Margaret also used the exact phrase "like-minded people" when discussing reasons why they participated at the centers or why the community at the centers was important. Several other respondents, including Carol, Marconi, and Gerald, expressed similar sentiments in different language. The frequency with which such sentiments were expressed suggests that being involved with others who had the same interests was a strong motivation for respondents to seek out and continue participating at Friends of the Heart or Chandrakirti Centre.

Few respondents had much contact with Buddhist sympathizers, those like-minded individuals, before stepping through the centers' doors. The fact that Gerald first attended a Buddhist center with a friend makes him a bit of an outlier among western Buddhist sympathizers. The majority of such people find their way to Buddhist centers on their own: few have friends or family members involved with Buddhist teachings or practices. Several respondents had friends or acquaintances who had at one time introduced them to meditation or Buddhist teachings, but most came alone to Friends of the Heart or Chandrakirti Centre. It was also rare to see family members participating together. Respondents Margaret and Marconi attended Friends of the Heart classes with their respective partners and Alan had introduced his daughter Bronwen to Chandrakirti Centre, and later, his wife. Friends of the Heart teachers interviewed included Joyce and Richard, a married couple. Friends of the Heart had been recommended to Gwen by another member, but Gwen first went to the center on her own. Catherine H., the one respondent whose family was Buddhist, sometimes participated at her family's Chinese Buddhist temple, but she started attending Chandrakirti Centre on her own. She later introduced her friend Brenda, another interview participant, and they attended together for a time. Of twenty-four total interview participants, then, only nine had originally come to Friends of the Heart or Chandrakirti Centre in the company of a friend or family member.

Coming with someone else to a Buddhist center or meditation group is, therefore, not crucial: being with others is. As Diane put it, "No one in my close circle is on the same path that I'm on," she said, "and so that's the other thing, I guess, is that I like being around people who are on the same kind of path. I can learn from them." Being involved with people who understood and shared their perspectives was clearly important for most respondents. Anna said, "I would say that I can find spiritual experiences anywhere. This just happens to be with like-minded people, that if I share what I visualize or experience in other ways, that they are open to it." Friends of the Heart thus provided an environment in which Anna felt she could safely share her experiences with others who would understand.

Shared understanding and experiences constitute one reason for the importance of a community. Another, as Gerald had pointed out, was the opportunity to socialize. It was, in fact, among his initial reasons for attending the General Program class. He found Chandrakirti Centre to be a warm and welcoming place. As a result, he continued even after the friend who introduced him to the center stopped participating. One of the Chandrakirti volunteers had made a lasting impression on Gerald when he first arrived. "She was so welcoming that it made you feel good and it made you feel you want to be there. So that was a good starting point right at the door." As noted, much of the socializing at Chandrakirti Centre took place following the classes in the basement common room. Gerald said:

> After the meditation, you're encouraged and invited to go downstairs and have snacks, usually cookies—delicious cookies, actually. Sometimes I think I go there for the cookies....And you can sit around in a nice environment and usually about half or a third will sit down and the teachers will sit there too and you can ask them anything you want, whether it's about the lecture that night or anything in particular.

Alan said something similar. "There's something about being in the center. . . . There's a little community afterwards, when you go downstairs. You can talk, or if you wanted to speak to the monk or the nun, you can do that." Socializing thus offers additional opportunities to learn, through informal discussions. For Bronwen, socializing offered the opportunity simply to meet and engage with others. "I love being with people because I live on my own," she said, "and it's a time to indulge a bit in the socializing after, just even the different age groups, just to meet people and explore other's lives and see what they're doing."

Being with like-minded people, however, did not necessarily mean seeking out a new social group. While nearly all participants indicated that it was important to practice with a group, some made it clear that they were not looking to socialize. Diane said that it was important to be in the company of others who were interested in the same subjects as she was. "But," she said, "I don't need to go to the center for a group of friends, if you know what I mean. I don't see that as the center of my social life. . . . The whole experience for me is the meditative one, so I haven't been particularly social [or] wanting to get to know people." John said that it was "nice to get out" when he practiced with a meditation group, but he still did not consider it to be a social occasion. When I asked if it was important to be part of a community, he replied:

> Not particularly, I would say. I like going to a group and doing [meditation], but I—it's funny, one of the people at this Mindfulness Based Stress Reduction [course] said that he had looked around at different groups to learn meditation before, but he couldn't find one that didn't involve potluck suppers as well. He thought that this hospital one would be a good one because there were no potluck suppers. No, I'm not really looking for community.

No potluck suppers: John offered this story to describe his own sentiments about becoming involved with a community. He was interested in meditation practice, and wanted to practice with others, but did not wish to become socially involved with others in the group. Some respondents who said they were not interested in socializing at the centers explained that they had other social circles and were not looking for another when they enrolled in meditation classes.

Although Alan appreciated the opportunity to socialize and ask informal questions after the class, he was somewhat wary of what he called "the business side" of the center. "I think there's a danger, in any of these things, of becoming part of an organization," he said. He spoke about a church he and his wife had attended which became structured too much like a business, in Alan's view. "I think it's likely to happen with all of these centers. They are a business as well. And [at Chandrakirti] you get a core: you see the people that show up all the time. I don't mind helping, but I don't want that becoming something I need to have: to go there as almost like a club." Alan preferred to keep his involvement at an educational and spiritual level, remaining apart from the social community and the core of volunteers at the center.

Several respondents noted another benefit of participating with a group. Practicing with others, they said, helped them develop and maintain their meditation practice. Nine student respondents emphasized the discipline and commitment involved in attending classes, qualities that they believed were less easily cultivated on one's own. Gwen, for example, said: "I may always need the sangha,[16] but right now I need it so that I can start to build, because I'm in the process of building that discipline." Speaking of participating with a group, Dennis said:

> It helps me stay disciplined. I know class is coming up, so I want to keep pace with the class. So I make sure I get my meditations in during the week. Yeah, just the support it gives. I had a couple of bad weeks where it just wasn't working out and I missed a couple of days and then I was kind of frustrated. And then Meg came with her analogies [i.e., for teaching meditative practices] and it helped that quite a bit.

Like Dennis, Margaret believed that the weekly reinforcement of attending the classes gave her the discipline to keep meditating. "I wouldn't maintain a home practice if I weren't doing something at least once a week that calls me in to a little more structure and encouragement and so on." Erin said: "I would imagine that once I stop this I'll probably find it harder to make the time and be regimented about it and actually do it. Practicing with other people is obviously the best way to do it." Marlon, Brenda, Anna, and Carol also indicated that practicing with others reinforced discipline for and commitment to keeping up the practice.

At Friends of the Heart classes, students were expected to discuss and ask questions about their daily meditation practice and were thereby encouraged to keep meditating at home. Chandrakirti question-and-answer sessions offered a similar opportunity to learn from other students and receive encouragement from teachers. John and Marlon noted that one could draw energy for meditation practice from the presence of others. Marlon said that the path to enlightenment takes a lot of energy. "And that's one of the purposes of practicing in the center. People have said that when they practice here they feel more motivated or that they have more energy and I guess the other one is the fact that it's good to have a community. Some people, they practice alone. They don't feel that motivated." Several respondents, therefore, believed that engaging and meditating with other meditators built commitment and motivation for keeping up with the practice.

The communities at Friends of the Heart and Chandrakirti Centre were thus important for some as a social group, for others as a support for their practice. As might be expected, the centers' memberships were not often characterized as religious communities. While John was himself not interested in finding a religious group, he speculated that that might be one motive for joining a meditation class. "I can see that some people would come looking for community. Some people will come looking for almost a religious community—sort of a clean slate religious community that doesn't have the baggage that their old religion carried with it for them." This is an informative remark. John was aware that some Buddhist sympathizers might have negative views toward their previous religious affiliations. He speculated that some might expect a Buddhist group to become a substitute religious community, one they hoped might be free of the problems they associated with other religious organizations.

Whether respondents were seeking a new practice, a new outlook on life, a new way of living, or just a healthful hobby or exercise, the majority of them said they had a variety of different motivations for enrolling in meditation classes. It is significant that respondents' stated motivations included a desire to gain new information or intellectual-level learning, an interest in exploring new attitudes, outlooks, and ethical perspectives, and the motivation to learn meditation skills and techniques. These particular interests correspond to different categories or domains of learning that meditation classes would, to one degree or another, provide. As respondents' experiences at Friends of the Heart and Chandrakirti Centre unfold in subsequent chapters, it will become evident that the learning that took place through formal practices such as meditation involved all of these domains of learning. But before investigating the patterns of learning that students experienced, it is first necessary to explore in some detail the events and practices that took place in the meditation classes at Friends of the Heart and Chandrakirti Centre.

3

Meditation Classes, Rites, and Ritual

BEGINNING IN SEPTEMBER of 2006 through to June of 2007, I participated at a variety of different events at Friends of the Heart and Chandrakirti Centre. The introductory meditation classes offered to newcomers were my main interest, but I also had the opportunity to attend higher level classes, some social events, prayer services, and empowerments. Over the course of my research I learned about Guru Yoga, Vajrasattvapūjā, a number of meditation techniques including insight, black-and-white meditation, and Tantric visualization, and was initiated into the devotional practices of Chenrezig, White Tara, and Je Tsongkhapa. At Friends of the Heart, I attended a number of different classes offered to newcomers and more experienced members; those who volunteered for interviews included participants from each. At Chandrakirti Centre, the General Program was the flagship offering for newcomers; all Chandrakirti interview participants, including the more experienced members, took part in General Program classes during the time I was conducting my field work. While the courses at the two centers were quite different in style and content, each involved similar elements, including lectures, group discussions, and formal practices like prayers, bows, offerings, and meditation.

In addition to the introductory courses themselves, the individual activities that took place in the classes (see table 3.1) bore certain qualities of ritual, and can thus be explored as ritual, or as a series of rites or ritualized behaviors. As noted in the introduction, rites and ritual are regarded here as existing on a sliding scale from less to more ritualized. Elements of the classes can be regarded as ritualized,

TABLE 3.1 Introductory Meditation Class Structure

Friends of the Heart	Chandrakirti Centre
Introduction to Insight and Calm and Clear	General Program
Entry, participants remove shoes	Entry, participants remove shoes
Meeting, greeting in the lobby (teacher present)	Meeting, greeting in the lobby (teacher not present)
Enter shrine room	Enter shrine room
Pull out cushions or chairs	Take seats in chairs or pews or on cushions
Teacher greets class	Teacher enters (some stand, perform prayer mudra), greets the class
Refuge prayer	Liberating Prayer
Teacher re-introduces last week's meditation technique	Teacher guides body scan and breathing meditation
Meditation, guided	Meditation, guided
Group discussion	
Movement: yoga, *qi gong* or walking meditation	
Teacher's talk	Teacher's lecture
Introduction to new meditation technique	Meditation, guided, often on lecture topic
Group discussion	Question and answer session, group discussion
Dedication of merit (always)	Dedication of merit (sometimes)
Parting: students and teacher informally exit	Parting: students stand, perform prayer mudra as teacher leaves, students follow
Individual questions with teacher, some students leave	Some students leave, some participate in social group in common room

to one degree or another, to the extent that they were repetitive, formal, stylized, embodied, and performed, special or highly valued, and, for some participants, spiritual.

The elements of the classes described in detail below are: rites of entry, opening prayers, meditation sessions, talks (Friends of the Heart) or lectures (Chandrakirti), discussion or question-and-answer sessions, and closing rites.

Alan Rogers, who has written at length on adult learning, claims that there are two different means of learning: formalized, which usually takes place in educational environments like classrooms, and experiential or "acquisition" learning.[1] The latter most often takes place in the midst of everyday activities as learners perform tasks and observe what is going on around them.[2] Experiential learning is task-specific, highly contextualized, and tacit, or that which we might not know we know: the type of knowledge required for riding a bicycle, for example.[3] Rogers's experiential learning, therefore, relates to the type of knowledge I described in the introduction as embodied knowing, the habituated schema inscribed on the body-mind, which we draw upon without conscious reflection.

Rogers describes formalized learning as learning-conscious-learning, in which students are aware of their activities as learning. Formalized learning most often involves receiving and remembering new knowledge or information. Overlaps occur when, for example, experiential learning takes place in formalized settings: a group of students is set a problem to work out. Further, formalized learning—memorized multiplication tables, for example—can become tacit knowledge and may develop into tools to be used in task-conscious-learning.[4] In this sense, intellectual learning or information may transform into tacit knowing. This is somewhat distinct from the embodied knowing I suggest derives from ritualization. While I do not mean to suggest that cognitive learning is not embodied, the concept of "embodied knowing" I derive from ritual and embodiment theorists refers to skills rather than knowledge. It has much more to do with riding a bicycle than memorized multiplication tables. Still, Rogers's reflections on learning sites are useful, here. As Rogers puts it, there are not two different sites of learning, but two different ways of learning which can take place in the same settings.[5] Similarly, there were overlaps between how and what students learned at Friends of the Heart and Chandrakirti classes. The range of postures, techniques, and effects of meditation, for example, was learned through lectures or talks, formal instructions, personal experience, observing and following others, group discussions, and personal insights. Lectures, formal instructions, and question-and-answer sessions were more formalized means of learning, whereas practice, observing and following others, and developing personal insights were experiential.

Within formalized and experiential means of learning there are three different types or domains of learning: the cognitive, involving the acquisition of knowledge or information; the affective which refers to changes in attitudes, feelings, and values; and the psychomotor, which entails movement and motor skills.[6] Formalized learning most often conveys information or develops cognitive abilities, but it can also be used to teach new attitudes and values as well as physical skills. Experiential learning is the means by which we most often gain new physical skills and attitudes. An example is found in Jennings's analogy about chopping wood: through one's arms, hands, and shoulders one learns about the ax, the wood and, to an extent, about the world itself.[7] Yet cognitive learning can also be applied in experiential learning: Learning about and then practicing meditation postures and techniques is an example. Like formalized and experiential means of learning, there are also overlaps between the types: cognitive, affective, and psychomotor learning. These domains will be explored in more detail in subsequent chapters. For now, it is important to distinguish between the various means of learning—the formalized structures in the classes and the ways students learned experientially—and the types of learning that students experienced: changes in knowledge, attitudes, and skills. All of the various elements of the meditation classes, described below, are formalized in the sense that they are parts of a formally structured class. Yet, most also involve experiential learning as students personally engage in the various learning activities. What follows is a description and exploration of all of the various means of learning, both formalized and experiential, that took place in the introductory meditation classes at both centers.

RITES OF ENTRY

What I am calling "rites of entry" at the Friends of the Heart and Chandrakirti introductory classes were a series of activities preceding the formal start of each class. At both centers, the first thing we participants did on arrival was to take off our shoes. Each center had shoe trays set out just inside the door where participants could leave their footwear. If newcomers arrived who did not know about this requirement, teachers or other members would point it out. Although removing one's shoes was a less formal activity than some of the behaviors performed on entry into the shrine rooms, it is still somewhat ritualized. Being asked to remove our shoes, or discovering through observation that we were expected to do so, students became aware that we were entering a space that was somehow special, that it was different from other public spaces. Meg, who taught Friends of the Heart's Calm and Clear introductory class, described removing the shoes as "crossing a threshold, creating a container, or creating a sacred space. Leave your worries behind you." Gerald said that taking off his shoes "initiates a sense of respect for the place, which is good. But it seemed foreign at first and I felt quite weird." Indeed, most Canadians are not accustomed to removing their footwear when entering a public place. Anna noted that taking off the shoes denoted a similar decorum to not wearing shorts in certain places. She agreed that it signified respect. "I like to think of that as a sacred space. So, that's what it does: it just reminds me to honor it. You know, when you're in sacred spaces I think you treat yourself and others more respectfully." The removal of the shoes, then, was a practice that taught something: The centers are places where a certain decorum holds. In Diane's view, removing the shoes had practical reasons as well. She said: "I love it. I ask people to take their shoes off in my house. It's pure cleanliness." There are, therefore, several meanings implied in the gesture of removing one's shoes in a public space, meanings that identify the space being entered as special or even sacred.

Further rites of entry took place as participants entered the shrine rooms. At Friends of the Heart, the entrance to the shrine room was an archway, bordered by two wooden pillars and draped across the top with colorful Tibetan prayer flags. At Chandrakirti Centre, participants stepped from the lobby through two wooden, glass-inset doors into a space that at that time still looked very much like a church. Participants who were familiar with customary procedures in these spaces placed their hands palms together in the *añjali* or prayer mudra[8] as they crossed the threshold into the shrine rooms. Newcomers observed as teachers and experienced members either performed one or more prostrations facing the shrine or bowed to the shrine, with hands in the prayer mudra position. Introductory students were not required or expected to perform such gestures, but some occasionally imitated others by performing the mudra and bowing. I did not observe newcomers performing prostrations at either center unless specifically asked to do so during empowerments or chanted prayer services. On arrival at introductory classes, most newcomers simply entered the hall and took their seats. At Friends of the Heart, rites of entry were fairly informal. Students filed in to the shrine area with the teacher, and would chat informally until the start of the class. A few minor rites sometimes preceded the class, such as lighting the candles on the altar, refreshing flower offerings on the shrine, and so forth. At Chandrakirti Centre, teachers spent time alone in preparation before the class and would therefore enter the shrine room after most students had arrived and taken their seats. The entry of the teacher was therefore more formal than it was at Friends of the Heart. Rites of entry changed at the General Program classes during fieldwork. When Zopa was teaching, he would enter, bow to the shrine, and take his seat while most students remained seated. With the arrival of new head teacher Gen Delek in February of 2007, General Program students would stand, perform the prayer mudra, and bow as the teacher passed. Observing experienced members, newcomers imitated this gesture of respect. The performance of this gesture continued for the remainder of my participation at the General Program classes. Carol, one of my interview participants, told me that Zopa did not want people to stand when he arrived to teach the General Program class. He wanted the class to be open to everyone, and felt that too much formality might be unwelcoming for newcomers unfamiliar with Buddhism. According to Carol, Delek was much more familiar and comfortable with ritual. The rites of entry, therefore, changed with the styles of different teachers.

OPENING PRAYER

At the start of each class, teachers at both centers began by greeting students and would sometimes introduce the topic for the evening. The greeting was followed by an opening prayer. The Refuge Prayer that was spoken at the beginning of all Friends of the Heart events was printed in the student handbook given to members when they enrolled. Having taken our cushions or chairs, and with hands placed in the prayer mudra, students either listened or followed along as teachers spoke the Refuge Prayer in a measured, low, and somewhat reverent tone of voice. The prayer included the traditional refuges of Buddha, dharma, and sangha along with certain resolutions to develop and perfect one's body, speech, and mind. At Joyce Allen's Introduction to Insight course, we were encouraged to bring our handbooks and read the prayer aloud at the beginning of each class. Meg's approach in the Calm and Clear course was to recite the prayer and encourage students to say it if we knew it or to just listen and contemplate its meaning. All teachers and more experienced members appeared to know the prayer by heart. The meanings of the prayer were expressed not only through the words spoken but also through the performance of the prayer itself, its formality, and reverential style. Like removing one's shoes, reciting the prayer served as a kind of threshold crossing: it was a signal not only that the class had begun, but also that this time and place was set apart from the everyday—it was special.

The performance of a prayer at the beginning of General Program classes at Chandrakirti Centre also began when Delek started teaching in February 2007. Called the Liberating Prayer, it was an homage to Shakyamuni Buddha. The prayer, written by Kelsang Gyatso, was sung accompanied by a recording on compact disc. Senior members handed out printed copies of the prayer at each class so that students could sing along with the recording. The prayer was sung in a light, lyrical melody. The music was western in style, in contrast to the resonant, almost-atonal chanting often performed by Tibetan Buddhist monks. In addition to honoring the Buddha and requesting blessings, the prayer also created a clear moment of separation from ordinary activities and a shift to the special activities of the class. Before the use of the prayer, the class began less formally—in a less ritualized fashion—with the teacher's arrival, greeting, and introduction to the lecture topic for the evening.

The sense of crossing a threshold to enter a special or set-aside time and place contributed to the ritualized nature of the meditation classes. In his writings on rites of passage, Arnold van Gennep explores the significance of literal and metaphorical threshold crossing. He argues that rites of passage have three distinct phases: separation from the ordinary space and time of everyday living; the transition or liminal period during which the rite takes place; and incorporation, the act of re-entering ordinary space-time.[9] Van Gennep called them, respectively: preliminal rites, liminal (or threshold) rites, and postliminal rites.[10] Naturally, not all rituals are rites of passage or initiation ceremonies, but many involve the three general phases of van Gennep's model. At meditation classes, there were threshold-crossing rites as participants arrived at the centers, removed their shoes, and stepped into the meditation halls. The spaces could be considered liminal; they were set aside for a special purpose during which participants' normal roles and activities were suspended. Turner, who builds on van Gennep's work, explores the transitional or liminal phase in more depth. He describes liminality as a state in which ordinary structures and identities are suspended, a quality that imbues ritual with its sense of being set aside or other than ordinary. Turner also documents a unique kind of bonding among participants in the liminal space-time of a rite, which he calls *communitas*.[11] It is important to note that Turner's concepts of communitas and liminality have been critiqued as being overly idealized. Not all rituals create anti-structure or strip participants of their normal status, for example.[12] Neither is the creation of social equality or an intense feeling of togetherness universal to all ritual enactments. Still, the general notions of liminality—a time and place regarded as qualitatively different from the everyday—and communitas—a degree of bonding between participants created through their shared experience—are features found in many services and ceremonies. Likewise, these elements can be found in the meditation classes at Friends of the Heart and Chandrakirti Centre. Several respondents said that sharing their learning experiences with others was an important part of participating at the classes, possibly indicating a kind of communitas or bonding between participants.[13] At Friends of the Heart and Chandrakirti classes, the rites of entry described above were one form of separation, the prayers another. By the time the prayers were recited, participants had fully entered the distinctive space-time of the class.

MEDITATION

Opening prayers were almost always followed by meditation. Teachers and students usually referred to meditation sessions as "sittings" or sometimes just "sits." Most classes involved two sittings per class. Teachers at all three classes introduced a variety of different meditation practices or techniques, beginning with some instruction on meditation posture. While traditional meditation postures such as the lotus—legs crossed with one or both feet placed on the opposite thigh—were not taught, at both centers we were always advised to sit with a straight back. In order that we remain awake and alert in meditation, teachers often advised us to keep our eyes half-open rather than closed. Alan noted that he was trying to follow this technique: "One of the things I've been trying is keeping my eyes half open. I've always closed my eyes, but I know when I close my eyes I end up dozing off."

At Friends of the Heart, most students sat or knelt on zafus on the floor. The primary objective for seated meditation postures was to achieve a stable, three-point foundation that would support the body during meditation. If, when seated cross-legged on the floor, our knees were raised off the ground, Joyce or Meg instructed us on the use of extra support cushions under the legs. Some participants used several support cushions to achieve the stability required. Those who sat in chairs were advised to keep their feet apart and firmly planted on the floor. While a few specific postures were taught and most students followed them, we were not given any strict rules or requirements for how to sit. We were, in fact, encouraged to experiment with different postures, including lying down. The overriding guideline on meditation posture was to find a position that was comfortable in which we could remain alert. The traditional lotus posture almost automatically provides a stable three-point foundation without support cushions because it levers the knees toward the floor. It was not taught at either center, however, likely because it is a difficult posture for westerners who are not normally accustomed to sitting cross-legged for long periods of time.

John described how Joyce instructed students on meditation posture at her first Introduction to Insight class:

> She went through all the different varieties of cushions that they had. It was pretty much make yourself comfortable, really. She was showing all the different [postures], kneeling. At that time, she couldn't do it cross-legged, so she was kneeling on the floor with the pillow between her legs, taking the round pillow on its end.... And then saying: if you're more comfortable in a chair, just sit in a chair. Try and keep your back upright. I don't recall her saying anything particular about the hands. She just ran through a few places you could put them, cross them or put them on your legs.

I asked Meg if it was important to teach newcomers formal meditation postures. She said, "I think they're very important. We are incarnate creatures. We are embodied." She said that personally she was very intellectual, so understanding the significance of the body in meditation came as quite a revelation. She therefore made a point to emphasize the body in her teaching. Still, there was a balance to be maintained, particularly with westerners who might find traditional postures painful or difficult to maintain. "Having said that, I'm wondering what we are actually teaching in terms of formal practices," Meg said. "Certainly, I try to take the middle road in terms of meditation posture. Anywhere from: at the end of the day, it's not that important to yes, it is important." Meditation posture, therefore, is one element of the practice for which teachers must attempt to find an appropriate balance between tradition and adaptation when introducing Buddhist practice to western practitioners.

At both Friends of the Heart courses, a few meditation hand postures, or mudras, were also demonstrated. Both Joyce and Meg showed us what is known as the "cosmic mudra": hands cupped together in the lap, palms up, with the thumbtips touching. Although this and other mudras were demonstrated, students were free to use them or not. Again, although there was some formality in terms of the postures and practices that were taught, the general approach in the classes was one of openness and experimentation.

Of course, meditation involves more than just figuring out where to place the hands, buttocks, and feet. After demonstrating various postures, teachers moved on to the concentration techniques. There was usually some formalized instruction given beforehand, but concentration techniques were primarily taught experientially through guided meditation. As we meditated, teachers gave slow, softly spoken instructions. For example: "Concentrate on your breathing; feel the sensation of your breath at the nostrils, the cool sensation as you breathe in and the warm sensation as you breathe out." In addition to instructions on posture and concentration techniques, teachers also gave us general advice on how to sit or how to concentrate, little tricks that some students found helpful. John described one such piece of advice that Richard gave the night he taught Joyce's Insight class. "Richard said something about: don't seek the breath, let the breath come," John recalled. "Which I thought was really good. That felt much better when I tried to do that. Little things like that, I think, are going to be helpful as you go down the road."

Each of the introductory courses presented a variety of different meditation practices: concentration techniques for engaging or training the mind during meditation. As the name of her course implied, the main practice Joyce taught was insight meditation, but she also introduced other practices as well. Over the ten weeks of the course, she added new practices and expanded earlier ones to include new techniques. The first meditation session at each of Joyce's Insight classes began with a body scan, as a prelude to other meditation practices. Beginning at the forehead and moving down through specific areas of the body (eyes, mouth, jaw, throat, arms, torso, hips, legs, and feet), we were asked to feel each area become relaxed, softened, and broadened. The body scan concluded as we widened the focus to take in all of the body.

The insight meditation practices Joyce taught began with developing an awareness of sensations in the body. She asked us to move our awareness through our bodies and search for areas of activity—pain, pressure, tension, and so on. Find one such area and label it as "touch," Joyce said. Stay with that area and be with the experience for a while. Then move on: find another area of the body that is either "touch" or "rest." Or we might choose to remain with the first sensation and refresh our awareness of it. Joyce asked us to concentrate on each of these areas for a time, noting what, if anything, the awareness did to alter the sensations. Later in the course, insight practice was expanded as we added the labels "feeling" and "peace" to "touch" and "rest." We were asked to pay attention to areas in the body with which feelings or emotions were associated. Where there were none, we were to label the area "peace." It was a difficult practice: many students, myself included, initially had trouble with the idea that emotions could be located in the body, and were unsure what we were meant to be seeking. Joyce advised that we could return to seeking out areas of "touch" and "rest" if this new practice was too difficult.

Joyce later taught an insight technique in which we paid attention to images behind our closed eyes or tried to determine the location of our thoughts. Labels used in these practices were "image active," "image rest," "thought active" and "thought rest." Each insight practice involved the same process: find, label, experience, then move on or refresh. The emphasis was on using neutral labels so as not to become overly concerned with whether the presence of tension, emotion, thoughts, or images was positive or negative.

Joyce also taught a basic breathing meditation. We were asked to count from one to ten on the out-breaths, returning to one again. Joyce suggested that this technique was good for students who had trouble sitting regularly or if other methods seem complicated or confusing. Finally, she taught metta or loving-kindness meditation. She gave us a print-out with three four-line verses:

May I be happy.
May I be peaceful.
May I be well and free from suffering.
May I be filled with kindness and compassion.
May you be happy..., etc.
May all beings be happy..., etc.

We began with the first verse, silently repeating it over and over again in our minds. Then Joyce guided us to the next verse: we were advised to think of an individual, someone we cared about. Again, after several silent repetitions addressing the second verse to that person, we moved on to the last verse, offering peace, happiness, and so forth, to all beings. Occasionally, Joyce guided us in directing the second verse to people for whom we had neutral or negative feelings. We were encouraged to make metta part of our regular practice.

As the Introduction to Insight course progressed, meditation sessions became gradually longer. We began sitting for ten minutes and were up to twenty-five or thirty at the end of ten weeks. Joyce thus guided us through a process intended to improve and increase our meditation skills and techniques as the course progressed.

In February 2007, the Introduction to Insight course came to an end and Meg Salter's Calm and Clear introductory class began. This course maintained much of the same structure as the first, but Meg introduced some different techniques. The first concentration technique she taught was a focus on good, relaxing feelings in the body. She asked us to allow the jaw to drop just a little bit and to feel how good that little bit of relaxation felt. We stayed with that for a moment, then she asked us to feel the good feelings moving out from there: What else in the head area feels relaxed? She slowly took our attention through other areas of the body, observing good, relaxed feelings in the neck and shoulders, down into the arms and hands, through the torso, hips, legs, and feet.

Other techniques Meg taught included a body scan while silently repeating the "mantra," as she called it, "letting go in the body." We were asked to imagine the awareness as a beam of light being shone throughout the body, melting areas of tension as if they were ice in a beam of sunlight. Meg also taught breathing meditation—counting from one to ten on the out-breaths and returning to one. A second kind of breathing meditation had us focusing our awareness on our breathing, first in the belly or chest and then at the nostrils. Meg's version of metta or loving kindness meditation had us recalling times when we had received kindness from others and then focusing on the feelings of happiness, gratitude, and kindness that the memory created. Meg also taught the same metta verses that Joyce had introduced. The last technique Meg taught was a visualization meditation. We were guided through visualizing a beach and a calm lake, and a pebble tossed into the water. This was a simple introduction to visualization, a meditation practice often used in Tibetan tantric or Vajrayana Buddhism. Once again, the meditation sessions were longer by the end of the course than at the beginning. Meg told students that the cycle of classes was designed to be open and available to people to join whenever they were ready, but she did want to move on with each class so that students would improve their meditation skills as the weeks passed.

At Chandrakirti Centre, introductory classes were not part of a one-time, short-term course. They were designed to be open to newcomers at all times. As it was always possible that people with no meditation experience were present, brief instructions on meditation techniques and postures were given at each class. Most participants sat in chairs or pews, and the sittings were relatively short, between five and fifteen minutes. Instructions on meditation posture at General Program classes were brief, often limited to the advice that students should keep their spines straight. Gerald described meditation instructions he had heard:

> You try to get a good posture, being a straight back. There's a position that you hold your hands in, and then you try to get as comfortable as you can wherever you are sitting. And then they try to get your focus on your breathing—breathing through the nose. If you're stuffed up—they always say this—if you're stuffed up, then through the mouth. Focus on the breath in and the breath out. And once they have that, they try to tell you to relax your body from top to bottom down to your toes, from the crown of your head down to your toes and back up again. Basically trying to relax and try to focus on your breath, keep everything simple, there's nothing mystical or magical about this. It's straightforward.

By far, the majority of students at General Program classes meditated in chairs or pews. I occasionally observed someone lying down in a pew during meditation. Mats and cushions were available, and a few students used them. I did not hear any instructions on meditation postures for cushions at the General Program classes, but Carol told me that such instructions were occasionally given.

When I asked Thekchen if it was important to teach specific meditation postures, he replied:

> Usually, in the General Program, we are sitting in chairs. I know that in some traditions it's on the cushion, and part of the practice is getting through the pain. Fair enough, but I think because I'm doing more contemplative, analytical meditation, rather than just sitting, I think it's important to be in a comfortable position so that I can just focus on first my breath and then on what I need to accomplish.

Under all of the General Program teachers I observed, meditation sessions generally followed the pattern Thekchen described: the first sitting normally began with a body scan for relaxation and then some kind of breathing meditation. The second sitting involved contemplative practices like metta or silently observing the mind, or an analytical meditation on the teaching that preceded it. Meditation techniques were easy to follow and many of the same techniques were used without much modification from class to class.

The first meditation session at General Program classes almost always began with a body scan: we were guided in concentrating our attention at the head and moving down through various areas of the body (head, neck, shoulders, arms, hands, back, abdomen, legs, and feet). Teachers asked us to take a little time to feel each area as relaxed and clear. At the end, we focused on the whole body, seeing it as relaxed and clear. The body scan was used as a prelude to other meditation practices. Another meditation practice taught at General Program classes was called "silent observer," in which we watched the processes of our minds as thoughts arose and disappeared like bubbles from a lakebed. Teachers asked us to be aware of our thoughts and observe them without judgment or attachment and then let the thoughts go without becoming distracted or carried away by them.

There were two different breathing meditation techniques that I encountered at General Program classes. The first was simple awareness of the breath, usually focusing on sensations at the nostrils, as described above. The second was sometimes called "black-and-white" meditation. Teachers asked us to imagine breathing out stress and negativity in the aspect of thick black smoke. We then breathed in goodness, light, or healing energy. As Gerald described black-and-white meditation: "While you're breathing, they try to make you visualize what you're doing with your breath. You're breathing in light and getting rid of tension with your exhalation." When Thekchen guided this meditation at one class I attended, he asked students to imagine that the light or energy we were drawing in came from the hearts of enlightened beings. The meditation thus became a means of receiving blessings.

Metta or loving-kindness meditation was practiced in different forms at different General Program classes. Examples were: (1) make a wish for all beings to be liberated and to find permanent inner peace; (2) concentrate on health and happiness, first for yourself, then for someone you know, then for all beings; (3) think about the people in your life and wish them well; (4) imagine that all other beings are your kind mothers.

Finally, analytical meditation involved reflecting on the teaching of the evening. This particular practice was reserved for the second meditation session. Students listened to the teacher guiding the meditation and concentrated on their feelings as the teacher reviewed the concepts covered in the talk. Topics frequently included compassion, kindness, patience, and gratitude, and how to develop these emotions or attitudes. Gerald described this kind of guided meditation as follows: "They'll try to get you to remember a feeling or a situation in your life which makes you feel compassion for something. They ask you to remember when someone was good to you to try to stimulate that feeling."

As part of meditation instruction, General Program teachers sometimes described one or more traditional mudras—usually the cosmic mudra described above. Thekchen told me that this mudra symbolized wisdom in compassion: the right hand represents wisdom and is cupped in the left, which represents compassion. The thumbs, he said, symbolize *tuma*, or inner fire. Two respondents, Gerald from Chandrakirti Centre, and John from Friends of the Heart, mentioned a more practical purpose of the cosmic mudra that they had learned: the point where the thumbs touch is a measure of a meditator's concentration and relaxation. If the pressure is too hard, the meditator is too tense, if the thumbs drift apart, the meditator is too sleepy. Thus, in the same gesture, we have symbolic (more ritualized) and practical (less ritualized) meanings.

All of the meditation practices described above were guided; that is, teachers gave verbal instructions for following the selected practices throughout every sitting. Guided meditation sometimes involved periods of silence where students carried on the practice on their own, but no sittings at any of the introductory classes I attended were completely silent. I will admit that this was one instance where my Zen training got in the way of my experience at these two centers: Accustomed to silent meditation, I often felt distracted by teachers speaking during meditation. Some of my interview respondents said the same, while others appreciated being guided. Catherine Rathbun told me that guided meditation was used for introductory courses and visualization meditation. "If you come to the retreats," she said, "you will find that they are silent."

Novice meditation students occasionally express a belief that the object of meditation is to silence one's thoughts completely. Some students at the meditation classes said that they were frustrated when unable to do so. Teachers usually responded by saying that it is impossible to completely suppress or eliminate thoughts. Even experienced meditators, they said, find that the mind tends to wander. The trick is not to silence the mind but to recognize the moment when it has wandered and "gently," as teachers often put it, bring the attention back to the practice. Thus an important goal of all of the practices described here was to develop concentration, the ability to stay with or return to the meditative focus, whatever it might be.

There were several additional objectives of the meditation practices described, some explicitly stated by the teachers, others left to interpretation. At Friends of the Heart, sittings often served strictly as practice, helping students develop the capacity to maintain a meditation posture and concentrate on the meditative technique. Other possible purposes of meditation practice, in my understanding, were: relaxation, resulting from body scan and breathing meditation; developing awareness of the body and the processes of the mind from insight meditation; generating gratitude and compassion from metta; developing detachment and becoming less judgmental from insight, metta, and others. Meditation sessions at Friends of the Heart, therefore, were aimed at helping students develop new skills such as physical flexibility and the ability to concentrate, new attitudes such as gratefulness, equanimity, or nonattachment, and, to some extent, an understanding of Buddhist values such as compassion.

The first sitting at General Program classes was often intended to help students relax and concentrate in order to prepare them for the teaching to follow. When the second sitting was dedicated to reflecting on the teaching, it appeared that the goal was to help students internalize and more deeply understand its meanings. Once, Zopa said that the meditation would help us "develop the mind of a Buddha," thereby hinting at enlightenment, a goal not often mentioned at introductory classes. Occasionally, the second sitting was given over to metta, a practice intended to develop gratitude and compassion for others and a frequent topic of the lectures. Because meditation practice was most often dedicated to preparing for or reflecting on the teaching, it seemed to be supplementary to the teaching, rather than a goal in and of itself. Chandrakirti meditation instruction, therefore, focused more on the development of new attitudes, values, and perhaps insights into Buddhist truths than on the physical or practical techniques of meditation.

Instructions on meditation postures and concentration techniques are a formalized means of teaching physical skills and techniques. They were means by which students learned about postures and techniques on a cognitive level, by gaining new information. Such instructions represent the "how" of learning to meditate. By employing the techniques, students later learned experientially how to perform them. The "what" of meditation—that is, what students learned through doing it—came with time and experience. The specifics of what respondents said they learned in meditation are explored in chapter 5.

Friends of the Heart classes always included some form of movement exercises following either the first sitting or the teacher's talk. These exercises either involved a few yoga postures, some flowing *qi gong* movements or walking meditation. The objective of the movement sessions was to stretch out the joints, get the blood flowing and, as most teachers stressed, to increase students' awareness of our bodies, thus indicating that meditation is also embodied rather than simply a mental exercise. Movement sessions were taught in a formalized manner as the teacher led the group and demonstrated the different postures and gestures, but students also learned experientially how to perform the exercises. For the most part, movement sessions primarily taught specific motor skills and techniques, but respondents indicated that their attitudes were also affected. All of the Friends of the Heart newcomers I spoke to said they appreciated the movement sessions because afterward they felt more alert and physically and mentally prepared for subsequent meditation sessions.

TALKS OR LECTURES

At Friends of the Heart, the teachers' talks preceded the second meditation session. Less like lectures, the talks were fairly short and somewhat casual. Teachers sat with students on cushions on the floor in a rough circle and students would interrupt to comment or ask questions. Talks usually had to do with meditation techniques and students' experiences meditating. Joyce dedicated several talks to concepts derived from a variety of Buddhist scriptures, although they were not always identified as such. In a talk on lasting happiness, for example, Joyce spoke about several qualities that corresponded closely to some of the six perfections (*parāmitās*) of the Bodhisattva path[14] in Mahayana Buddhism—generosity, virtue, patience, strenuousness, concentration, and wisdom. Joyce did not mention the six perfections, however, or the source of the concepts she taught. Given the center's eclectic, lay-oriented character, I was not surprised that the introductory teachings did not go heavily into Buddhist doctrine. Talks at Friends of the Heart also avoided references to metaphysical concepts such as karmic rebirth. Some of the topics Joyce covered were: reducing stress, the nature of being versus doing, generosity and gratitude, developing equanimity, and happiness. From these talks, students gained some new factual or conceptual information and had the opportunity to discuss, analyze, and evaluate it. While talks were a formalized means of learning, they were not intended to impart a great deal of new information to be memorized. Rather, their objective was more along the lines of generating certain attitudes and feelings and learning ways to reinforce those attitudes and feelings through meditation. Most of the talks were given in direct relation to the meditation practice taught in the same evening.

Some talks introduced values traditionally associated with Buddhism. Joyce spoke about generating compassion and sympathetic joy, of letting go of attachments and desires, and of the impermanence of the self. In week ten, she introduced a path for applying the practice to the life of a householder. The path Joyce laid out involved the following steps: committing to meditation practice; building insight into impermanence and no-self; letting go of attachments; developing equanimity; and ripening wisdom, ethics, and compassion. Although Joyce did not identify the specific sources of these teachings, which have their origins in Theravada and Mahayana schools, she did indicate that they were generally Buddhist. The ritualized setting in which the talks were given and the association of their topics with traditional spiritual teachings imbued the teachings themselves with certain ritual qualities: several respondents regarded them as specially meaningful or elevated.

Meg's class introduced some of the same concepts, although her talks tended to focus more closely on meditation techniques and the processes of the mind involved in meditation. Instead of presenting a prepared talk every evening, Meg sometimes introduced a topic and gave us time to discuss it among ourselves in pairs or smaller groups before relating our reflections to the whole class. The talks she gave included the following: the myths about meditation; the immediate effects of meditation (slowed breathing as an example); concentration; and meditation as a means of healing. In order to explain the concepts she introduced, Meg often used colorful analogies. She referred to the mind as a wild horse running in an open field, for example: Meditation helps us build a secure corral in which to contain the horse and keep it from wandering too far. Once she compared meditative concentration to a microscope: With practice, we can refine its focus. These analogies gave students new and memorable ways of understanding the practice and the goals of meditation. Months after the class concluded, Dennis, who had been a student in her class, remembered Meg's wild horse analogy. Student discussion groups were a means of exploring the topics Meg introduced through our personal experiences and reflections within a formalized learning structure. Again, the learning gained through Meg's teaching methods had more to do with changes in attitudes and values and gaining new skills than acquiring a lot of new cognitive data.

In their lectures, Chandrakirti teachers used many direct references, not only to the Buddha and his teachings, but also to the more religious or nonempirical concepts of traditional Buddhism such as karma and rebirth. They did not shy away from introducing these concepts, even when teaching newcomers. Teachers often insisted that a full understanding of the Buddha's teachings depended on an understanding of karmic rebirth. Kindness and compassion for all beings, for example, resulted from the understanding that every being has at one time been our mother. At one of the Runnymede library classes, a man in the audience asked if the rebirth cosmology was important. He said he was more interested in meditating in the here and now. The teacher, Chogyan, replied that one could use meditation to feel happy just in this life but, as he put it, "it's like using a Rolls Royce to haul manure." He said that without the rebirth cosmology, we cannot use meditation practice to its full potential. Chogyan urged us to put our doubts aside and keep our minds open to other possibilities.

Because of this resolve to teach karmic rebirth even when it did not appeal to some newcomers, my impressions of the General Program lecture topics were that they were more religious, metaphysical, and philosophical than those I had experienced at other western Buddhist centers, including Friends of the Heart. Even so, Chandrakirti students frequently asserted that the lectures were presented in such a way as to be practical and applicable to their personal situations. Gerald said that "the examples that they offer, when they try to explain the teachings, it's very practical. They try to root it in the world in everyday examples." Despite this focus on practicality, Gerald admitted that the teachings "can be quite theoretical and metaphysical." Carol said that the focus on "practical applications of Buddhist thought" was what appealed to her about the General Program lectures. "They'll address a particular topic, but usually the focus is on the practical terms." Practical applications of the teachings were sometimes assigned as homework: try being generous to people around you, Marlon suggested at a General Program class he taught, and let someone else have the best seat on the subway. Alan remembered and recounted this homework assignment in his interview.

General Program lectures were usually about one hour in length, and Chandrakirti teachers spoke without notes, although they sometimes read from Kelsang Gyatso's texts. The majority of people who teach in the NKT follow the Teacher Training Program, and it was clear after attending classes with several different teachers that they had been well instructed in NKT topics and teaching styles. Many of the same topics were covered by different teachers, sometimes using the same wording. All teachers also tended to use plural pronouns together with single nouns: our body, our mind, our self. This style is used by Kelsang Gyatso in his commentary texts.

General Program classes were formally structured. Teachers sat alone at the front of the room and students were seated in rows facing the teacher but not one another. Teachers would usually speak uninterrupted until formally concluding their talks. A few times, teachers asked questions of the class during the talk and students seemed reluctant to reply. Thekchen said he regretted students' reluctance to interrupt. He told me he would prefer it if students would ask questions and challenge him. It seemed to me, however, that the formal structure of the lectures was what discouraged students' comments and questions.

Each teacher had different techniques for making the concepts they introduced memorable. For example, Chogyan often referred to desires to have "a cottage by a lake and a yellow Hummer," lighthearted yet pertinent examples for illustrating attachment and impermanence. Gen Sanden had a humorous way of speaking in which he would parody a contrary position and then deconstruct it in his teaching. Another effective pedagogical technique used at the General Program classes was simple repetition: teachers would often present the same concepts in a few different ways over the course of a lecture.

The long, detailed lectures at Chandrakirti General Program classes do not lend themselves easily to a brief summary. Topics and key concepts that were frequently reiterated included the following: the need for spirituality to overcome material desires and suffering caused by impermanence; karmic rebirth cosmology and the idea that all beings have at one time been our mothers; the need to reduce anger, attachment, ignorance, and self-cherishing; the need to be kind and generous to others; developing inner peace; and developing compassion for all beings as necessary for achieving enlightenment. The topics presented were always plainly identified as Buddhist teachings and principles, although their specific sources in

Buddhist texts or specific schools were rarely mentioned. While there was a great deal of new information to be learned, and some students told me they wished they could remember more of the lectures afterwards, my impression was that teachers were not concerned about how much detail students remembered. The lectures primarily referred to attitudes and emotions and were obviously intended to encourage students to find ways of changing their habitual perspectives and behaviors in accordance with Buddhist values. Once again, the formalized structure of the lecture, the ritualized setting, and traditional spiritual sources of the teachings, along with the monastic status of most of the teachers, gave the teachings a sense of authority or sanctity.

GROUP DISCUSSION AND SOCIALIZING

All of the introductory classes had time set aside for group discussions or question-and-answer sessions with the teacher. At Friends of the Heart, there was usually more than one discussion session in a class. Teachers led discussions about meditation practice following each sitting and there were discussions during the talks. Discussion groups at Friends of the Heart generally focused on students' meditation experiences and techniques. At Chandrakirti Centre, there was typically one question-and-answer session near the end of each General Program class following the lecture. The question-and-answer sessions were usually centered on philosophical questions about Buddhist ethics and principles, often regarding karma and rebirth. Rarely were questions asked or experiences shared about meditation practice in the General Program classes I attended.

Several respondents indicated that learning through group discussions was an important part of their experiences at the meditation classes. John, for example, said:"Going to a group where other people come and talk about their experience: You learn that whatever difficulty you're having, other people are probably having it too and it's quite normal. Everyone's mind wanders. That will go on as long as you have a mind. That's definitely a good thing to learn." Several other respondents also said that hearing that others shared the same difficulties or experiences was helpful and encouraging. Discussion groups allowed students to share their confusions and work some of them out together. Dennis, for example, said: "You get to hear how people are doing, how well they are doing or not. You just sort of learn from that.... Most everyone in the class is at the same stage. Almost everyone is a beginner, so you get an idea of how they are dealing with the same roadblocks and the same problems and the same successes here and there." Carol said, "I found the questions were always quite amazing because people would ask things that you had thought about, but didn't make an effort to ask, or questions that you hadn't thought about. And you thought: yeah, what about that?" Group discussion sessions thus afforded the opportunity for students to learn what other students were curious about, and hear answers to questions that they may have had without being aware of them. Brenda said that one of her most significant learning experiences resulted from someone asking "big, thoughtful questions" at the General Program classes. "It's Gerald who asks good questions," she said. "He just asks the most amazing questions. And I started to learn. I've learned from him."

While discussion groups included students' reflections on their experiences, they were not themselves means of experiential learning. They had a fairly formalized structure in which teachers led the discussions and students were given an amount of time to speak or respond. The discussion sessions provided new knowledge about meditation, Buddhist teachings, and what other students had learned through their meditation practices. For the most part, such sessions explored and reiterated, through students' queries and shared experiences, the received attitudes and values learned in the classes. Discussion groups helped reinforce many of the shared, modernist notions about Buddhism so often found among adoptive Buddhists and sympathizers: the centrality of meditation, for example, as well as the therapeutic or psychological aspects of Buddhist practice, the compatibility of Buddhist teachings with science, and the perceived differences between Buddhism and religion.[15] Occasionally, a newcomer at a General Program class would challenge the teacher on the topic of karmic rebirth. People asking such questions appeared to be seeking more psychological or scientific explanations of the concept, but Chandrakirti teachers held firm: belief in karmic rebirth was a strong foundation for their teachings on Buddhist ethics.

CLOSING RITES

Following the last discussion session of the evening, Friends of the Heart teachers concluded the class by reciting the dedication of merit, a short prayer which also appeared in the student handbook: "May any merit that has been raised here for the good and the wholesome be shared forth now to help all beings who are suffering."[16] This prayer concluded with a mantra—*idamtepunnya-kammanasvaki-yavahanhotu* [sic]—which teachers and experienced members repeated three times. Although the mantra was printed in the handbook and transliterated for ease of pronunciation, few newcomers recited it, as it was spoken very quickly. Joyce told me that the mantra meant the same in Pali as the line in English that preceded it. It was the only use of the Pali language in the Friends of the Heart introductory classes. Like the refuge prayer at the beginning, the dedication of merit was accompanied by the prayer mudra. On the last recitation of the mantra, some students imitated teachers and experienced members as they opened up their hands, palms up in front of the body: a gesture that symbolized distributing the merit to others. Following the dedication of merit, a few students sometimes stayed behind to ask questions of the teacher. Most filed out to the lobby, put on their shoes, and left.

In the General Program classes, a dedication of merit was sometimes spoken as a separate prayer at the end of the class, but was more often included in one of the meditation sessions or as a separate, less formal statement made by the teacher at the end of the class. For example, Zopa concluded one General Program class in January 2007 with a dedication of merit that was performed as part of the teaching. He asked us to reflect on any good energy that we had developed through our attention and our efforts that evening and to dedicate that energy to those in our lives—family or friends—who might be having difficulties.

At the conclusion of General Program classes, teachers usually invited students downstairs for tea and cookies. Then the teacher would stand, bow to the shrines, and exit down the main aisle of the meditation hall. The gestures performed on the entrance of the teacher were repeated. That is to say, before February 2007, there was little by way of formality on the exit of the teacher. Beginning in February 2007, students stood, performed the prayer mudra, and bowed as the teacher passed on the way out of the hall.

The formal activities that ended the classes wrapped up the teaching and returned participants to ordinary time and space. As noted earlier, a sense of respect, for the space, the teachings, and the teachers, is what students said they learned from the decorum of the entry and closing rites. Traditional gestures like the prayer mudra, the use of the Pali mantra at Friends of the Heart, and the dedication of positive energies to others completed the framing of the classes as special, set aside, and elevated.

RITUAL AND INTRODUCTORY MEDITATION CLASSES

Teachers and students alike regarded the classes offered at Friends of the Heart and Chandrakirti Centre as learning environments rather than rituals, although students attended in order to learn, among other things, certain ritualized practices. Even so, the overall structures of the classes did have a number of ritual qualities: they were enacted, embodied, or performed; they were communal; they contained symbolic elements and sometimes referenced the transcendent—karma, rebirth, enlightenment, and enlightened beings, for example. Some aspects were spontaneous, others were formalized and repetitious.

Moreover, the classes took place in undeniably ritualized settings: that is, in the presence of shrines adorned with offerings, Buddhist icons, devotional paintings, bells, candles, incense, and other religious symbols. The main spaces in the two centers were variously called shrine rooms, meditation halls, or sometimes Buddha halls. The same spaces in which the introductory classes were held were also used for empowerments and chanted prayer services. Events in these spaces, including some of the introductory classes, involved the use of *sādhanas*, a word used at both centers to describe prayer texts, and were sometimes conducted by ordained people wearing monastic robes. As mentioned, Chandrakirti Centre held some of its General Program courses in other, more secular spaces such as libraries and coffee shops. I attended two classes at a library where the only ritual objects in the room were the teacher's robes. At another General Program class, this one in a spare room above a coffee shop, a temporary shrine was set up with a Buddha statue, a painting of Kelsang Gyatso, a painting of a *stūpa* (a Buddhist burial shrine), and a small vase of flowers. While General Program classes that took place in these public spaces were less ritualized than those held in the shrine room at the main center, they were ritualized nonetheless.

Some ritual theorists have investigated links between learning and ritual by examining education itself as a form of ritual. Peter McLaren, for example, studied the ritual elements of a Catholic high school in Toronto. He discovered that there were several different states, spaces, and times that were more or less ritualized in the course of a school day. Schools, like ritual spaces, are "temporally insulated just as they are spatially insulated from the rest of society."[17] Classrooms are places where students' everyday roles or identities are suspended (or, rather, subsumed by the student role), and they exist in a kind of liminal state. McLaren regards the overall structure of the school day as a macro-ritual, whereas micro-rituals are the individual activities that take place during the day: the morning prayer, the lessons, the prayers before and after lunch, the act of contrition at the end of the day, and so on. His reflections on how ritual structures and symbols influence learning can illuminate how and what meditation students learned. I have observed, for example, that the ritualized structures and spiritual sources of the teachings at Friends of the Heart and Chandrakirti Centre served to legitimize and elevate them. Similarly, McLaren finds that the symbolic dimensions of Catholic-school culture, along with its ritual structure, create "the deep codes that provide the blueprints for how students come to know and react to various situations"—a kind of learning he calls "ritual knowledge."[18]

Whereas McLaren explores education as ritual, I am examining ritualizing as a means of learning. Nonetheless, some of his insights are applicable to the "classrooms" at Friends of the Heart and Chandrakirti Centre. The repetition of lecture topics at Chandrakirti General Program classes had something of a ritual formality. So, too, did many of the class activities. Each time classes were held, similar elements were performed in a similar order. Hence class structure, like that of the school day in McLaren's study, is the macro-ritual. Nested within the larger ritual of the class itself were several smaller micro-rituals. Meditation is an example: the practice sometimes began or ended with the ringing of a bell, a symbolic gesture constituting a framing rite. It also included any or all of the following: the assumption of specified back, leg, and hand postures, guided meditation instructions spoken slowly and softly by the teacher, and the performance of specific practices like scanning the body, repeating a mantra, controlling or concentrating on the breath, and so on. Hence, inclusive of all of these activities, meditation itself can be regarded as a ritual since many of its individual elements are ritualized to one degree or another. Moreover, all of the rites that make up the ritual of meditation involve ritualized behaviors or movements that we can further classify as either ritualization or ritualizing.

RITUALIZATION AND RITUALIZING

Ritualization, in its generic sense, refers to a process by which acts take on the qualities of ritual: They become ritualized. In a study of the Jain pūjā, for example, Caroline Humphrey and James Laidlaw present ritual as "a quality that action can come to have" and "ritualization is the process by which normal, everyday action is endowed with this quality and becomes ritual."[19] The bulk of their text is dedicated to an illustration of what it is that makes actions ritualized. There is, in their view, a subtle transformation of an actor's intention in acting which distinguishes ritualization from ordinary, everyday actions. They claim that in ritualization, actors are aware of their actions, but these actions are also perceived as "objects" that are "encountered and perceived from the outside."

> Instead of, as is normally the case in everyday life, a person's act being given meaning by his or her intention, with ritual action the act itself appears as already formed, almost like an object, something from which the actor might "receive." In this transformed situation, the intentions and thoughts of the actor make no difference to the identity of the act performed. You have still done it, whatever you were dreaming of.[20]

It may appear that the opposite is the case in meditation practice: following the breath, focusing on an object of meditation, or performing a complex tantric visualization must certainly require that one not be daydreaming. What is going on in the mind must be significant, and thus the meditator's thoughts and intentions must make a difference. But the distinction is this: For meditative concentration practices, it is not necessarily what is going on *in* the mind, but what is going on *with* the mind that is important.[21] The way meditators direct and focus the mind is the key—it does not matter that there are thoughts also taking place, and it matters even less what those thoughts are. So, in a sense, Humphrey and Laidlaw's insights about the separation of act and intention do apply to meditation: The difference is that the entity that is acting without normal intention is the mind, not the hands, feet, or voice. Teachers at Friends of the Heart and Chandrakirti Centre often underscored the idea that sitting, making the attempt to meditate, *counts*. Experienced meditators know that their minds will wander. For some, the goal—at least the initial goal—is to develop the ability to recognize when the mind has wandered and then bring it back to the object of meditation. In this sense, then, it does not matter if one is daydreaming, as long as the ritualized act is performed: the conscious, stylized, received (and given-as-traditional) act of drawing the attention back to the object of meditation. Mindful attention to the mind is, in this case, the ritualized act or the rite that the mind performs in meditation. If, however, one is daydreaming and does not bring the attention back to the meditative focus, then this is a much less ritualized act than would be a more focused meditation.

In any case, I am less interested here in Humphrey and Laidlaw's ideas about intention than their idea that ritual actions are not created by those who perform them, that such actions can be regarded as pre-formed objects. They claim that "the peculiar fascination of ritual lies in the fact that here, as in few other human activities, the actors both are and are not the authors of their acts."[22] Ritualists perform actions that they learn from other ritualists, that they and others have performed perhaps many times before. They may experiment with them, or change them over time, but the behaviors are first received from external sources. Roy Rappaport reflects this idea in his definition of ritual, "the performance of more or less invariant sequences of formal acts and utterances not entirely encoded by the performers."[23] Respondents involved in this study performed formal practices that were not entirely their own, practices that have a history, long-standing objectives, and complexes of symbolic meanings attached to them. This perspective on the qualities of ritual action is therefore significant for this study.

Humphrey and Laidlaw's view of ritualization—as a process by which actions take on the quality of ritual—refers to ritualization in its generic sense, noted above. But this conception misses an important aspect of ritualized behavior, one that Grimes points out in his text *Beginnings in Ritual Studies*. Grimes asserts that ritualization is "the stylized cultivation or suppression of biogenetic and psycho-somatic rhythms and repetitions."[24] In this view,

> the grounds of ritualization as a human necessity are ecological, biogenetic, and psychosomatic. We cannot escape ritualization without escaping our own bodies and psyches and thus rhythms and structures that arise on their own....Among the modes of ritual activity, ritualization leaves us the least choice. Whether we are involved in ritualization is not ours to decide. We can only choose whether to be attentive or repressive in the face of actions that compel and surround us.[25]

Ritualization, therefore, is unavoidable. It is dependent on our physiology, but it includes the symbols and meanings we attach to the movements we enact. Ritualization is performed whether we like it or not; it is the preconscious enact-ment of our bodily movements. It is performed by the socially informed body and its complexes of symbolic meanings are unconsciously interpreted, reproduced, and reinforced by others around us.[26]

Ritualization is the first of six "modes of ritual sensibility" identified by Grimes. The others are decorum, ceremony, liturgy, magic, and celebration.[27] While it is a category of its own, ritualization is not entirely separate from the other five, but is present in all of the other ritual modes.[28] It is found in a wide range of phenomena, not all of which fall under the term "ritual"; ritualization is found in activities ranging from day-to-day interactions to secular performances to high religious ceremonies.

Rituali*zing*, by contrast, is a more deliberate activity. Grimes notes that it is closely related to ritualization, but the two terms are distinguished by their degrees of consciousness and intention. "Ritualizing is an attempt to activate, and become aware of, preconscious ritualization processes."[29] Ritualizing can also refer to the act of creating new ritual. Thus ritualizing, in my view, refers to behaviors that are cultivated and sometimes invented or experimental, and that also bear a number of other ritual qualities. This perspective draws attention to the fact that ritual is not static; it can change, and it can be reformative as well as conservative. Grimes's list of the qualities of ritual asserts that rituals (not ritualizing) are not usually regarded as invented, spontaneous, improvised, and the like. But ritualizing, as emergent ritual, may eventually become more formal, repetitive, and stable. With time, it can become ritual.

Grimes notes that establishing a hard-and-fast definition of ritualizing would be to arbitrarily set distinct boundaries and perhaps fail to recognize connections to significant elements outside those boundaries. He accordingly offers the following "soft" definition of ritualizing, a behavior that, in his view, is characterized by boundary-crossing: "Ritualizing transpires as animated persons enact formative gestures in the face of receptivity during crucial times in founded places."[30]

The shrine rooms at Friends of the Heart and Chandrakirti Centre are founded places, as are the centers themselves. Tuesday or Wednesday evenings at 7 PM are not necessarily crucial times, but they are special, set-aside times when participants gather with like-minded others to learn meditation and Buddhist teachings. Students participating in order to learn something new may naturally be in a receptive frame of mind. But the teachings, practices, and ethics they learn are also rooted in Buddhist cosmology, something that transcends the immediate and everyday. In the context of a study of meditative practices, terms such as "animated," "enact," and "gestures" require a little conceptual tinkering, which will ensue. For now, I wish only to note that the above description and the notion of ritualizing as consciously cultivated ritualization are the connotations with which the term is used here.

To summarize: ritualization refers generally to the process by which behaviors take on ritual qualities. More specifically, it refers to the stylization of our preconscious or unexamined bodily movements, those programmed by our anatomy but also influenced by our social and cultural conditioning. It is the way we relate to the world as bodies in that world. It is taking place all the time, and it may or may not develop into regular rituals. Ritualization becomes ritualizing when it is developed into a more conscious, intentional process, one in which we become aware of and experiment with ritualization. It is sometimes playful, often tentative or experimental. Assembled together, behaviors involved in ritualizing can produce new forms. Ritualizing becomes ritual when those forms are developed and sustained.[31]

According to this characterization, meditation postures and practices taught at Friends of the Heart and Chandrakirti meditation courses are examples of ritualizing. They are pre-formed, even traditional behaviors that are received by the students who perform them. Having learned them, they are encouraged to experiment with the behaviors to determine which ones work best. Postures and practices were thus adapted by students to fit their individual preferences or needs. Teachers indicated that it was important for students to find a comfortable, sustainable, and personally relevant practice because the primary goal was to be able to meditate every day. Thus ritualizing—experimentation with ritualized behaviors—was intended to become ritual—daily meditation practice.

Several respondents indicated an appreciation for the adaptability and experimental nature of the practices taught. Erin and Diane noted that counting the breath was their preferred meditative focus because it allowed them to concentrate better than did other techniques. Diane was happy to learn she could meditate sitting in a chair rather than having to sit on the floor. Tanit said that she had been worried about her inability to sit still for long. She was relieved but also surprised when Joyce advised students to move if they became uncomfortable. "It's funny how you have this perception of: you will not move at all during meditation," Tanit said. I asked why she believed that, and she replied: "I think it has a lot to do with how meditation is portrayed in films and that we see monks who are meditating and they are not moving. And meditation is associated with stillness. I think, somehow we make this connection."

In fact, many interview participants made some associations between meditation and formality, along with a range of other ritual qualities, even though most, when asked, did not consider meditation to be a ritual. While meditation postures were not strictly standardized at any of the classes, most students did adopt some kind of special posture, such as the straight back or a traditional mudra. At Friends of the Heart, most participants, encouraged by the majority, made an effort to sit on the floor, even when it was not comfortable to do so for long. When speaking about meditating at home, respondents always related some kind of formal practice that they would repeat each time. Alan, for example, made what he called a "ceremony" out of his home meditation practice. To begin, he would light a couple of candles. Then, he said, "I have a sort of a shawl that I put on. And I sort of put that on in a way that I'm trying to make it more of a spiritual thing—or maybe not spiritual. It's a structure....I noticed that there is a ceremony—that's the word I'm thinking of—you create a ceremony around it." Despite the flexibility and encouragement to experiment with different postures and practices, students did associate meditation with formal structures, standardized or traditional practices, repetition, and consistency. They implicitly, if not consciously, associated meditation with certain qualities of ritual.

PERFORMANCE THEORY AND RESTORATION OF BEHAVIOR

Schechner describes the process of receiving, adjusting, adapting, and experimenting with behavior in order to create new forms as "restoration of behavior." As a performance theorist and theater director, Schechner has written extensively on the intersections between ritual and theater, along with other kinds of cultural performance. In Schechner's view, performance entails all forms of activity that show or display, including the performative behaviors of humans and animals as well as the performing arts.[32] Performances are behaviors that are embodied and enacted. Not limited to the fictive or make-believe, they include everything from the ordinary activities of daily life to sporting events, theater, and ritual.

Performance theory, therefore, is a method for investigating ritual by exploring its correspondence to other performances.

Schechner's description of restoration of behavior is an important contribution to performance theory and the study of ritual. He describes it as a process by which physical or verbal actions are deconstructed into small strips or "bits" of behavior that can then be rearranged and assembled into new actions, like editing together strips of film.[33] It is behavior that is "not-for-the-first time, prepared or rehearsed."[34] Schechner regards restored behavior as the root of all theater and ritual, and claims that it is the same process in both.[35] His characterization of restored behavior has significant parallels to both ritualization and ritualizing. Schechner writes:

> These strips of behavior...are independent of the causal systems (social, psychological, technological) that brought them into existence. They have a life of their own. The original "truth" or "source" of the behavior may be lost, ignored, or contradicted—even while this truth or source is apparently being honored and observed. How the strip of behavior was made, found, or developed may be unknown or concealed; elaborated; distorted by myth and tradition. Originating as a process, used in the process of rehearsal to make a new process, a performance, the strips of behavior are not themselves process but things, items, "material."[36]

Like Humphrey and Laidlaw's ritual actions, restored behaviors consist of actions that do and do not originate with the performer; they are actions that are received, independent objects or materials. In theater workshops and meditation classes, performers are aware that they are experimenting with different behaviors and developing them into something new. In that sense, then, restoration of behavior is similar to ritualizing as I have described it above: formative, experimental ritualized actions.

In theater, restored behavior takes place primarily in the workshop-rehearsal process. Workshops, Schechner claims, are the most ritualized elements of the theatrical process. A workshop is a liminal space where performers' normal roles are suspended and their usual behaviors are broken down and reconstructed. Performers enter a workshop as "fixed or finished beings."[37] In the liminal environment of the workshop, behavior is broken down into bits, what Schechner calls "the smallest strips of repeatable action."[38] Then begins the work of rearranging and reconstructing the bits into something new.

Meditation classes, like performing arts workshops, were sites of experimentation. Students were given certain practices to perform. They repeated the behaviors to become familiar with them, but were also encouraged to try different forms. If sitting cross-legged on a cushion was not comfortable, they could try kneeling or sitting in a chair. If insight practice was too difficult, they could switch to watching or counting the breath. Any one of the different practices students learned could

be dropped, combined with others, or reconfigured as they tried to find the practice that worked best for them. Several students also added practices they had
learned elsewhere. Like theater workshops, the classes were intended only as a
beginning: Students were expected to take what they learned and develop from it
a regular meditation practice.

Schechner makes a direct connection between performing artists and certain
ritualists. He writes that "performing artists—and, I would say, meditators,
shamans and trancers too—work on themselves, trying to induce deep,
psychophysical transformations either of a temporary or permanent kind."[39] If we
see ritualists as performers, then we may see the students at introductory
meditation classes as performers in training. It should be understood that this is
not merely an analogy: Students at introductory meditation classes were learning
to perform what they were taught.

CONCLUSION

Meditation classes provided spaces for restoration of behaviors like meditation postures, gestures, and concentration practices. They were also sites for discussing and
assessing Buddhist teachings, ethics, and worldviews. Each of the various elements
of the class was an opportunity for gaining new knowledge, attitudes, or skills
through different means: either direct, formalized teaching or through experiential
learning. Each of the elements of the classes was also, to one degree or another, formally structured, or standardized; they involved received practices and teachings
originating in an historical spiritual tradition; many were symbolic, valued highly,
and so on.[40] Ritualized learning, therefore, is learning whose settings, content, or
activities bear several of the qualities commonly associated with ritual.

With its formal structures and embodied patterns of action,[41] ritualizing in
meditation classes has the unique quality of combining formalized and experiential forms of learning. It takes place in formalized educational settings, but it
involves the learner experientially. By sitting cross-legged and concentrating my
mind on an object of meditation, my body-mind teaches me how best to sit and
concentrate. In the context of a formalized meditation class, I am aware that what
I am doing is learning the best ways to sit and concentrate. Moreover, the ritualized nature of what I am learning has important influences on *how* I learn. As the
discussion of respondents' learning experiences progresses, it will become clear
that certain patterns of learning developed which included gaining new knowledge,
new attitudes and values, new skills, and new insights. Before explaining that
pattern in more detail, however, it is first necessary to establish what each of these
different types of learning entails.

4

Beyond Knowledge

PARTICIPATING AT THE meditation classes, I experienced first hand the different ways in which Friends of the Heart and Chandrakirti teachers taught meditation and Buddhist philosophy. But I was also interested in students' own reflections on what they had learned. In the interviews, I asked students several questions designed to get them thinking about their learning: What is the most important thing about the class? Why do you attend? How do you learn what to do, where to sit, what to sing? Do you gain any new knowledge or understanding through the lectures? Through group discussions? Through the practices? Can you teach me something you were taught? This chapter draws on insights from ritual scholars and learning theorists to explore students' responses to these questions and more.

One of the first observations I made was that interview participants made clear distinctions among a number of different spheres of learning. The following interview excerpts supply some examples, taken from responses to the question: Why do you attend meditation classes? Diane's response highlighted cognitive learning:

I attend because I want to know more. So in addition to practicing I get some very concrete teachings which I really like.... So, what I like about the Tuesday night [at Atisha Centre] is that there's a significant teaching. It appeals to the cognitive part of me that wants to understand. I'm a head person, I want to understand it in my head. I wish I were more of a heart person and I could just take in the stuff

at a heart level, but my mind is like: What's that? Why are we doing this? . . . So I
have that bit of a barrier. So, the intellectual and the meditation, the combination
of those two appeal to me.

Although Diane sometimes wished she could take in the teachings on a more experiential or emotional level, she claimed she was more interested in gaining new
knowledge; an intellectual understanding of new material. She more often
responded analytically to what she was learning. Her response suggests that her
need for cognitive understanding is partly due to her aversion to organized religion: She does not wish merely to accept the teachings without evaluating them
first. This is quite a common theme among western Buddhist sympathizers: Many
point to oft-repeated translations of the *Kalama Sūtra,* in which the Buddha advises
followers not to rely on tradition or devotion to a teacher, but to assess the value
of a teaching for themselves. In interviews for this and other projects, I have often
heard this sūtra or its sentiments cited by adoptive Buddhists and sympathizers as
one of the key reasons that Buddhism appeals to them. McMahan, among other
scholars, confirms that a preference for "free inquiry and self-determination" is a
common feature of modernist Buddhism.[1]

When I asked Catherine H. why she attended Chandrakirti classes, she also
spoke about learning new knowledge or information. She said that she had gained
the use of a new kind of language, one that aided her relationships with her hair-
dressing clients.

> It's really giving me a language to communicate with my clients. As a hair stylist,
> we are so close to people, physically, mentally, in all different aspects of their
> lives: personal life, romantic life, family life. So everyone goes through a struggle,
> and I'm able to communicate how to become more compassionate for their
> struggle. And I found that people have actually been able to hear what I was try-
> ing to say. Whereas other times, I didn't have the language before.

Catherine's learning was not only intellectual or analytical. She had also gained
new communication skills. Moreover, the new language she had learned was based
in an increased awareness of compassion, helping her respond to her clients with
increased empathy.

Bronwen noted that learning meditation was important, but she also spoke
about the teachings she heard at Chandrakirti Centre.

> I like the lesson. I should say I always love it. I find I really liked just all the
> thoughts. I really like what they say. My father and I walk down from the center
> to Bloor Station afterwards, and it's a long walk. And we talk and we talk, and

I just feel fresh or just amazed about the thoughts that come out of people's minds, the things that I had never thought of before.

Bronwen was intrigued by the new perspectives she and her father encountered in the General Program classes. She noted that the discussions with her father usually focused on the teachings' ethical dimensions.

Margaret claimed that meditation gave her a kind of skill or technique for focusing on peacefulness and happiness, things that she otherwise overlooked in her daily life.

I guess why I'm drawn to the Wednesday night class and therefore subsequent activities is this search for some kind of groundedness and peace. The meditation that we do when we talk about: May I be happy, may I be peaceful; that embodies what I'm looking for. It's almost like a pause where you start to actually pay attention to those sorts of things that in my day-to-day life get ignored way too often.

Margaret thus highlighted changes in attitudes and emotions that she was developing through meditation practice. Similarly, Gwen spoke about gaining a deeper understanding of herself through meditation, enabling her to be less self-focused and more compassionate. She believed she was learning new ways of relating to those around her.

I believe that it makes me just a little more aware of the depth, the space inside of me and it gives me an opportunity I guess, in that meditation, to explore that, which in turn has all sorts of emotional and psychological benefits. It sort of de-personalizes me on some level....I think it helps to make me more compassionate. Really and truly, I think it helps me particularly in my work to be as connected to my heart or my feelings as I am to my mind.

Gwen's response indicates emotional and psychological changes as well as a degree of spiritual insight. Others described gaining new knowledge, discovering new perspectives or outlooks, and developing skills or techniques for altering habitual emotional responses. Some spoke of the practicalities of posture and meditation technique, learning that strictly focused on how to meditate. Respondents often distinguished intellectual or cognitive learning from that which took place in meditation. These responses indicated, therefore, that there were several qualitatively different types or spheres of learning that took place at the introductory classes.

Dennis's response is interesting because it refers to a number of different types of learning in a few short sentences. When asked why he attended the

Friends of the Heart Calm and Clear class, Dennis said he attended the class "just to try to develop a good meditation practice, and to help me develop a good meditation practice and to learn how to develop a good meditation practice, because the ten weeks will be up soon. You sort of have to learn how to do things. You learn from going to class, but then the class teaches you how to learn, how to do things." Dennis's response at first appears simply repetitive, as though he was trying to gather his thoughts. But on reflection it shows that he was aware of different aspects of learning meditation: his own trial and error, the support he gained from others in the class and the specific techniques he learned. Dennis also noted that the class helped him learn how to learn. He was thus aware of learning on a macro level, or learning itself as a skill that is learned.

The range of different terms respondents used to describe their learning fell into categories such as: intellectual, attitudinal, emotional, ethical, physical, practical, and spiritual. The previous chapter showed that similar descriptors applied to respondents' motivations for attending the courses and hence their expected learning outcomes. Naturally, none is an ideal category: Most interconnected and overlapped with others. But this range of descriptors suggested that respondents' learning went beyond gaining knowledge.

All of this leads us to an important question: What do we mean by learning? Acquiring new information or knowledge by way of studying is one common interpretation of the term. Learning may also involve gaining new skills for assessing, organizing, and relating bits of information to each other. These are intellectual processes. Some interview participants distinctly referred to this kind of learning. It took place chiefly through listening to lectures, reading, discussion groups, and asking questions. This perspective, however, refers to one specific type of learning: knowledge or cognition. When respondents spoke about discovering decorum in the shrine rooms, learning meditation postures and practices, developing concentration, becoming compassionate, finding out about themselves, or uncovering new ways of being in the world, they were speaking about types of learning that are not strictly intellectual or cognitive. We therefore need a broader definition of learning if we are to understand all of the ways in which students at Friends of the Heart and Chandrakirti Centre learned.

In its most basic terms, learning refers to change.[2] Rogers defines learning as "changes in knowledge, understanding, skills, and attitudes which lead to those more or less permanent changes and reinforcements brought about in one's patterns of acting, thinking, and/or feeling."[3] This definition pays attention to processes as well as results of learning. Like the respondents quoted above, Rogers highlights the fact that there are different attributes that change during the learning process: specifically, knowledge, understanding, attitudes, and skills. These changes, in turn, affect the way one acts, thinks, or feels.

The learning attributes Rogers notes in his definition correspond to the categories set out in an influential learning model called Bloom's taxonomy. In effect, three of the four terms Rogers uses in his definition—knowledge, attitudes, and skills—correspond to Bloom's main learning domains.[4] Bloom's taxonomy is a useful framework for analyzing learning in meditation classes. I will show that two of Bloom's domains, the psychomotor and the affective, entail learning processes reminiscent of Schechner's restoration of behavior and are therefore applicable to ritualized learning.

BLOOM'S TAXONOMY

First published in 1956, Bloom's taxonomy identifies three distinct learning domains: the cognitive, which involves mental or intellectual learning and is associated with gaining and employing new knowledge; the affective, which relates to attitudes, emotions, and values and the ways in which they affect behavior; and the psychomotor, which refers to physical abilities, movement, and motor skills.[5] Under each domain is a list of related learning processes which are arranged hierarchically, illustrating the movement from simple learning tasks to those that are more complex. Benjamin S. Bloom and colleagues published handbooks on the cognitive and affective domains[6] but none on the psychomotor domain, citing a lack of secondary school– or college-level teaching of physical skills.[7] Since the original taxonomy was published, revisions and additions have been proposed. Anita Harrow, for example, set out an expanded taxonomy for the psychomotor domain in 1972, and in 2001 a group of educators led by Lorin W. Anderson constructed a revised taxonomy of Bloom's cognitive domain. The purpose of the taxonomy was to help college-level educators plan learning objectives, but it is useful here because it elaborates on different types of learning and their associated learning processes.

COGNITIVE LEARNING

The cognitive domain entails knowledge in terms of information or content. It includes activities such as remembering or recalling, along with abilities related to working with that knowledge. Learning activities in the cognitive domain begin with the basic task of gaining and remembering factual, conceptual, or procedural knowledge.[8] More complex cognitive learning tasks include: interpreting, analyzing and evaluating information, and using it to create something new.[9]

Among Friends of the Heart and Chandrakirti respondents, cognitive learning involved gaining new information about meditation (its purposes, potential bene-fits, and its different postures and techniques) as well as knowledge of Buddhist terms, some of its teachings, but mostly its values and ethics. Respondents gained such knowledge through listening to lectures or meditation instructions, discuss-ing concepts and experiences with others, asking informal questions of teachers and other students, and through reading books or internet sites on their own. Students' cognitive learning also involved analyzing, interpreting, and evaluating the new knowledge they acquired.

At first-round interviews, several newcomers had already learned some common Buddhist terms such as dharma and sangha. By second-round interviews, a few had learned some less familiar terms like *bodhicitta*.[10] Gerald had learned enough to explain placement and analytical meditation (described below). Other factual knowledge included: the names of different Tibetan deities, the terms for practices like insight (known to most respondents by the Pali, *vipassanā*) or black-and-white meditation, metta or loving-kindness meditation, and the names, functions, and meanings of certain mudras. A few students had also learned the names of various ritual objects, as well as their uses, symbols, and meanings, even through this information was not usually given in introductory classes.

Neither was it the objective of introductory classes to provide students with factual data about Buddhist traditions, their history, schools, texts, and so on. Even the talks or lectures did not cover much information of this kind. What respondents did learn about Buddhism as either a philosophical tradition or world religion came mostly from self-directed reading or internet research, and sometimes from informal questions of teachers and other members. When I asked if they had learned about Buddhist history, philosophy or doctrine at the Friends of the Heart class, both John and Dennis said not much. Erin said, "No, not really. Really basic knowledge....Nothing that I could even speak of." But then she said, "Maybe I have, but...haven't really known it as such." Erin suspected that some of Meg's talks were based on Buddhist teachings, without being identified as such. Meg affirmed that the material she used was from a variety of sources. "In this class, I will certainly utilize concepts of ethical precepts. But we don't learn the noble path...[11] we don't learn any of that....So, they don't learn Buddhist stuff. I might use analogies, stories from the Buddhist tradition. But then I might use stories from other traditions as well, but they are from the sacred traditions." Historical Buddhist concepts were introduced but not explicitly identified in Friends of the Heart meditation classes. While such teachings were sometimes mentioned in General Program lectures I attended, specific Buddhist terms such as "Four Noble Truths" were only occasionally used. What might be regarded as technical terms were kept to a minimum so as not to confuse or alienate newcomers. Because Friends of the Heart teachers drew on Buddhist sources without identifying them, students were, in fact, learning more about Buddhism than they were aware. In any case, the teachings emphasized ethics and practices rather than factual details about history, philosophy, or doctrine.

Diane said that Atisha Centre was where she encountered the most "real teachings," those that appealed to her desire for cognitive learning.

> Sort of like Buddhism 101. Where do we go to get that? That's why I like the woman who's teaching at Atisha, because at least I'm getting some of that. It's not at an academic level, which is not what I really want either, I don't want to get a degree.... Certainly, the Wednesday meditation class [at Friends of the Heart] is not a place where you learn about those things, because the purpose of those classes was insight meditation.

I asked Diane if it was important to know about the history of Buddhism, its philosophy, or its teachings, and she replied:

> To a certain extent. I'd like to understand the framework.... I don't really want to delve into all of the history, but just generally to understand what it means to be a Tibetan Buddhist or Vajrayana Buddhist.... And I don't know why there needs to be so many Buddhists out there. I guess I don't know enough about the differences that you need to have so many different kinds of them around the city.

Like many newcomer respondents, Diane was unaware of the varied cultural influences over extensive geographical regions that had created the many diverse Buddhist schools.

In the interviews, I noticed other bits of information that respondents had learned. When speaking about his meditation practice, for example, Alan said: "I can always go home and drink a glass of wine. But I can't do that now, I've got to meditate first." Alan had learned that drinking wine before meditation is, as he put it, "a no-no." He said that this was "their idea," indicating that he had heard about the restriction on alcohol from General Program teachers. The fifth of the five Buddhist precepts, traditional guidelines for laypersons, advocates against the consumption of fermented drinks.[12] When I asked Alan if he had heard of the five precepts, he said he was not sure. "Are they things to give up?" he asked. I described them to him, and he said that the teachers at Chandrakirti Centre had mentioned them from time to time. "Observance of them increases your merit for a good rebirth," Alan said, "a better life the next time around. They hold them up as good things to do, but they don't tell people they should do them." Hence some of the factual information Alan had learned included one of the precepts' restrictions, but no specific knowledge of the precepts themselves.

Several respondents said they did not consider cognitive learning, in the sense of an intellectual understanding of new material, to be important when learning about Buddhism or meditation. When asked about what they were learning, six of the students interviewed said they would rather avoid what they considered to be too much information or analysis. Gerald, for example, said he was willing to familiarize himself with basic principles, but did not want to read any interpretive information about Buddhism.

> Personally, I prefer not to read. I have the most basic [book]—it's like the Dr. Seuss of Buddhist books, *What the Buddha Taught*.[13] It doesn't go off anywhere except for basic principles. I try to stick with that only because I don't want to come in there with something I've picked up and think it's my question. I want to go in there, at least for the first year, for the first introduction, knowing that my questions are my own, that I haven't picked it up somewhere. And that's important....I wanted to just have that initial reaction to it myself, uneducated.

Gerald thus felt that gaining too much knowledge in advance might impede his personal reactions to and interpretations of the teachings. Similarly, Priscilla said, "I think you can get confused if you read too many different commentaries on texts." Alan distinguished between learning in the sense of gaining information and discovering ways to improve himself, the latter being more important in his view. "I think at this stage of the game," he said, "because there's a lot of work I have to do myself, I don't need to get tons of information." John, notably, contrasted meditation to learning new concepts. "I'm sure you can go into Buddhism and find vast concepts to try and get your mind around, but you don't do that during meditation. At least, not any meditation that we've been taught. It's the very opposite." Finally, Brenda expressed a similar sentiment:"I've learned by not rushing to learn, which is how I would normally do things. I turn most things into research projects, so this one I thought: You can't do it. You just have to be with it. Just allow it to be as it is and don't analyze it....I need to treat this as an experience, not an intellectual exercise."

In fact, these comments reflect an interpretation of learning that is also found in Buddhist sūtras or canonical texts, where cognitive learning or intellectualizing is regarded as an obstacle to putatively higher levels of wisdom. Commenting on this perspective, Étienne Lamotte writes, "A person may become convinced that dedication of a purely intellectual order is sufficient, but this is far from the truth. The direct view constitutes true wisdom [*la vraie sagesse*] and this is what is necessary for salvation."[14] In this view, intellectualizing is merely a first step; it may, in fact, hinder deeper understanding. Although the majority of students to whom I spoke were not familiar with the scriptural sources for these ideas, several students from both centers expressed a preference for domains of learning other than the cognitive.

Another indication that cognitive learning was not of primary importance came, notably, from the one respondent who claimed to be most interested in cognitive learning. Diane said:"I really like the meditation classes that we did [at Friends of the Heart], the meditation part of it, but I would like a little more teaching about what it is that we were looking for. Maybe that's not good for me, because it's too much in my head, but [I prefer] a little bit more of a cognitive component to it." Diane frequently described her learning preferences as cognitive or intellectual. "I live pretty much from the neck up," she said. "It's at Atisha, really, where the most concrete learning has been. You know, like: What is the mind? What is concentration? I feel like a bit of a sponge. I'm doing a lot of reading and trying to understand." Diane felt it was important to learn new concepts from knowledge-able teachers, and she was most interested in cognitively exploring those concepts. "It appeals to the cognitive part of me that wants to understand. I'm a head person, I want to understand it in my head."

Despite her interest in the cognitive aspects of learning, Diane said she would rather be able to respond differently to what she was learning at Atisha Centre and Friends of the Heart: "I want to understand conceptually but that's not my ultimate goal. My ultimate goal is to live my life a bit differently, with more meaning." She said that intellectually understanding the concepts she was learning was appealing, but her main objective was to make some more substantive changes in her life. "Who am I?" she had been asking herself: "And that brought me back to wanting to meditate and that's why I was interested in insight meditation, because I wanted to find out more about who I am." While she recognized that she was "a head person," she also said, "I wish I were more of a heart person and I could just take in the stuff at a heart level." In Diane's view, her preference for cognitive learning influenced the quality of learning she experienced. "So I have that bit of a barrier," she said, an indication that her desire for intellectual learning was an obstacle for experiencing learning on the "heart level." "So, the intellectual and the meditation," Diane said, "the combination of those two appeal to me."

Thekchen also indicated that a cognitive or intellectual understanding of the teachings was not sufficient. He said that sometimes students at the General Program classes respond a little too easily to certain concepts.

I give a teaching on challenging your self-cherishing mind: That [self-cherishing mind] is your entire basis of reality and of being. And for people to just sit there and go: Yeah, makes sense—I don't think it got in. I just challenged every single belief system you have. Either you took it on an intellectual level and you're not taking it in, which means you're just going to keep on being self centered, or … you want to soak it in a little bit before asking a question.

In Thekchen's view, then, some of the concepts he taught required something other than cognitive comprehension. He was, in fact, referring to the need for an affective understanding of his teachings.

AFFECTIVE LEARNING

The term "affective" refers to affections or emotions as well as changes that affect behavior. Learning on an affective level begins with sensitivity and attentiveness to new emotions and attitudes. As affective learning progresses, the learner responds to the new emotions and attitudes, "valuing" or attaching value to them, and then either rejecting or accepting and committing to them. Acceptance and commitment create a new value system by which the learner begins to voluntarily adjust his or her behavior. With time, the new value system may be internalized to the point at which it influences behavior, in predictable ways, at a less conscious level. Bloom and colleagues referred to this last affective process as "characterizing values."[15]

Nearly all of my respondents, teachers and students alike, indicated that affective change and reinforcement was the core of what was taught and learned at Friends of the Heart and Chandrakirti Centre. Most respondents actually indicated that the primary purpose of cognitive and psychomotor learning was to support the affective changes that they sought or experienced. Gwen, for example, described her learning process in terms very similar to affective learning processes, especially changing emotions and accepting new values.

I can see the transitions as you progress through life. … It's not that I have rubbed away emotions. I'm probably better at sitting with them. I'm probably not as reactionary as I used to be. I have the ability to respond, I think, in a way that I didn't feel like I had to do. I feel like I settle in a different way, sitting. I also feel I'm connected to something really good in the world. Something that I believe is good.

Gwen believed that her emotional responses had changed over time, and that the new responses were being repeated and reinforced as she practiced at Friends of the Heart. She said she had gained new values that she wanted to put into practice. The affective changes she described were, in her view, the result of meditation practice. Her strongly positive description of her learning emphasizes the fact that she highly valued and had committed to the teachings and practices that she had learned.

Another question I put to respondents was: can you teach me something you were taught? The question was intended to draw out the most significant or memorable elements of respondents' learning. In response to this question, experienced Friends of the Heart member David said, "What's coming to mind is not so much of a teaching, like a technique or something. It's more knowing that we have the potential, we have the ability to have peace, a great deal of happiness, acceptance. So that's something very deep I've learned from Friends of the Heart." Note the distinction David made: He declined to speak about a particular technique, emphasizing instead a change in perspective, the belief that it was possible to be happier and more peaceful—an affective change. Respondents used a range of similar or related terms to refer to what I am calling affective learning. Margaret, for example, believed that learning meditation at Friends of the Heart helped her become more grounded and at peace. Anna also spoke about feeling more peaceful. Catherine H. said that Chandrakirti lectures highlighted compassion, kindness, and giving. Brenda spoke about compassion, patience, wishing others well, being in the moment, and being respectful. She said that her practice was loving kindness, and that the General Program classes helped reinforce and remind her of that practice. Tanit spoke about compassion, patience, spirituality, and virtue:

I'm beginning to realize that, as I travel this journey, there's something else, that spiritual thing. And I don't even know how to define that. I understand that being compassionate, having patience, these relate to spirituality, but it's almost like they are symptoms of it, but not it. So, I don't think I can define it. I just have the sense to recognize that there is this spirituality, of being concerned about virtue, about your word being true.

Alan emphasized generosity and honesty. He said he used to think of generosity in terms of giving time or money, but now regarded being generous as being more caring or thoughtful. He also talked about giving things up, being happy with less, and letting go of attachments. Carol, who also participated at Chandrakirti Centre, spoke of compassion and selfless love. Among Friends of the Heart students, Dennis spoke about equanimity and balance, and Diane believed that affective change meant learning nonattachment, selflessness, and aspects of Buddhism's eightfold path: right thinking and right behavior were the examples she gave.

To summarize, attitudinal changes that respondents described included becoming more generous, selfless, or less attached. Emotional responses included gratitude, love, sympathetic joy, equanimity, happiness, and feeling calm, grounded, or at peace. All of these attitudes and emotions may also be regarded as values, since they were generally highly esteemed or "valued." In meditation classes, teachers held up such values as positive means of counteracting negative states such as selfishness or self-cherishing, materialism, anger, impatience, attachment, or stress. The values emphasized in the lectures, talks, and meditation practices were usually inspired by Buddhist teachings: truthfulness (one of the Buddhist precepts), interconnected-ness, and cherishing others were among them. Compassion, which is often described in the Buddhist perspective as a virtue rather than an emotion,[16] was mentioned most often in classes and interviews.

The reason affective learning was important for most respondents had to do with their motivations for enrolling in meditation classes. Most of those to whom I spoke described learning goals that corresponded to affective changes. Alan, for example, enrolled in meditation classes because he wanted to be happier. Tanit, who had been intrigued by the idea of enlightenment, spoke often about learning meditation techniques, but most strongly emphasized the new outlooks and values she believed meditation practice had inspired in her.

By contrast, John was not expecting to change his attitudes or values in a significant way when he enrolled in meditation courses. He was interested primarily in learning meditation techniques, and he emphasized skills and, to a lesser extent, intellectual learning, over attitudinal changes or changes in values. When I asked John if he thought he had developed any new attitudes from the practice he said no. He said that meditation affected his mood, an affective change, but he primarily spoke about meditation techniques as the results rather than a means of learning. Dennis and Erin were the other two respondents whose primary interest was in learning how to meditate. When speaking about the results of the meditation course, Dennis said he thought he was better able to concentrate and to be more efficient at his job. Erin said she felt less stressed, and was better able to calm her mind. Significantly, both said they could not conclusively attribute these changes to the meditation classes, but believed that there may have been a relationship. Dennis and Erin spoke about the techniques they were learning and the ways they cogni-tively understood the purposes of those techniques more than any attitudinal or emotional changes they experienced. Motivations for attending the classes, there-fore, corresponded to, and may have influenced, learning outcomes. Friends of the Heart students John, Dennis, and Erin were exceptions overall: most respondents highlighted affective change as the most important aspect of their learning.

Another question I asked in the interviews was: Does learning at the meditation classes differ from learning subjects at school or job skills? This question was intended to encourage respondents to reflect on the types of learning they experienced. In most cases, students contrasted learning meditation or Buddhist teachings to learning on a technical or cognitive level.

When I spoke with Tanit, much of her conversation concerned various skills and techniques involved in learning meditation: its postures and how to sit comfortably; its meditative practices and how to concentrate; and so on. Even so, when asked to compare learning at Friends of the Heart to learning job skills, she made a distinction between what she called technical skills and the skills used in meditation.

> It's interesting because I'm learning about Buddhism right now and I just got into a series of classes on CAD, which is a computer program. Somehow, there's a difference about learning a skill. CAD is out here [Tanit gestured in front of her]. I'm on my mouse and I'm controlling a screen and I'm drawing something. And meditating is inside. It's more profound in some way than learning CAD. And I enjoyed learning CAD, too. But I'm not thinking about how it connects me to my world, how I see.... It's a different consciousness. Because, interestingly enough, I draw and paint and that is more connected to the Buddhist practice of meditation because I'm thinking about what I'm doing and I'm laying down a piece of paper or a color and then I'm thinking, okay is that where it should be? And it's completely personal.... So, there's this internal questioning—is this right? Does it need to be here?—which I find in the meditation. You know, is this right for me? It doesn't matter about the autoCAD standards, it's not applicable. So I find the meditation has more to do with creating than learning technical skills.

In this response, Tanit was referring to the overall processes and effects of learning meditation, rather than learning its individual skills or methods. She was drawing a distinction between the objectives of learning autoCAD and those of meditation: learning the computer program had specific external results, while meditation's effects were internal and "more profound." Despite the fact that autoCAD is a computer drawing program, Tanit distinguished it from other forms of drawing and painting, which she said were more creative and personal—qualities that she associated with meditation. The distinction she drew thus highlighted the affective elements of learning meditation—values and attitudes—rather than physical abilities or motor skills.

Marlon referred to the intellectual activity of the mind as a skill, and contrasted it to learning through meditation, which he saw as a way of gaining an understanding of how the mind works.

> The other types of learning that I have encountered, say in a job or even in the regular education that I had in school, they often asked us to use our mind to achieve something. You know, if you're in a job, you work out a certain skill; you

use your mind to do that. Here, the learning is inward. The other type of learning that I had was that we use our mind to achieve something, like a skill, or construct certain things. Here...we learn about ourselves, in particular our mind, and how our mind works and how to produce positive minds and how to get rid of negative minds.

In this speech, Marlon makes a distinction between learning new applications of the mind and understanding its underlying processes. He describes the latter as more holistic and spiritual: It creates a deeper understanding of the self, and creates more positive, more valued states of mind than does learning particular mental skills. While Tanit contrasted meditation to technical skills and Marlon contrasted meditation to cognitive abilities, both regarded learning at the meditation classes as more inward—more about the self than the sensory world—than learning at school or on the job.

Like Marlon, Gwen indicated that learning about meditation or Buddhism was distinct from the intellectual kind of learning that takes place at school. She said that learning about Buddhism entailed discovering and exploring the processes of the mind rather than adding to its content. Gwen also compared learning Buddhist practices to practicing t'ai chi. She said:

I think learning Buddhism is a bit like a learning how to think, like in philosophy. So, if you think: I'm studying a way of being in the world. You can do that through philosophy right? This is my philosophy of life. Or you could do it through t'ai chi for a while. I did it through t'ai chi: What does it mean to recreate balance and harmony over and over again? Buddhists [ask]: What does it mean to be a compassionate human being? And continuing to develop in that way is bigger than understanding Math 101 or geography. Because I think it gives you a framework in which to view things. So everything that you're viewing, you view through a particular heart-mind sort of connection. So I think it's different, I think it is bigger than one little subject.

Like Tanit and Marlon, Gwen indicated that learning Buddhist meditation had a more holistic effect on the learner than gaining knowledge or skills related to a particular subject. Gwen spoke of creating balance and harmony and learning to be compassionate—affective processes of internalizing and enacting new attitudes and values. These students are describing what McLaren calls "deep codes": frameworks for understanding and for changing the ground upon which other knowledge, experience, and skills are founded.

Like Gwen, several other respondents distinguished the heart from the mind or brain. Diane, as quoted earlier, distinguished between head-level and heart-level learning. Anna associated learning with the mind or intellect while describing her experiences at Friends of the Heart as heart-felt. She said "I think because the practices there that I have seen, they sit with my heart so readily that I don't really think of it as learning." Anna thus affirmed the common association of learning with what goes on in the mind.

In Alan's view, learning about Buddhism also had wider effects and applications than learning job skills. "I think there's a huge difference. I think with the Buddhism, it's really changing yourself. For example, if you try to get a new skill or a new trade, it would be all about you, the idea of gain, or whatever. The Buddhism, to me, actually is giving up. It is giving up what you might have thought. It's like changing a lot of what I would have thought." There is an interesting contrast here: learning on the job consists of gaining something, a process that is more individual and, in Alan's view, more selfish. Alan believed that Buddhist concepts were about letting go, being selfless, less attached. Still, Alan is describing the affective process of receiving, valuing, accepting, and enacting new ethical perspectives on being a better person, living a happier life. Margaret also contrasted learning, in the sense of gaining something, to learning meditation, which meant letting go.

> I guess much of the formal learning that I have done has been book learning. You know, applying your mind, trying to fill your mind with information. Meditation for me, initially anyways, is about emptying my mind and there's also the kind of mind/body connection. That's quite different from my formal education experiences. It's also more about me as a person rather than me as a worker or task kind of person. . . . It's very apparent to me that that is a place that's values-driven and has a spiritual component to it. And, to a large extent, it is a place for personal, inner kind of work as opposed to a club or a library or whatever, where it's either very social, not about looking inward but interacting with people, or acquiring book knowledge.

Margaret, like Marlon, Tanit, and Gwen, associated other kinds of learning with the intellect and meditation with inward processes affecting larger aspects of the self including values, ethics, and spirituality. The majority of student respondents, in fact, described learning meditation or Buddhist concepts in terms that corresponded to Bloom's affective learning tasks.

Students' emphasis on affective learning may have been influenced by the objectives of the teachers, who also stressed affective outcomes. Catherine Rathbun expressed what she believed was the most important learning gained at Friends of the Heart: "What they take away, I hope, is courage, the ability to find their own strength, the ability to develop compassion, and see how those things—their skills and their compassion, their courage, and their convictions—can be used in the world to help others." Thekchen described the General Program classes as "a place where people can come, develop an inner peace through meditation in a safe environment, question and talk about things, and discuss and listen to other perspectives and different methods that come from a different source." As already noted, the talks and lectures at both centers highlighted attitudes and values based in Buddhist teachings. It was clear that the objectives of the teachings, together with the meditation practices, were to help students: moderate emotions by developing equanimity and nonattachment; change attitudes by listening to teachings or meditating on generosity, sympathetic joy, or cherishing others; and begin developing a new value system based on Buddhist principles of compassion, impermanence, and no-self.

The ritualized nature of the classes, their settings and teachings, also influenced students' affective learning. Chandrakirti Centre was the stronger example. Its setting, the formal character of the class, the role of the teacher—who was not only a teacher but often an ordained monastic—the traditional source of the teachings and their religious or spiritual content: all of these elements were strongly characterized by various ritual qualities, that is, they were formal, special, set aside, elevated, and so on. In his study of Catholic-school instruction, McLaren argues that ritual structures and symbols sanctify the learning process, and tacitly shape the ways in which students learn.[17] Like Friends of the Heart and Chandrakirti courses, the Catholic-school classes McLaren studied had elements that were formal, repetitive, communal, elevated, spatially and temporally separated from ordinary activities, and so on. McLaren argues that these qualities served to instill ritual knowledge, the deep codes that act as the foundations of learners' understanding of the world and of their reactions in various situations.[18] His description of ritual knowledge brings to mind the last learning activity in Bloom's affective domain, by which the learner develops characterizing values that predictably influence his or her behavior.[19] Ritualized structures invest teachers and teachings with heightened affective qualities: attitudes, emotions or values that are, in a sense, sanctified by their association with the ritualized structures and settings in which they are encountered.

Even so, there were limits to this legitimizing effect. Many respondents, especially newcomers, were not ready to accept the more metaphysical aspects of Buddhist teachings, particularly those related to karma and rebirth. Unlike Friends of the Heart and several other western Buddhist centers I have encountered, Chandrakirti lectures did not shy away from karmic rebirth cosmology. Students heard about the different realms of rebirth—heavenly, human, animal, and hell realms—and the belief that our actions have lingering consequences that, if unfulfilled at the time of death, cause us to be reborn. While teachers sometimes softened these concepts with metaphorical interpretations—realms of rebirth likened to emotional or psychological states, as noted earlier—they were rarely apologetic about interpreting these doctrines literally. McMahan points out that a number of contemporary westernized Buddhist organizations are "retraditionalizing" in this way: teaching literalist interpretations of Buddhist metaphysics as a means of establishing authenticity through references to the past.[20] Chandrakirti's literalist presentation of karmic rebirth follows this trend.

Even so, several Chandrakirti participants I spoke to were uneasy about karmic rebirth. Alan, for example, said he had read an article by Kelsang Gyatso in which he wrote about discovering his mother reborn in the child of friends living in England. Alan said he could not bring himself to accept, logically, that reincarnation occurs as Gyatso described. But Alan also said that such beliefs were not an obstacle to his participation in Buddhist-based practices or at Chandrakirti Centre.

At Friends of the Heart, Meg noted that her students were often doubtful about karmic rebirth.

> We never taught reincarnation. Never. Personally, because I'm a little bit wavering myself on that concept. And secondly, because it just puts people off, and it's just plain not relevant at this stage....I'm a little cautious about that, because I think it has been treated in a new-agey way that is inappropriate....We won't necessarily talk about karma. We will talk about action and reaction. Sure. We get that. As westerners, we really get that.

An understanding of karma as the law of cause and effect is another way of reinterpreting Buddhist metaphysics. But such metaphorical shifts were not necessary if the concepts could be avoided altogether. Few Friends of the Heart respondents expressed concerns over karmic rebirth, for the simple reason that it was not taught at the classes. Friends of the Heart student Diane, who had learned about karma at Atisha's General Program classes, said: "I have to say I was a bit disturbed about karma." Gwen, who had twenty years' experience learning and teaching t'ai chi and had encountered many eastern religious concepts, said that she was still working out her feelings about karmic rebirth. "Do I really believe in reincarnation? I don't know that it matters yet. Certain questions don't matter yet. The truth of the practice and the fact that it's good for myself and the rest of the universe, and I believe that, is what matters. Whether I come back again, I don't know." While teachings regarding karmic rebirth may have caused concern, most respondents did not regard them as a barrier to their participation at Friends of the Heart or Chandrakirti Centre. Naturally, newcomers for whom such teachings were an obstacle would not have been around long enough to participate in interviews, so it is impossible to say how many people may have been discouraged from participating. These responses do show, however, that ritual legitimation of teachings did not overcome most respondents' preferences for a rationalist, demythologized expression of Buddhism.

To better understand what students had learned, I also asked them what they had not. Were there any questions they still had? Was there anything they found confusing? Responses to these questions illuminated the content and purposes of the meditation classes. They also highlighted the limits of learning through ritualizing.

When I asked John what he had not learned, he said he was curious about some of the symbolic elements at Friends of the Heart:

> I suppose it would be interesting just to have someone who knew all the details about the statuary and the symbols on a lot of things. I think there are probably a great many more symbols on different tapestries that are on the walls that Buddhists would look at and say: Oh, yes, that's such and such. That represents this, that, and the other. I'm seeing them and not knowing what they are.

While this statement indicates mere curiosity on John's part—he made it clear he was not interested in Buddhism as a religion—it is an indication of something that was not explained at the Insight meditation class. Students engaged in ritualized practices, but were not always informed about the ritual objects or symbols present in the meditation halls.

Other respondents suggested there were some gaps in learning about particular meditation practices, the correct ways to do them, and what their benefits were. Dennis felt that the teaching at the Friends of the Heart class had been very thorough, but he sometimes wondered if he had learned enough about meditation.

> What I'm sort of wondering is if there is ever a point where it all sort of clicks. I guess I sometimes you wonder if you're doing things right and if you're getting the full benefit. That might be a bad way to put it, but at the end result, when you've got a lot of experience and you've been doing it for a while, what does that feel like? So I'm wondering, will something sort of click where you know you've [got it]. So, that's sort of a wondering going forward, I guess.

Dennis understood that a certain amount of practice is required in order to know the "right way" to meditate and to experience its benefits. He had learned that the goal was to keep practicing and evaluating his practice until it began to feel right. While he had questions about how to get to that point, he also believed that such questions could not be answered by someone else, and that the answers would come through experience. Dennis, therefore, was aware of the value of experiential learning: practicing, adjusting, and perfecting his skills and abilities. Friends of the Heart classes were not meant to be the end of the learning process. Commitment to a regular personal meditation practice was seen as the next step.

Several students from both centers expressed a kind of equanimity about questions they still had or things they had not yet learned. In their view, learning would take its own time. When asked if he still had questions, for example, Alan calmly said: "The questions I have, I will find the answers to." Brenda said that she learned by "not rushing to learn." Although Carol was aware she was missing the detailed study of the Foundation Program, she said she was content with her current level of participation: "I'm not getting as deep as I could and maybe my little brain is happy to be there at the moment. This is where I am along that path." Gwen said that she thought she should have questions, but she did not. "And that's like how I approach t'ai chi. I do it, and we shall see what comes." Tanit said that she did not understand the practice of seeking feelings or emotions located in the body. But, she said: "that's okay. I think that's probably what I'm enjoying about it [the class] so much. It sounds a bit trite, but everything is right....Everything you don't understand, this is fine." Tanit was confident that the answers would come in their own time. "I think there's a lot that's unanswered, but I am really comfortable with that....I feel that I'm on a journey, and I'm enjoying the journey."

This equanimity attests to respondents' receptivity in the context of learning meditation and Buddhist teachings. Allowing answers to come in their own time and avoiding seeking out too much cognitive knowledge may indicate a preference for affective learning tasks: valuing, absorbing, and gaining a deeper appreciation over time for new outlooks and orientations. But unconcern over things yet unlearned also suggests that some things can only be learned with time and experience, that learning through practice was more important than gaining knowledge.

PSYCHOMOTOR LEARNING

The third of Bloom's domains is the psychomotor, which has to do with developing and refining motor skills, physical activities, and co-ordination. The learner begins by observing and then imitating new movements or physical abilities, developing the rudiments of skills. Skills improve with practice and repetition, and finally the learner adapts and fine tunes the skills in order to perfect them.[21] In a later addition to Bloom's taxonomy, Harrow listed the kinds of skills that are learned and perfected in this domain. Her list begins with reflex movements which are not learned, but are the building blocks of other physical skills. In Harrow's account, psychomotor learning involves fundamental movements like walking and grasping, physical abilities like strength and stamina, and more complex abilities she calls skilled movements. It also includes nondiscursive communication such as body language.[22]

Several students described meditation techniques in terms of the skills that they developed. When I asked John if learning meditation was different to learning on the job, he significantly compared meditation, including its concentration techniques, to learning physical skills. "Oh, well, it's very different than that. It's much more like a physical activity. Oddly enough, for being as mental, for sitting still, it has much more in common with physical activities, in terms of practicing and doing it over and over and not being very good at the beginning and getting better as you do it." John is actually describing the type of learning that takes place in the psychomotor domain: meditation involves the repetition of received activities (physical-mental skills in terms of postures and concentration techniques) and refinement of those activities through practice. In John's perspective, then, meditation—even in its mental aspects—was more comparable to a physical than a cognitive activity.

Dennis also compared learning meditation to developing physical skills.

I'll give you an example. I joined a running club with a friend of mine. You meet every Monday and then you have to get your runs in every week, and if you don't do that you sort of fall behind. So, jogging, I guess is the same thing as meditation in that you have to do it at regular times throughout the week instead of on one day, do a run for an hour or something. So, from a discipline aspect I would say the two are similar. Yeah, with other things, too, it's a skill. I look at it as a skill you have to learn and develop over the time.

Dennis chose a strongly physical activity, running, as an analogy here: he likened meditation to training, perfecting a skill through disciplined repetition of performance. Following the above remarks, I asked him about learning from an intellectual perspective: Was learning meditation like mathematics classes at school? He replied:

Well, I wouldn't say so. I mean, in the sense of the learning process where you read something for the first time, think about it, and then maybe read it again and then maybe discuss it with somebody, it's the same thing that we're doing in meditation class. You might read about something, try it out, and discuss it. So, I guess that process in learning might be similar. And I guess, also, if you don't do something for a long time the skills get rusty, so if you don't meditate for a long time you get rusty. At the same time, if you're out of practice at doing math and problem-solving, you can get rusty with that as well. So, I guess there are some similarities.

Dennis points out that, in the meditation class, there are cognitive processes of learning going on: students take in information, mull it over, and perhaps discuss it with others. But learning *through* meditation practice itself is not the same as learning *about* meditation in class lectures and discussions.

Now, it could be argued that the skill learned through meditative concentration techniques is a cognitive one. Certainly, the cognitive domain does depict a similar pattern of learning tasks: acquiring information, becoming familiar with it, refining our skills of analysis and comprehension through discipline and familiarity, and so on. The process undeniably involves the development of cognitive skills for evaluating and analyzing information. But rather than concluding from this that meditative concentration techniques are strictly cognitive, I would argue that some psychomotor learning—the improvement of performance—also takes place concurrent with cognitive learning.[23] I find it significant that many respondents differentiated gaining, memorizing, and manipulating new information from learning, repeating, and refining concentration skills. The important feature here is how the mind performs meditative focus, not how it manages content.

While Bloom and colleagues did not elaborate on the psychomotor domain, Schechner actually offers a detailed vision of this type of learning with his description of restoration of behavior. Restored behavior refers to "organized sequences of events, scripted actions, known texts [and] scored movements" existing separately from those who perform them. As such, it can be "stored, transmitted, manipulated, transformed."[24] Like psychomotor learning, restoration of behavior is a process wherein behaviors are observed (that is, received from the outside and transmitted), imitated, repeated, and adapted. In theater workshops, Schechner notes, performers break down behaviors into the smallest repeatable "bits."[25] Not likely as small as Harrow's reflex movements, Schechner's bits would probably fall under her "fundamental movements" category. Bits are then experimented with, rearranged, and restored into new, longer strips of behavior. Workshops and rehearsals are sites in which performers practice skilled movements until they gain the stamina, strength, agility, and familiarity required to perform the new actions expertly. Harrow, in fact, lists performing arts under skilled movements in her taxonomy. As Schechner writes: "What was rote movement, even painful body realignment, becomes second nature—full language capable of conveying detailed and subtle meanings and feelings."[26] With repetition and refinement, physical skills become embodied to the point at which they act as a kind of tacit knowledge on which the performer can draw without explicitly thinking about it. This is just the kind of ritual knowledge or "embodied practical reason," as Crossley calls it, that develops through ritual activity.[27]

Schechner notes that restoration of behavior is a process that is virtually the same in ritual as it is in theater; and it is in theater workshops that ritualizing is most prominent.[28] In ritual and in theater, the performer is first separated from his or her ordinary state. Schechner claims that performers become a tabula rasa on entry to the workshop space, thus becoming receptive to new learning. Receptivity means that there is always something being received by someone.[29] That someone is either the performer him- or herself, a group of primary or secondary performers, or an attendant audience, be it human or divine.[30] For performers to become receptive they must first be separated from familiar surroundings, which is why restoration of behavior and ritualizing often take place in special, liminal, or sacred spaces. Note, however, that separation is never complete: performers bring with them their prior knowledge, attitudes, and skills. The liminal space and time enables them to work with those preexisting attributes, creating something new through the work of ritualizing or restoration of behavior.[31] The last phase of the workshop process is reintegration, in which the performer rehearses the restored behavior until it becomes second nature. The outcome of a theater workshop is a new theatrical performance. Schechner makes it clear that similar processes takes place through ritualizing, which is the means of creating a new ritual or of updating an old one.

The behaviors that performers acquire and begin to adapt in workshop settings are received from a particular source, which may be a text or a previous performance or ritual.[32] Schechner argues that, while source material is often believed to be drawn from historical events or ancient tradition, much actually derives from earlier performances, what Schechner calls "nonevents."[33] Meditation postures, gestures, and techniques are examples of behaviors that may be received, repeated, and refined. The mythic origins of these behaviors—the Buddha seated under the bodhi tree, the saffron-robed monk or nun deep in meditative absorption—can influence attitudes or emotions concerning them, and may connect them to a value system that is itself (believed to be) traditional and therefore special. Meg, for instance, spoke of the connection between her meditation classes and the traditional origins of Buddhist practice:

> I guess my own personal goal in this is to give some robust, effective, time-tested (like 2000 years of time-tested) tools that they [students] can work with, which if they work with will yield benefit now, but will yield benefit deeper and deeper and deeper as they proceed with it. And if they choose to proceed, it's not up to me. It's up to the dharma. I'm just a servant. I'm just a tool of the dharma in that sense.

In actual fact, Meg's teachings were adapted each time she offered them, quite consciously so. She presented what worked best, in her experience, for her particular audience. Still, she maintained that there was an important link to Buddhist tradition, a link that, in her view, made the practices special.

Meditation classes I attended had phases similar to those of Schechner's theatrical workshops. We students, performers-in-training, stepped out of our everyday routines on entering a shrine room. Formal practices performed on entry helped us accept, if only for a time, the values expressed by the setting and the group. We then received instruction on meditation, its postures and particular meditation practices; or we listened to a talk on Buddhist ethical teachings and worldviews. Guided through meditation practice, we learned new ways of sitting or maintaining a particular posture, new ways of breathing, of directing and holding our awareness, or of reflecting on the meanings of a teaching—all very basic, fundamental behaviors performed in new ways. Our learning involved restoration of behavior: We received the different postures and techniques from teachers and then repeated them over and again, refining them in order to achieve familiarity and the capacity to maintain postures and concentration. Note the correlation to psychomotor learning tasks. We were encouraged, especially at Friends of the Heart, to combine, experiment with, and adapt the postures and techniques we learned: Try this gesture, that posture, teachers advised. Try it again. If it does not work, if there is too much pain or discomfort or you cannot concentrate, try something else: adjust the support cushions, kneel, or sit in a chair. Students tried different postures and supports at home: Tanit tried sitting on a sofa cushion, which was lower than the zafu, for example. Using a short stool was never suggested at the classes, but this was Alan's choice for his home meditation practice. Joyce and Meg both conducted lying-down meditation in their classes, having us lie on the floor with our knees up and hands on our abdomens. This posture was taught as an alternative: try it out if seated meditation is not working. At more than one of the Chandrakirti General Program classes, I observed students lying down in the pews during some meditation sessions, even though there were no instructions from teachers to do so.

Postures constituted only one set of behaviors with which we experimented. There was actually more encouragement to experiment with the concentration techniques we were taught. Try beginning with a body scan, teachers advised: relax the tongue, the muscles around the eyes. Look for other areas that are tense, if that works better. Turn the body scan into insight meditation, seeking out areas of touch or rest in the body. Add the search for images or thoughts; if this becomes too complicated, just go back to observing the breath. We were introduced to several different techniques, and encouraged to combine them or to set aside those that did not work. At one Insight class, for example, a young woman who had fidgeted through the meditation sessions said she liked the concentration techniques she was learning, but she had a hard time sitting still. She preferred to perform the concentration exercises while walking. This was her way of "restoring" the meditation "behavior." There was, therefore, a wide range of adapted behaviors going on both within and outside the classes.

If classes were workshops, then rehearsals began with our daily meditation practice. We were encouraged to meditate each day—Friends of the Heart students were asked to meditate for longer periods each week—to find the best techniques and keep them up until we gained facility and familiarity with the practices. The final performance was the hoped-for outcome of meditation practice: long-lasting behavioral change resulting from emotional and attitudinal changes such as stress reduction, calmness, equanimity, or increased capacity for kindness and compassion. Ideally, students would begin performing ordinary activities in accordance with the new values and attitudes. Several respondents indicated, however, that such behavioral changes tended to drop off once they had discontinued their home practice, their involvement at the centers, or both. Even so, students' engagement with meditation classes and personal meditation practice appeared to link the development of new skills with attitudinal change, thus connecting psychomotor and affective learning.

Restoration of behavior, like affective learning, involves willingness, attention, and awareness. There is an interesting reversal between Schechner's approach to restoration of behavior and the affective learning tasks described by Bloom and colleagues. Bloom's taxonomy suggests that changes in attitudes, feelings, emotions, or values lead to changes in behavior. Behavioral changes are initially conscious and voluntary. With time, driven by the new value system, they become stable, predictable, and characteristic of the learner.[34] Such behavioral changes are not necessarily things learned; they are results of learning—Rogers makes a similar point in his definition of learning. For Schechner, however, behavior is an object or material that may first be experimented with, something that one takes apart and reconstructs, distancing oneself from one's behaviors in the process. This is not behavior in the sense of the outcome of attitudinal change: It is closer to the motor skills and activities of the psychomotor domain. In Schechner's view, it is the manipulation of behavior that changes attitudes, not the other way around.[35] Experimenting with, practicing, and adapting behaviors may affect attitudinal change which, in turn, may lead to long-term, less conscious behavioral change. As Schechner notes, the work of performing artists along with ritualists like trancers, shamans, and meditators is to effect permanent or temporary "psychophysical transformations."[36] Schechner's perspective thus links psycho-motor and affective learning.

If learning activities consist of conscious experimentation with culturally and biologically conditioned behaviors, affective and psychomotor learning have simi-larities to ritualizing and restoration of behavior. All of these activities lead to change: something new built from breaking down and reassembling something old. Like ritual activity, psychomotor learning processes are repetitive, enacted, and embodied. Psychomotor learning tasks that are more ritualized—that are also considered to be elevated, special, traditional, or spiritual, for instance—may influence changes in attitudes, emotions, and values. That is to say that the stronger the ritualized qualities of the learning, the more likely they will lead to affective change. Students may value them more highly, commit to them more readily, and be more likely to change their behaviors accordingly. While it cannot be concluded from this that learning is equivalent to ritualizing, the premise that ritualizing bears similarities to recognized learning activities, especially of the affective and psychomotor types, is a significant point for investigating the ways in which ritualizing contributes to new learning.

A FOURTH DOMAIN?

Bloom's taxonomy is informative because it describes different types of learning that correspond to respondents' learning experiences. But it does not fully account for all types of learning or change that respondents indicated in their interviews. A fourth category, which I label "insight," is also suggested. It is a type of change that much of Buddhist scripture indicates is a valued goal of Buddhist practice. To the extent that this category is drawn from Buddhist sources, it is specific to the kinds of practitioners studied here: namely, participants involved in Buddhist based practices and teachings.

Several Sanskrit and Pali sūtras refer to something akin to different domains of learning, which the texts refer to as the development of wisdom.[37] The three wis-doms, as they are called, are "the wisdom gained by listening to expositions of the dharma, the wisdom gained by contemplating the truth, [and] the wisdom gained by the cultivation of meditation."[38] This is the usual order given in Sanskrit and secondary sources, but the three wisdoms appear in the Pali Canon's Dīgha Nikāya sūtra,[39] or the Collection of Long Discourses, as follows: "Three more kinds of wisdom: based on thought, on learning [hearing], on mental development [meditation]."[40] According to Buddhist scholar Brian Nichols, Sanskrit sources indicate that the three wisdoms form a hierarchical sequence: "One hears the dharma, one thinks about it, one meditates; each stage generates a higher level of wisdom."[41] The development of wisdom is intended to change one's perception of the self and the world, in the end eliminating delusion and suffering.[42] Developing wisdom is thus intended to change one's patterns of acting, thinking, and feeling, the kinds of changes that constitute learning in Rogers's definition. Where Rogers specifies that these changes are the result of changes in knowledge, understanding, skills, and attitudes, Buddhist doctrine speaks of wisdom.

According to Powers, the first wisdom, which arises from hearing, refers to a surface understanding gained through someone else's teaching.[43] In this sense, it corresponds to Bloom's cognitive domain: receiving information, which is change on an intellectual level. Lamotte, however, suggests that the first wisdom also relies on faith: if one does not understand the teachings one hears, then one must take them on faith until understanding develops.[44] The second wisdom, which arises from thought or reflection, means considering the significance of the teaching and coming to a deeper understanding of it.[45] The second wisdom may correspond to the affective domain, since it refers to developing new attitudes or values inspired by the dharma or Buddhist truths. Even so, the second wisdom is still analytical or cognitive to some degree. Lamotte suggests that wisdom arising from reflection refers to a personal reaction that is still intellectual, and is not true wisdom.[46] True wisdom is that which arises from meditation. In Lamotte's view, the third wisdom is a direct, autonomous realization of the truth of Buddhist teachings.[47] Because the third wisdom arises from meditation, it would involve certain formal practices and techniques which may be developed through psychomotor learning processes. But the third wisdom primarily refers to developing a type of understanding that transcends the ordinary. It is understood as a fully internalized conception of that which one has pondered, and is regarded as a type of realization that surpasses conceptual understanding.[48]

Thus, while Bloom's categories have some correspondences to the three wisdoms, the third wisdom points to a type of development beyond any of Bloom's domains. In order to draft a model with which to explore what meditation students were learning, I therefore propose adding a fourth category to Bloom's three domains. The four categories that encompass potential learning or change taking place through meditation classes are: cognitive, affective, psychomotor, and insight. These categories are consistently found in respondents' reflections on what and how they learned at Friends of the Heart and Chandrakirti Centre.

While most newcomers spoke about learning in terms that matched Bloom's domains, several respondents made references to types of learning similar to the three wisdoms. Learning through meditating on Buddhist teachings was described most clearly by Marlon, an experienced member and occasional teacher at

Chandrakirti Centre. I had asked him how he learned about Buddhist practices, teachings, and history, and he replied: "There are classes that teach us. Or you can read about it. And then the other thing is that you can meditate. I think in meditation, you learn about more and the teachings go in further.... Without the meditation, the practice wouldn't get far. You can read something and quickly forget about it." Another experienced Chandrakirti member, Priscilla, said that the Foundation Program involved reading, thinking about and meditating on Kelsang Gyatso's texts. "When we do FP, we only do maybe six pages a week," she said. "We're supposed to read the six pages in advance and really contemplate and meditate on them and have questions ready for when we go into class." Experienced members involved in higher level classes had therefore learned something about the three wisdoms. But some Chandrakirti newcomers also spoke about different levels or types of understanding.

Reflecting on what he had learned in the General Program classes, Gerald identified hearing, thinking, and meditating as parts of his learning process. This was at his first interview, only four months after he began attending General Program classes at Chandrakirti Centre. Gerald said:

> There is an emotional awareness that's stimulated by intellectual observing. There is observing your process of mind which in turn affects your emotion. So, that mechanism there, I'm deeply interested in and it seems a healthy approach Buddhism has to getting the gears of that mechanism moving, not to shut them down and just accept a given thing. I say I have faith, but faith in the mechanism, speculation, and observing.

Gerald speaks about the learning process as a mechanism that moves from one element—emotional, intellectual, and meditative—to another. I asked him if what he meant by faith was faith in the practice. He replied, "Certainly, yeah. Faith in the practice of inquiry." Gerald said that he had learned certain principles from his readings, in particular the idea that self-responsibility derives from the notion that you are what you think. Having learned this principle, he said he could then ponder it on his own, an inquiry process that was a significant part of his practice.

> So, from understanding more of the principles through a book, the idea of self responsibility being that you are what you think, you are who you think you are, and basically all of your actions are a result of your own choices and your own other actions. That seems so simple but it's really got an enormous depth to it. So the more I ponder some of the principles, the broader the space becomes between being able to meditate.... Some of the principles are like a Mobius strip, I find. You can start

and then go a long way and then come back to the simplicity of it. It's really intriguing. It's like a little adventure in your mind. You can see where this will go. And then once you start to observe yourself it's amazing to see how accurate they are.

Gerald said that observing the processes of his mind affected his emotions. Moreover, exploring the principles he learned intellectually and emotionally related to his meditation practice: The process of inquiry helped him observe himself, gave him what he called a "broader space" in meditation for further exploring the principles he had been taught. Gerald believed that observing himself in meditation affirmed the accuracy of the teachings. He said he was able to develop what he regarded as a deeper understanding of the teachings by reflecting on them and, in a sense, testing them in meditation.

Are these the three wisdoms of the Dīgha Nikāya? There are some similarities. Intellectual awareness, Gerald said, stimulated emotional awareness. By emotional awareness, Gerald was referring to an understanding that was more intrinsic and less strictly cognitive. He also said that reflecting on such principles on his own increased his understanding and, perhaps, added to his meditation practice. Although unfamiliar with the concept of three wisdoms as described in Buddhist scripture, Gerald's responses suggested two, and possibly all three.

Different levels of wisdom corresponding to the three wisdoms are also indicated in a meditation practice found in schools from the Theravada, Mahayana, and Vajrayana branches of Buddhism. This practice has two dimensions. The first is stabilizing meditation (śamatha), often called calm abiding, the objective of which is to generate mental tranquility. The meditator concentrates on a particular object of meditation such as the breath, the elements, various colors, loving-kindness, compassion, and so on in order to induce single-pointed concentration; the ability to remain focused on an object of concentration without interruption.[49] The other dimension is analytical meditation (vipaśyanā), which refers to developing insight.[50] It is intended to help the practitioner develop personal, intuitive insight into the nature of reality; specifically, Buddhist truths concerning impermanence, suffering, and no-self.[51] The meditator begins, for example, with a conceptual understanding of emptiness, the lack of inherent existence of all phenomena. He or she then analyzes emptiness from the state of calm abiding in meditation. Priscilla gave an example of analytical meditation taught at Chandrakirti Foundation Program classes: Practitioners reflect on the emptiness or lack of inherent existence of various parts of the body and of the self: the emptiness of the eye, of the mind, of the body. The latter is considered as neither equivalent to nor independent of any one of its parts. Priscilla said that, through such analyses, the meditator may begin to experience the emptiness of the body.

Analytical meditation is not cognitive analysis, although it may begin at that level. The meditation is intended to result in a deeper sense of the absence of inherent existence. The meditator then concentrates on that sense of absence. Insights developed in this way are thus taken as subsequent objects of stabilizing concentration. Stabilizing and analytical meditation are first developed separately, but the goal is eventually to unify the experience of calm abiding and insight to the point at which the results of analytical meditation themselves generate calm abiding; an experience which leads to what is called "higher insight." Higher insight means achieving a deeply felt—as opposed to intellectually grasped—realization that all phenomena are by nature inherently impermanent, empty, and unsatisfactory.[52]

Calm abiding and insight meditation, respectively, were the core practices of the Calm and Clear and Introduction to Insight courses at Friends of the Heart. Describing the alternating course schedule, Meg said:

> I think of it as two wheels: one is śamatha practice, calm abiding…only it is put in more secular terms. And then, once you have a stable base—once you have a clearer lens, you can look. If the lens is shaking you can't see anything. So, which comes first? I think that they are two sides of a coin. They are both needed. The question becomes: what is a suitable entry point? The thought has always been that people need calm first. In our society, people need calm first. Which is why the Wednesday night has been more śamatha-oriented practice. Because if people get nothing else, there are going to get stress reduction.

Hence introductory students at Friends of the Heart did learn stabilizing and analytical meditation practices, albeit at a preliminary level. Several Friends of the Heart students to whom I spoke reported increased calm and concentration as well as insights into their reactions to sensations in their bodies. Insights at this preliminary level, however, are more akin to affective change than the deep intuitive realization Powers describes as "higher insight."

Chandrakirti students also learned about stabilizing and analytical meditation practices, which Kelsang Gyatso translates as "placement" and "analyzing" meditation. In his description of them, the practices correspond to the three wisdoms of the Dīgha Nikāya. Placement meditation, he writes, depends upon analytical meditation and analytical meditation depends upon listening to or reading spiritual instructions."[53] Chandrakirti teacher Thekchen offered what I found to be the best description connecting the three wisdoms to stabilizing and analytical meditation.

> You listen, or you read. That's the wisdom arising from listening or reading. And then, in meditation you do contemplation. So, that is where you integrate more from your own experience or other examples, and you're applying it and contem-

plating using the reasoning, until you arrive at a new understanding....And that meditation, that wisdom arising from that meditation, is coming because your mind is becoming more familiar, more embodied with the truth, with that understanding. I think, technically, wisdom arising from meditation occurs at a very advanced level. Once you have developed what is called tranquil abiding, perfect concentration, you can focus on the object for days, months without any distractions....You are able to concentrate, mountain-like concentration, and analyze at the same time....It's called superior seeing, and once you get to that level, your mind and the image of the truth, let's say emptiness, you are analyzing and concentrating at the same time. And that's what leads to direct realization, a nonconceptual realization. I think wisdom arisen from meditation occurs when you can analyze and concentrate at the same time.

Thekchen described highly advanced stages of the practice, where placement and stabilizing meditation are no longer separate, but which are believed to generate the third wisdom alone. It is believed that novice meditators can experience insights through which they begin to understand emptiness, but most initial realizations are still of a conceptual—what Bloom and colleagues would call a cognitive—sort.

Even so, a few respondents reported having experiences that corresponded to Buddhist descriptions of insight. Some described them as little "aha" moments or what might be explained as brief mystical experiences. Teachers indicated that such experiences were encouraging signs of development in students' practice. Marlon, for example, said:

Now, the deepest learning is what is called realization, when there is something that goes on in the mind which allows us to directly access what Buddha talked about. That is called realization. That is something that is, well for myself, hasn't happened a whole lot yet. It takes time. Often I wish those would happen more. But those are things that are quite rare. I guess in other religions or other traditions, we would call it inspiration or something like that. Often I hope those would happen more often.

Marlon's description of what he calls realization corresponds well to the description of the third wisdom, above: realization which happens in rare moments of direct experience of the Buddha's teachings.

Respondents' descriptions of such experiences were few and often vague, which is not surprising, given that insight experiences of this sort are said to be ineffable or beyond words. Tanit attempted to describe one such moment. She had been experimenting with different meditative concentration techniques, including the insight meditation Joyce had taught, a relaxation body scan and another technique from her book on Daoism.

And I got this incredible, I don't even know how to describe it, it almost felt like there's this wave of something. I don't even know what to describe it as. And I [thought] what was that? And then I kept trying to do it again, and I think it was almost like I was too conscious....And then it would only happen almost if I did it obliquely. I don't know how to describe it.

Tanit felt that this experience pointed to the possibility of more frequent and deeper experiences of the same kind, and that it was the sort of thing she should try to develop through meditation practice. As she pointed out, however, conscious efforts to initiate such experiences almost always fail.

Gwen said: "When I have an awareness of what it means to be empty—not what it means, experience of emptiness or experience of this precious moment, this one right here. How do I sustain that? And I think, yeah, practice." With this statement, Gwen indicated that she had had more than one such experience in meditation. Her clarification is significant: She believed that she had achieved not an understanding of the meaning of emptiness, but a direct experience of emptiness itself, an immersion in the present moment.

Carol also touched on insight when she spoke about "going beyond imputed reality," by which she was referring to Buddhist teachings on what is real and what is illusion. Insight into such principles, many meditators believe, requires more than attitudinal or behavioral change: It is defined as an experiential realization of emptiness, impermanence, or no-self. Respondents who described insight experiences said that they *resulted* in affective changes: subsequent changes in attitudes, emotions, and values. But insight experiences themselves were not the same as affective change.

While it is difficult to describe internal experiences, never mind analyze them, I believe that it is important to acknowledge the possibility of such insights as well as the emphasis placed on their role within Buddhist traditions. I include these examples here because respondents considered insights to be possible, important, and even necessary experiences when learning meditation. I follow my respondents in acknowledging the possibility of a type of change that is neither cognitive, affective, nor psychomotor. The three wisdoms doctrine and the practices of stabilizing and analytical meditation indicate that achieving insight includes development in all three of the other domains.

"PRACTICE" AS CHANGING BEHAVIOR

In chapter 5, I will explore learning through practice, with an emphasis on meditation and other kinds of rites. Before concluding this chapter on learning, however, I want to touch on another perspective on practice.

Teachers at both centers indicated that "practice," the repetition of new behaviors and reinforcement of new attitudes, was the best way to learn. There were, however, different perspectives on what constituted practice. At Friends of the Heart, where the focus was on learning how to meditate, students generally referred to meditation as their practice. Teachers at both centers often encouraged students to turn everyday situations into opportunities to enact the ethical perspectives introduced in the classes, but it was at Chandrakirti Centre that doing so was considered the main "practice."[54] Rarely did Chandrakirti respondents speak about meditation as their sole practice. Meditation was, rather, a device for understanding and reinforcing ethical teachings. Many General Program students thus regarded their practice as the everyday activities that they conducted with mindful awareness of values such as compassion, kindness, selflessness, and so on.

For two Chandrakirti members, Catherine H. and Brenda, sitting in meditation was not a regular practice. But each had her own formal practice and her own ways of experimenting with Buddhist teachings. Each had made certain behavioral changes in her everyday life. Catherine, as mentioned, had changed the way she related to her clients. Brenda said she was trying to turn her whole life into a meditation. "It's about being in the moment and being respectful and about seeing the beauty that lives in the world," she said. One of the manifestations of this attitude was the way she swept up seed pods that fell from a tree in her yard. "I used to do that job and rail against it and end up with a sore back and I would be whinging away. And then, when I turned it into a meditation, the job is done and none of my bits hurt." In this way, Brenda had ritualized the act of sweeping up seed pods. Like focusing the mind on the breath or returning the wandering mind to an object of concentration, formality, stylization, and mindful attention to ordinary activities can transform them into rites. Rather than an ordinary chore, Brenda began to regard sweeping as a practice, attaching value to it and regarding it with spiritual significance. Through this kind of practice—a deliberately cultivated meditative activity—Brenda believed she was learning to change her habitual attitudes and reactions.

When I asked Alan to describe what he had learned at the General Program classes, he spoke of a new value or ethic he had learned and immediately began describing ways he considered changing his behavior in response.

I learn that the only path is to give up thinking about yourself. Which is so hard to do, when you spend so much time generally thinking about yourself. I could say: well, I'm only going to open [the store] three days a week and . . . go and work for charity. But, for me, I have to find the balance: what do you need to support yourself, what are your needs? You could sell the house. There's lots of things you could do. It seems to me there's a balance with the attachment that you have to things, that it wouldn't be wise to be too radical. You have to really be able to change your mind rather than quickly change your circumstances. I'd like to be happier with less. That's my goal.

The idea of being less self-centered appealed to Alan. He had assessed and valued it, and had begun to look for ways to change his behavior accordingly. He considered the possibility of making far-reaching changes to his lifestyle, but recognized that it was more important to change his mind—that is, his attitudes—than to change his life radically. He decided to instead find ways to live with less. I asked if he thought he was learning ways to that goal. He said:

> Yes, first of all there's the giving and sharing, which I've never been good at. It's never been my lifestyle. I've always figured it's important to be self-sufficient.... I won't ask you for anything and you won't ask me for anything and we'll get along fine. But, I realize that it doesn't work like that.... I wasn't happy living that type of life. So, you try and change it.

The new values Alan encountered in the General Program classes suggested that he should rethink his position on being charitable. When I asked Alan how he learned these new values he indicated an immediate connection between changing his values and changing how he behaved.

> Practice, I would say. I now make a point of giving, say, to my wife. Not in what I would normally think of as giving, [for example], money or time. But every week now I buy flowers so when she comes home they're there. And I realize she gets so much pleasure out of that. I end up getting it back in the pleasure she receives from it. Just being more thoughtful with the children. And I've even been taking my daughter Bronwen, introducing her to something that at a young age she might recognize will give her happiness.

Alan had an interesting perspective on what practice entailed. It primarily consisted of his conscious efforts to enact the new values he had learned; to be more generous and giving in his everyday life. In fact, what he regarded as the more profound changes in attitude followed from his behavioral changes. He had learned and accepted the idea that selflessness led to happiness, he then enacted new behaviors in accordance with that idea, and the behaviors, he believed, then began to affect his emotions and attitudes. Speaking of practicing generosity, Alan said:

> I think, what it does for me, is it makes me look at things differently. Whereas before I might have looked at it one way, and thought: oh, I'm very logical about

that, I've done the right thing and I'm doing the right thing. And then suddenly, it's like an "aha." You've had a shift, because there's a different way of looking at it. Giving, for example, when I see people sitting on the streets...I [used to] automatically say: you know what, all I'm going to do is give you money and you're going to go off and buy a drink. Going to the lessons has changed that. I shouldn't be attached to what they're going to do with the money. The idea is just to give.

When interviewed again several months later, Alan said he was better at examining his instinctive reactions in order to refrain from being as judgmental as he had been previously. He said he was operating based on his "insights" rather than "automatic drive." "I give money to panhandlers without attachment. I make sure I have loose change." Alan had begun this shift by setting aside his initial instincts and deliberately giving spare change to panhandlers, an activity he regarded as part of the "practice" he had learned at Chandrakirti Centre. Like Brenda, Alan was transforming something ordinary into something special: He had ritualized the act of being generous to strangers. With time, he believed, the behavior had changed his attitudes toward giving and toward those to whom he gave. He also experimented with different ways of being generous.

Practice, like rehearsal, involves a conscious awareness of the behaviors being repeated and refined. Alan was trying out new behaviors, becoming increasingly familiar with them and with their results. It was through the practice, through a deliberately reconstructed behavior, that Alan learned something about himself and about a different way of being in the world. "It makes you feel better," he said. "It's a good feeling to give rather than always think about what you can get." His learning process had some similarities to Schechner's restoration of behavior, in that his consciously reconstructed behaviors led to attitudinal changes, which in turn reinforced the new behaviors. Alan thus described a kind of cyclical link between affective and psychomotor learning. The fact that he, like other respondents, spoke about his experiences in such positive terms is another indication that he had experienced affective learning: He had highly valued the lessons he received at Chandrakirti Centre, choosing to commit to them and to adapt his behaviors accordingly.

For Chandrakirti students, changes in everyday behaviors like those Alan described were the primary tool for implementing affective changes. Meditation, another formal practice and psychomotor means of learning, was regarded as a means of reinforcing the changes initiated by the formalized lectures and experiential learning in daily life. Alan, who said he meditated twice every day, regarded meditation as a reminder, a means of refreshing the learning, and a means of making him, in his words, "sharper" at what he believed was the real practice, the changes in his everyday activities.

CONCLUSION

Cognitive learning only went so far in the meditation classes. A few respondents were uncomfortable with some of the information they encountered, others were unconcerned, and still others felt that too much cognitive knowledge could be a hindrance to other, more important goals. Several respondents felt there was a transformative quality to learning meditation or Buddhist teachings; that they were learning life-changing views and practices. Overall, respondents identified learning at meditation classes more often with learning on the affective level—in terms of a value system that changes attitudes and behaviors—and the psychomotor—in terms of the physical techniques or concentration practices. While few of them explicitly referred their learning as ritualized, several of the responses included descriptions corresponding to ritual qualities: learning about meditation or Buddhism was somehow special, it was valued highly, and it had aspects of spirituality because it related to the experience of the whole person.

Bloom's taxonomy helps us recognize and analyze distinct types of learning. More significantly, it describes learning processes that have notable similarities to ritualizing and restoration of behavior. Learned ritualized behaviors—that is, behaviors that are received as an object or material from a source other than the performer and then experimented with—fall under the psychomotor domain. Moreover, psychomotor learning—whether it is consciously altered behavior in daily life or meditation postures, gestures and concentration techniques—initiates affective changes. The next chapter, which explores learning through ritualizing in more depth, will develop a better picture of the pattern linking learning domains.

5

The Ritualizing Body-Mind

MEDITATION, WITH ITS silence and stillness, is not as explicitly performative as other forms of ritual activity. Yet, as a practice, it bears many of the qualities we often associate with ritual: it is traditional, formal, standardized, and repeated. While often solitary, it frequently is performed as part of a community. Many meditators regard it as special, elevated, spiritual, or religious. This chapter will explore the ways in which practice, especially meditation, contributes to participants' learning. Meditation, however, was not the only ritualized practice introduced at Friends of the Heart and Chandrakirti meditation classes. Students also observed and performed practices such as bowing, prostrations, mudras, and chanting. These practices, too, contributed to students' learning about Buddhism and about themselves.

Among the interview respondents, few newcomers spoke about prostrations, mudras, and chanting of their own accord, a fact that indicated that they were less interested in formal practices other than meditation. I made a point, however, of asking respondents whether they thought prostrations, chanting, and the like contributed to learning. Some respondents did not think that they did. John, for example, said: "No, I wouldn't say so. I don't think they do. You learn that they exist, that people are saying this and are doing this." John's primary interest was in meditation, and he had little interest in the other practices he encountered at Friends of the Heart. With respect to such practices, he gained a bit of new information—knowledge of their existence and purposes—but no more.

Tanit spoke about the prayers recited at Friends of the Heart.

I'm trying to learn them right now, and I realize actually that's the part that I'm not aware of. I'm thinking: oh, I don't know it, and will I ever have to learn that? Have to. Oh, the language choices are so interesting. So, I've allowed myself, at the sessions, to simply listen to it....So that is not something I'm specifically aware of yet. And I realize, when I meditate at home, it doesn't even cross my mind. I don't do that part of it....So, yeah, that's not integrated for me at this point. But it makes sense...that you are consciously making a decision to think about enlightenment, truth, changing, using awareness. And that you are truly capable of enlightenment. That's pretty phenomenal.

While Tanit had some reluctance toward learning the prayers and was more concerned with getting her meditation posture and techniques right, she did indicate that, with time, she might learn the prayers and begin to understand their meanings. Many of the adoptive Buddhists and sympathizers I have spoken to have said they are not interested in prayer, or that they do not associate it with Buddhism.[1] Those who regard Buddhism as nontheistic believe that this trait obviates the need for prayer. Experienced members and teachers, especially those involved in Tibetan-based expressions of Buddhism, often speak about the importance of prayer and of receiving blessings from spiritual beings, while newcomers sometimes find these elements difficult to accept. This suggests that, with time, practitioners may develop familiarity with and acceptance of prayers and deities. Tanit said: "By repeating the refuge each time, you have a different response to it each time. For me, right now, it's kind of a bunch of words and I don't know them. But I recognize that that will change, that it's a kind of a formalization: I'm about to meditate, I'm about to think about things, I'm approaching a sacred space, all of those things. And it's very helpful." Tanit said that what she understood of the Friends of the Heart Refuge Prayer "made sense," particularly its references to a commitment to follow the path to enlightenment. She regarded it as a formal statement of that commitment rather than, for example, a prayer spoken to a deity. She said that one of the meanings she attributed to the prayer was the idea that the goal of enlightenment was possible. At this early stage, however, the prayer served a different purpose: It set up her meditation practice, she said. She associated the prayer with the start of meditation; reciting it or listening to it gave her a sense of the sacred space that she was entering. With this statement, Tanit was referring either to the shrine room or to the internal "space" she would generate in meditation.

In fact, many respondents claimed that practices such as prostrations, bows, mudras, and chanting primarily acted to give them a sense of the setting, the practices, the teachers, and the teachings as something special or worthy of respect. For instance, when I asked Nicolette if postures, gestures, or chants helped her learn anything, she responded: "Learn about what? Well, they certainly help me learn how to do postures, gestures, and chants." But then she said:

Beyond that, if I'm in the right mood they can teach me things like: how to be a good student, which is actually a useful thing; and all the things that are around that like how to be patient, how to be a good listener, those kind of practices; and then beyond that, if you're doing prostrations, which is the weirdest one for me, once you learn physically how to do it without keeling over, then the visualizations that you're supposed to be doing can teach you about who your teachers are, how you feel towards them, what they've given you; hopefully it can teach you how to engender feelings of gratitude and generosity. So, that's the kind of thing you can learn.

Nicolette's response touches on several key aspects of learning: how to be a good student, which is effectively learning about learning; learning patience, which is an affective type of learning; and learning skills like how to perform prostrations or visualization techniques. Nicolette also suggested that the formality of practices like prostrations generated a sense of respect and gratitude.

When asked if formal practices helped him learn in any way, Alan said:

I don't think they would really, but I think what it would teach me is to respect the teacher, the teacher has the knowledge. The teacher's earned the right or the status.... So taking the shoes off is part of that and the bowing and prostrating, whatever they call it. I probably wouldn't do that but that depends on the level that you probably put this person up on. Because by going down as low as you can, you are obviously raising... you should always keep them higher than you. But I think it's probably just showing respect. They don't seem to be bothered, it seems to me, the monks and nuns, one way or the other. I think it's more of the student showing respect. That's how I sense it.

Both Alan and Nicolette initially said that no, the formal practices do not lead to learning, then revised their statements by indicating that certain practices might teach students to respect their teachers. Their responses indicate that developing a sense of respect is not something they readily connected with learning. Even so, several other respondents agreed on the point Nicolette and Alan raised; that prostrations, bows, mudras, and chants conveyed a sense of respect. This is because we interpret formal postures such as these as a kind of decorum.

RITUALIZING AND DECORUM

Ronald Grimes lists decorum as one of six modes of ritual sensibility.[2] It takes place when the stylized movements that constitute ritualization become part of a "system of expectations" to which we, as members of a common culture, feel

we ought to conform.[3] At meditation classes, respondents observed or practiced the bows, prostrations, mudras, or chants: Through these observations or
practices, they gained an understanding that the space, the teachers, or the
teachings were considered to be special, elevated, or even sacred. This interpretation raised certain expectations of behavior that should or should not be
exhibited in the space. Grimes points out that decorum is often invisible to its
performers,[4] but we become acutely aware of it when it is breached. Our enactment and interpretation of decorum depends on embodied knowing, the stylized and symbolic ways we use and communicate with our bodies. Decorum, the
expected appropriate behaviors in the shrine rooms at Friends of the Heart and
Chandrakirti Centre, hinged on what students learned about those spaces while
there.

Carol said that newcomers sometimes observed teachers and experienced members bowing, performing the prayer mudra, or performing prostrations at the
General Program classes. "By example they [newcomers] see how things are. And
it's almost like a given, that you just behave. . . . It was like everybody understood.
It comes with an innate understanding of how you conduct yourself there and the
respect that was generated." Carol made an important point: People (and this
would be especially true of adults) do not learn the expected decorum on entering
a space like the Chandrakirti shrine room. The ritual setting and formal practices
performed within it tell us what kind of a space it is; with that knowledge, most of
us have an understanding, likely derived from experiences in other, similar settings, of the expected behaviors in the new space. For instance, Diane said: "No
one has ever said this to me, maybe I read it somewhere. The space where the altar
is is somewhat sacred and you behave in a way that is in keeping with being in
somewhat of a sacred space. So you don't yell or boisterously laugh or call out to
each other." Without being told, Diane knew the kinds of behaviors that would be
inappropriate in a Buddhist shrine room. Similarly, Gerald made his own
assessment of decorum in the Chandrakirti shrine room when he complained that
another student wore a hat in the class. As Gwen put it, "The energy of the space,
with the altar, it begs for a certain kind of respect and humility when you enter
into it." Once a sacred space is created and recognized via its ritual objects and ritualized activities, our cultural expectations inform us of the appropriate decorum
for that space.

Another way of learning about expected decorum is through various prohibitions. For example, Chandrakirti members Carol, Marlon, and Priscilla mentioned
that the prayer booklets should not be placed on the floor, nor should Kelsang
Gyatso's books. Catherine Rathbun noted the same prohibition at the Tibetan
meditation classes: Even though the prayer texts that we used were photo-copies

held together by paper clips, they were reproductions of ancient and revered texts, she said, and the protocol was to keep them off of the floor. Another rule of decorum was to avoid pointing one's feet in the direction of the teacher or any of the icons. Gwen had learned this rule on a Friends of the Heart retreat when she lay with her feet pointing toward Catherine, who then corrected her. At Chandrakirti Centre, Marlon also mentioned the rule about the direction of the feet. Most newcomer respondents were unaware of this prohibition, indicating that it was not a concern at introductory classes. Decorum, therefore, includes ritualized treatment of texts and the body.

Performing prostrations, bows, removing shoes, and keeping texts off of the floor initiated an affective learning process. These practices suggested that the space, and the teachers and teachings associated with it, were worthy of respect. Students then assessed that sense of respect and interpreted it through their preexisting understanding of decorum, and adjusted their behavior accordingly.

PROSTRATIONS

Prostrations were rarely performed at introductory classes, but many newcomers had learned about the practice or observed others performing them. Some had attended more formal rituals at the centers, such as prayer services and empowerments, where all participants were encouraged to either bow or prostrate to the shrines or the teachers. Diane had encountered prostration practice at the Chenrezig and Tara empowerments at Friends of the Heart and the Heart Jewel prayer service at Atisha Centre. I asked her if she thought it was possible to learn about prostrations simply through performing them. She replied:

> I have certainly read that people do learn through performing them. Prostrations in particular. Because it is very difficult for western people to do that. So, in stuff that I have read, I have read other people who, through that process, have come to learn something. But I'm not interested—it doesn't mean that I won't in some—I have a fairly prescribed interest right now. I don't know where that will take me, but right now it's in meditation, it's not in any of the—I don't even know what I would call them—rituals.[5]

While Diane's motivations for coming to Buddhist practices were in part spiritual, she was not immediately willing to engage in most of the ritualized activities she encountered. Consequently, she had had no personal experience with prostrations. "Personally," she said, "I have an aversion. It means bowing down to a god or to something. That's the other thing about Buddhism. There is no god in a sense. We can all be a Buddha, and we are." Although she hinted that her interests might change, for the time being Diane regarded Buddhism as nontheistic and strictly meditative, and felt that prostrations were extraneous. Like many other adoptive practitioners, Diane felt that devotional practices were unnecessary in what she regarded as a nontheistic tradition.

Many western Buddhist sympathizers are emphatically unsympathetic to prostration practice. They give several reasons for this view, from the physical to the ideological. Prostrations are a repetitive weight-bearing activity that can involve considerable physical exertion. To perform a full-body prostration, the practitioner begins in a standing position, usually with the hands in the prayer mudra, and then kneels to the floor. Placing the palms down on the floor, the practitioner then stretches full out face down on the ground, stretching the arms above the head. Sliding the hands back along the ground, the practitioner then kneels and returns to the standing position, replacing the hands in the prayer mudra. Together, these movements constitute one full-body prostration. The process is almost always repeated at least three times, but some practitioners perform hundreds of prostrations at a time. It can be quite a workout, and some people find it very hard on the knees, hips, back, or lower legs.

Most adoptive practitioners who object to prostration practice do so not because of physical difficulties but ideological ones. Reasons for this likely stem from Judeo-Christian prohibitions against worshipping or bowing before idols. Like Diane, many westerners assume that prostration practice signifies the worship of a deity. Tanit expressed the same view. She said she did not perform bows or prostrations.

> For me, somehow that is not important. I think what attracts me so much to Buddhism is that it isn't about a god. That is not the central aspect, and that is exactly what attracts me. Now, I understand the concept of working with devotion. For example, I was reading recently that maturity is behaving as if there were gods, knowing that there are not. And I think there's something really interesting [to that]. You know that there is no god figure up there saying: you need to be a good human being, but you behave that way because you believe that that is valid and important.

I then asked Tanit if bowing necessarily had to do with a deity, and she paused for a moment. "Okay, yes," she said. "In my mind it does. Interesting. But, for me, absolutely it does. So, that's something to consider." Tanit was not unwilling to perform other devotional practices like reciting the refuge and merit prayers, but the prostrations, in her mind, signified worship of a deity, a practice that did not appeal to what she regarded as a mature spiritual ethic.

Gwen also said she had not incorporated prostrations into her regular practice. "That comes from Catherine saying to me once: you don't have to say or do anything that you don't understand. Ever. If it doesn't make sense to you, or you don't understand it, just leave it alone. So, I feel really good about that." As Gwen's comments indicate, part of the problem with prostrations is that adoptive practitioners are not familiar with the practice. Powers notes that in Tibetan culture, prostration practice is very popular with monastics and laypeople alike. People are often seen in large numbers prostrating before religious sites or important religious figures. Many practitioners circumambulate religious sites by performing full-body prostrations. Some have even gone on long pilgrimages by performing prostrations, beginning each new prostration at the point where the fingertips rested with the last.[6] Prostration practice is believed to be valuable, as a vigorous physical activity, for overcoming negative karma.[7] It is also intended to counteract false pride, since the practitioner completely lowers him or herself to the ground. Prostration is also a means of requesting the aid of Buddhas and Bodhisattvas. Hence, in traditional expressions of Tibetan Buddhism, prostration practice is both devotional and theistic.

For adoptive Buddhist students to accept prostration practice, however, teachers often find it necessary to find new interpretations of the practice. Buddhist teachers in the West often assure their students that prostrations do not involve bowing down before an idol or a deity. Some teachers, for example, advocate it as a means of grounding oneself,[8] or as a repetitive physical activity that can produce meditative mind states. Catherine Rathbun said that full-body prostrations "de-armor the body" and open up its energy centers or *chakras*. "That's something that I found doing them," she said. "It's not part of the traditional teaching. That's my own experience." This is an interpretation of prostration practice by an adoptive Buddhist teacher for her adoptive Buddhist students that does not involve devotional practice or deity worship.

Some of the experienced members I interviewed had a positive outlook on prostrations. Marlon felt that they were a very important part of his overall practice and had no problem with them. Although Priscilla said she had problems with her knees and feet and could not physically perform prostrations, she defended their use as a gesture of respect for the teachings. Marconi did prostrations every day and said that they felt "pretty cool." He described a guru-yoga[9] visualization that he incorporated into his prostration practice, "and I go through that visualization before I start my prostrations and I'm now able to have a deeper and a clearer and a far more interesting connection." Marconi thus discovered that combining the visualization with the physical activity of the prostrations gave him a sense of mental clarity and a deeper, more personal response to the practice. Prostrations also helped Marconi develop an increased awareness of his body. While he said that the practice was sometimes painful, he regarded the pain as a learning experience. "Where does it hurt?" he asked himself, "and what are you holding there?" Pain, Marconi believed, resulted from tensions or negative emotions being held in the body, and prostration practice helped him recognize such areas and reflect on what was going on in his body. Marconi was able to reflect intellectually on the experience, but he was also aware that the practice was generating a deeper understanding of the body through its own physicality.

David was the only experienced member of the four interviewed who said he disliked prostrations. Laughing, he said: "I can't stand prostrations. It's interesting talking to people, because some people are totally fine with prostrations. And then, it's like, I can't stand it.... It's just weird. I think definitely there's something physical and there's something mentally uncomfortable about it too, that somehow I find very oppressive. So I don't like it." David was working through the Tibetan foundation practice under Catherine Rathbun's guidance. Foundation practice, which consists of the Tibetan ngöndrö or preliminary practices, includes the performance of one hundred thousand full-body prostrations, and David was working his way toward that goal. Even though he said he could not stand doing prostrations, he still performed them, hundreds of them in fact, every day. "You know," he said, "I think the prostrations are working on me because I'm having some sort of really strong effect, something that I'm trying to step back from. So, let's step toward it and see what happens." In effect, David treated his own mental resistance to the practice as a learning experience. His response reflects a conviction that Catherine had expressed. "We learn the best," she said, "when things go wrong or when things are difficult."

Aware of the aversion that westerners often have to prostrations, most teachers at Chandrakirti Centre gave students the option to perform prostrations or not. They were never required at General Program classes, but the chanted prayer services usually began with three prostrations facing the shrine. At one Heart Jewel service I attended, an experienced member, recognizing me as a newcomer, told me: "we do prostrations; you don't have to if you don't want to." Like experienced members at Friends of the Heart, however, some Chandrakirti members chose to undertake foundation practice and worked toward completing the requisite one hundred thousand full-body prostrations.

At Friends of the Heart, I asked Catherine Rathbun about the importance of persisting with prostration practice in the West. She replied:

It's up to the teachers to teach them. If you expect people to do something without explanation, you deserve the resistance you're going to get. So, you will hear me sometimes say at the beginning of class: we will now do prostrations. If you are following this discipline, and are instructed in this, you should do three prostrations now. If you're not, don't worry, simply be aware, or imagine that you're coming into the presence of your teachers, and then sit down. So, in other words, bringing [students] back to the idea of what it is that is being taught, rather than having people look around and trying to do something they don't know what they're doing.

Catherine thus suggested that students need to be taught about the symbolism or the meanings of prostrations before being asked to perform them. Then, through the action, through the practice, they may learn other meanings.

Catherine was clearly aware that prostration practice did not appeal to many of her students. At a Tibetan Meditation class I attended, she mentioned the need to find an alternative practice for westerners. She said that a Tibetan might brag about having a great uncle who performed hundreds of thousands of prostrations until his knees bled. But, she said, her western students were going to their doctors and telling them what they were doing, and the doctors would say: "You're doing *what*? Stop it!" Prostrations, Catherine said, ruin westerners' knees. Because of this, she had developed an adapted form of prostration practice which she said was specifically suited for her students. Rather than kneeling down to the floor, practitioners remained standing, bowing at the waist, and placing their hands palms down on the knees. Then, turning the hands palms upwards, practitioners bowed more deeply before returning to the standing position, placing their hands in the prayer mudra.

Diane told me that she more readily accepted the adapted prostrations Catherine taught than the to-the-floor prostrations she saw performed at Atisha Centre. "Somehow it didn't seem so bad to do because I guess what we were doing with Catherine the other day was the same thing, only in a different posture. . . . But the concept should be the same. I didn't have a problem with it standing up and bending over. . . ." Diane was aware that the full prostration and Catherine's bowing prostration were similar symbolic actions: She was not certain why she had an aversion to one and not the other. Her discomfort with prostration practice derived from a perceived connection to theism and religious devotion, and the adapted prostration should have carried the same meaning. For Diane, however, it did not. Perhaps this was because it was physically less difficult, as Catherine indicated, but Diane's aversion was more likely due to a sense that going all the way down to the floor seemed a more strongly devotional act.

Catherine was aware of more conservative teachers' insistence on preserving ritual forms. She discovered, however, that it was necessary to adapt certain practices, particularly prostrations, in order to make them accessible to her students. There was a precedent for adaptation, Catherine believed, in Buddhist tradition itself, in the principle that everything changes. Catherine found that adapting the form of the prostrations helped overcome her students' physical barriers to the practice, while adapting its meanings, particularly by downplaying its devotional associations, overcame ideological barriers. Adaptation of traditional ritual—in essence, transforming stable practices into a form of ritualizing or experimental behavior—thus made certain practices more accessible to new learners.

LEARNING, EXPERIMENTATION, AND INVARIANCE

Respondents indicated that creativity, adaptability, and experimentation supported discovery and new learning for other reasons as well. Tanit, for instance, spoke about the ways she had experimented with her home meditation practice. At Friends of the Heart, she said, she followed the specific practices that Joyce was teaching. But at home, Tanit added a visualization practice that she had learned from a book by Lama Surya Das, an American-born Tibetan teacher in the United States. The practice involved, as Tanit described it, listing and putting down all of the things one does not need. Describing how she adapted this practice, Tanit said:

> I'm not sure how it developed, but my image of myself is sitting on a little island and there's water all around me and I'm going through letting go of all of my things. And it's everything: my clothes, and I imagine my clothes lying on the water and floating away. But it is not only things. It's stuff like anger too, and actually trying to define the anger, what it is specifically and what it is triggered from and then: okay, acknowledge it, that's good. And now: put it on the water.

In this response, Tanit describes a unique visualization practice that she learned and then developed in her own way. The activity through which this new learning occurred was an example of ritualizing or restoration of behavior: Tanit combined and reconstructed techniques she received from various sources. In essence, she was constructing her own ritual. Having the freedom to experiment in the early stages of learning meditation thus enabled her to create a practice that was personally relevant and meaningful.

Jennings argues that a ritual's openness to novelty is necessary for new ritual knowledge to develop.[10] There is evidence, despite what participants think, that rituals change considerably over time and across cultures. Jennings interprets the fact of change as an indication that rituals are a search for meaning or understanding of how to be in the world. In his view, without experimentation, variability, and novelty, ritual would not be a source of new knowledge; it would simply repeat and transmit what is already known. Tanit, in fact, affirmed this view. Speaking about the yoga postures Joyce taught at Friends of the Heart, Tanit said: "Some of the poses are a little bit different than I have been taught in other places. So, that is actually helpful because it makes me more aware of what I'm doing, physically, because if it's exactly what you know, you just do it by rote. And this is helping me not do that." The variability of the practices helped Tanit learn them better because it demanded greater awareness and attention than rote repetition. For the same reason, Catherine Rathbun told students in one of her Tibetan Meditation classes that she sometimes changed the sequence and some of the words of the prayers she led at Friends of the Heart. Small changes such as these can help maintain a ritual's vitality by refreshing participants' attention and awareness. In this view, too much habituation can render a ritual meaningless.[11] Popular conceptions of ritual often identify it as being rote and meaningless: This is one reason why many adoptive Buddhists, raised with western, Protestant-influenced worldviews, reject ritual altogether. But Jennings's argument and Tanit and Catherine's observations show that ritual can involve innovative, adaptive, and mindful practices.

Williams and Boyd argue against Jennings's position, asserting that formality, repetition, and invariance invest ritual with an "aura of necessity" and a sense that rituals should not be changed.[12] In this view, experimentation, adaptation, and novelty are not what lead to the acquisition of new meanings: quite the opposite. Long-term and stable repetition of a ritual creates a steady horizon by which participants orient themselves and which draws them onward to new understandings and behaviors.[13] Of course, like Jennings, Williams and Boyd recognize that rituals do change over time. But in their view, it is the appearance of stability, and participants' belief that the ritual should not change that creates new meanings for the participant, thus inspiring change in the participant rather than in the ritual itself.

Although Tanit and other respondents suggested that experimentation and adaptation helped them learn, some also indicated that repetition and practice were necessary as well. Training necessarily involves an amount of repetition: through it, the body is familiarized with movements, skills, and techniques, thereby creating a foundation of tacit knowledge that supports practitioners as they continue to perform and transform their rituals. Additionally, the fact that the practices are viewed as traditional, time-tested techniques influenced participants' willingness to engage in and commit to the practices. Several respondents said that meditation connected them to traditional Buddhist wisdom. They thereby gained the benefits of stability as well as change.

The counterargument to both Jennings and Williams and Boyd, of course, is the possibility that ritual does not lead to new learning or knowledge; that it is not a means of inquiry or discovery. Ritual may become so stultified that there is no possibility for something new to come out of it. Underlying many westerners' customary suspicion of ritual is, perhaps, a concern that it may merely affirm the status quo, or even act as a kind of exploitation or oppression. Living rituals are those with which practitioners connect and make sense of their worlds. As Tom F. Driver puts it, "pompous repetitiveness" leads to "ritual boredom."[14] When rituals become redundant as a result of true (as opposed to perceived) invariance, they fail to connect meaningfully with participants, resulting in meaninglessness and rote, mechanical behavior.

This is a description of ritual, however, that is void of the creativity of ritualizing. Neither Jennings nor Williams and Boyd imagine that it is a condition of all or, indeed, most rituals. Stagnant ritual is not likely to befall Friends of the Heart or Chandrakirti meditation students. They tended, rather, to err on the side of too much experimentation and adaptation, to the point at which a number of participants did not develop a stable, ongoing meditation practice. If adaptation and experimentation are too strongly emphasized over invariance and repetition, stable ritual may not emerge, and the behavior may never develop into that touchstone that Williams and Boyd describe, the model by which participants measure and change themselves. Even Jennings argues that ritual imparts knowledge of "the right" way of doing things, of being in the world. But as Tanit described learning at Friends of the Heart, the experimental quality of ritualizing suggests that there are innumerable "right ways," that each participant has a right way of doing things. Tanit had read a book about meditation that described standard meditation postures. But at Friends of the Heart, she saw that Joyce was kneeling rather than sitting cross-legged, and others assumed a variety of different postures. Tanit said: "You don't get that from a book. You don't get that everybody is sitting differently. They are working out what they need to do. Being in a group situation and seeing that, it opens up that idea that there isn't *the* correct way." The meditation classes, therefore, taught participants to work out the correct way *for them*: Emphasis on ongoing experimentation thus led to a personalized, individualized practice that may or may not become stable ritual.

Still, ritualizing is an important first step. It allows for the creation of an appealing, relevant, more viable practice to which practitioners may consequently commit. Tanit's island visualization, for example, might work so well that she may continue to practice it regularly, without variance. It may become her own ritual.

Yet it might be limited in what it can tell her about her world. As a personal, individualized practice not performed among others it is not likely to connect her to a community or to phenomena beyond her personal experience of the world. For this reason Tanit, and most other participants, noted that it was important to practice with a community where the practices were formalized and repetitive: in short, where familiar practices were shared. Ritualizing as creative and generative is an important part of ritual, but so, too, are stable and repetitive ritual forms. As Driver puts it: "Without its ritualizing (new-making) component, ritual would be entirely repetitious, and static. Without aiming at the condition of ritual, ritualizing would lack purpose and avoid form; it would fall back into that realm of informal, noncommunicative behavior from which it arose."[15]

COGNITIVE LEARNING AND RITUALIZING

Experimentation and adaptation were not enough to make all formal practices accessible to all students. Few newcomers who participated in this study were interested in learning to perform ritualized practices other than meditation. While most newcomers followed along with prayers, mudras, and bows performed at introductory courses, most also explicitly or implicitly indicated that they were not much interested in such activities. Some were put off by the ritualized nature of the classes or the space itself. Meg told me that she had seen some people, on arriving for a first meditation class, walk into the meditation room and walk out again because of its strongly ritualized décor. "It's the shrine that does it," Meg said.

Diane stated several times that Buddhist rituals, particularly devotional rituals involving gurus or deities, did not appeal to her. She was willing to follow along with some of the rites at Friends of the Heart and Atisha Centre but, she said, "If I'm going to be doing it, I'm not going to be doing it as a sheep. I want to know what it is that I'm doing and why I'm doing it, to make sure that this is something that I want to be doing." In Diane's view, then, understanding the practice averts the danger of mindless repetition.

Several other respondents also noted that they wanted to intellectually understand rites such as prayers, mantras, and prostrations before engaging in them. Such claims stood in interesting contrast to the fact that, when it came to meditation, many insisted on avoiding intellectualizing. This is another indication that respondents more readily regarded meditation as nonritualized. According to our model, meditation is perhaps less ritualized than prayers, mantras, and prostrations. The latter may be regarded as more religious since they are typically associated with devotion to deities. But meditation is still formalized, repetitive, traditional, and, many would say, spiritual. It is interesting to note that respondents did not fear falling into mindless repetition in their meditation practice, but they were concerned about following other rites without first understanding why they were being performed.

Carol said that when she first began participating at Chandrakirti Centre, she had been concerned about the rituals at the center. Her initial attraction to Buddhism had been inspired by the Zen aesthetic, which is stark and simple. Then she started participating at Chandrakirti Centre where, she said, "the simplicity was becoming not so simple any more: the statues, and the offerings and all those kinds of things." In spite of this concern—in fact, because of it—Carol decided to learn about the symbols and ritual activities she encountered at the center. "So, just to educate myself, I started participating in the rituals. And I became more and more involved. I still evaluate it every time I do it. . . . I'm still evaluating that." Carol not only needed to know why the rituals were done, she also needed to re-examine their meanings with each performance.

Respondents who sought intellectual understanding of the rites were apparently trying to gauge whether or not such activities were too devotional, theistic, magical, or superstitious for their comfort. At Chandrakirti Centre, teachers were not reluctant to present students with the nonempirical elements of Tibetan-based Buddhism, and there was some tolerance of the religious and theistic aspects of the center among newcomers at General Program classes. Still, Thekchen told me, many westerners do have certain preconceptions about ritual. He said that members who were learning how to change the water offerings on the shrines appreciated knowing about the symbols, intentions, and meditative practices that accompanied them. Although deities and devotion to those deities were involved in making the water offerings, Thekchen pointed out that having the symbolism of the water offering explained made performing it more acceptable to Chandrakirti practitioners. "That's what I really appreciate and I think that's what people in the West really appreciate," Thekchen said, "is explained ritual. . . . I think people from other religious backgrounds love the fact that every aspect of the ritual is explained. There is no part of ritual that is: just shut up and do it." It would appear, therefore, that gaining a cognitive understanding of the rituals made them accessible to some respondents in the face of their reluctance or skepticism: Without first learning about the purposes or meanings of the offerings and the symbols involved, they might not participate at all. Some cognitive learning, therefore, may be a necessary first step for adoptive practitioners, a means of overcoming their initial wariness or skepticism.

Catherine Rathbun said: "many westerners actually have a reaction against ritual because they come from one of the Christian churches that use a great deal of ritual without explanation." At one of the Tibetan Meditation classes she gave a brief talk on ritual. She said that mysticism can disappear under the weight of formal ritual, like ancient sacred sites underneath churches. Ritual, she said, is calming if you understand it. In the Géluk school of Tibetan Buddhism there is a great deal of ritual and teachings that surround it. Catherine noted, as an example, the formal practices enacted before the shrine, and the precise movements that are performed. "This is outer training," she said, "it teaches you to be calm, it teaches respect, it teaches presence. But for westerners, it becomes something that keeps us away from its intent." Excessive ritual, she believed, is a barrier for westerners. This talk is itself a cognitive means of teaching about ritual, an attempt to open up students' acceptance of rites through intellectual understanding.

When Gerald first attended Chandrakirti Centre, he was a little wary of formal practices like bowing before the teacher and the offerings and statues on the shrines. He was reassured by one monastic that the offerings and the statues did not signify the belief that deities were actually present (despite the fact that most experienced members and teachers to whom I spoke said that receiving blessings from deities was a key element of the practice at Chandrakirti Centre). Gerald was reassured to learn that making offerings and bowing to the shrines were simply regarded as mindful gestures and did not constitute deity worship.

By the time of his second interview in May of 2007, Gerald had become very involved at Chandrakirti Centre. He had been asked to come in once a week and change the water offerings on the shrines. He said that being given that responsibility gave him a sense of connection with the center. "Since they asked me to do the water offerings," he said, "I consider myself a member. I think being asked to do that really brought me into it. Otherwise I would have felt I was still along the outside looking in."

Gerald described what he did when he performed the water offerings, beginning with pouring the water in the offering bowls into a special bucket. "Well, not special," he said; "it's just plastic, but it's only used for emptying the water [from the shrines]." He then emptied and cleaned each bowl, placing them upside down on the shrine until turning them right side up again, one at a time, to refill them. "With each process, you're supposed to try to think with a certain amount, as much as you can, of pure thoughts, which made me nervous at first. Oh, man, where am I going to get these?" Gerald said, laughing.

> But I lightened up somewhat since doing it. Just doing that, I try to be as honest as I can. For me, coming from a Catholic background, I use it as a confessional. Not that I stand there and tell them my sins, but I just try to be as honest as I can.

It's like a one-on-one kind of thing, just for the half-hour or however long it takes. So, it's sort of an intimate, tactile introduction to the rituals there.

Gerald was initially given some instruction on how to perform the water offering but not much detail on the symbols involved or their meanings. By simply performing the offerings, he developed an appreciation for the physical nature of the activity, and felt it was a unique way of coming to know about the center and some of its practices. "It's just a tactile approach, rather than having the ideas all abstract. It's just a tactile, hands on. It's the ritual." Up until the time he was asked to change the water offerings, Gerald had only attended the General Program classes at Chandrakirti Centre and had not learned about any of the center's more formal rituals. "They are heavy on the rituals, and I wasn't aware of that at first." He initially felt uncomfortable when he realized how "ritual heavy" the center was. "I thought, at some point, I would break with it once it strayed from the philosophical, the intellectual ideas. I thought that if it got into rituals, I probably wouldn't embrace it, but the more the ideas meant something to me emotionally, the more I was willing to embrace the rituals." Gerald's talk about performing the more strongly ritualized activities had thus changed since his initial interview—he had moved past the need for intellectual understanding to accept the process of learning through the physicality of performance. Being asked to perform the water offerings created an affective connection to the center, drawing him more strongly into the Chandrakirti community. Making the offerings also made the center and its rituals more accessible to him. "It's a daily, practical function that I think symbolizes or represents the community in maintaining the connection within the community. It's an important maintenance. It's important, and it's simple, and it just feels kind of nice."

Gerald definitely regarded the water offerings as a learning experience.

It's a chance to learn about the deities, about the symbolism involved in Buddhism and have a hands-on practical application of all the beliefs, to see how it feels. And also, I did it because mainly I work from the intellect, so I'm pretty suspicious of symbols and things like chants and rituals. And there's no reason for that, other than that's the way I see myself. So I wanted to break that down, and see how I felt. And it still feels kind of funny, but it's a good funny. It's like pushing outwards what you think you are. So, doing the water offerings, I get the chance to just feel myself a little, doing something I'm not that comfortable with. So, it's good. And I know it means something, it has a special function within the Buddhist ritual system.

Gerald's experiences are a significant example of learning directly through ritual. First, performing the water offerings helped him overcome his wariness of deity worship, and increased his awareness and understanding of the deities symbolized on the shrine. The learning process he described was personal and experiential: learning about the ritual through performing it, and through pushing against his initial skepticism by choosing to accept the ritual. Gerald also noted the fact that performing the water offering broke down his tendency to intellectualize and gave him an opportunity to reflect on that tendency. In so doing, he also learned about himself.

The tactile experience of performing the water offerings altered Gerald's emotional responses to the ritual itself, to the symbols involved, and to the Chandrakirti community. Performing the water offerings also taught him the potential importance of ritual itself. I asked Gerald if he regarded the rituals as important. He said: "Now I do, only because the ideas have become more emotional based." Gerald's experience of the water offering, therefore, is another example of psychomotor learning—observing, imitating, and refining physical activities (such as emptying and refilling offering bowls)—that led to affective learning—in this case, Gerald's awareness of emotional changes in himself.

Gerald also described the ways in which his attitudes had changed, in a speech that illustrates an intriguing process of embodied learning.

> By getting your hands involved...it's easier to, say, have focus on meditation, because you are more willing to do it. More of your experience of yourself is involved. It's not just part of your brain, now it's the experience of actually doing it with your hands. It's like a consensus within yourself, that's agreeing with everything. And there's less doubt and less criticism directed to it. And when the criticism does come, it's more balanced; judging about whether this works or not works. Because there is still criticism of the ideas.... [The offerings are] mind based, but they have some feeling attached to them because you start putting these ideas into daily practice in ordinary life and you realize: (1) they're beneficial and (2) they're difficult. So, you learn to serve the ideas rather than have the ideas serve you. You realize that they have the power to help you, but in order to do that, you have to give them a power because they're hard. They're difficult to do. It's easy to think about, as if they're science-fiction ideas and say: ooh, yeah, it's kind of cool, rebirth. But to really try to be in the present, it's quite humbling. And not to conceptualize, but just to put it into practice. Maybe if I do embrace them more, and you want to embrace them more, maybe I will have more of the strength because they go out from your head into your hands.

Gerald speaks about giving up control, allowing the practice to change him. Like many adoptive Buddhists, Gerald was uncertain about the more metaphysical aspects of Chandrakirti's teachings. Karmic rebirth, the example he gives in this speech, is an idea that many sympathizers from non-Buddhist backgrounds reject.

Yet Gerald felt that the offering rite made him more willing to embrace such ideas because he was able to make a shift from the conceptual to the physical. Gerald thus indicated that participation in the rite increased acceptance and deeper levels of understanding beyond the intellectual. He felt he had gained an emotional understanding through the tactile experience. Gerald was describing a kind of knowing that is situated in the body rather than that which is stored in the brain. Theorists like Jennings and Schilbrack describe this kind of knowing as ritual knowledge.[16] More than simple muscle memory, this kind of embodied knowing is closely tied to affective response because it develops in and through the elevated activity of ritualizing.

While performing the offering rite, Gerald tested out the ideas involved, entering a state of receptivity in which he provisionally accepted and explored concepts like the presence of deities and karmic rebirth. Afterward, he was free to reflect on the ideas, analyze them, and make his own rational conclusions about them. Some of what he understood about the offerings did develop with later reflection, but much of what he learned about and through the ritual took place simultaneously with its performance. While he was free to reject any of the meanings he perceived, repeated performances of the offerings evidently did increase his acceptance over time.[17] Gerald's experiences with the water offerings indicated that learning through ritualizing has the advantage of being tactile, personal, and intimate; it engages the whole body-mind in the learning experience.

By contrast, Carol, who had participated in some of the empowerments at Chandrakirti Centre, said that she was still uncomfortable with "serious rituals."

> Some of the empowerments and those things...because they are using the *vajra* bells and all those kinds of things and they have different meanings. I don't understand all of those things....And I appreciate that they have significance, but I don't feel compelled to be a participant in those things. It's probably just a comfort level, because I haven't grown up with that or something. I haven't been exposed to it enough. And there's still the question of: How much ritual does one require?

Carol indicated that her discomfort with highly ritualized activities stemmed from a lack of understanding of their meanings. She made an important observation: She had not grown up with the rituals and symbols of Tibetan Buddhism, and believed that this was why she was uncomfortable with them. Richard Hayes, a Buddhist scholar and practitioner, expresses the same thought. Hayes notes that the rituals and symbols of an "exotic" religious tradition one adopts in later life will always feel foreign, and that one's feelings for the new rituals and symbols remain only superficial.[18] Hayes suggests that it requires the imagination and fantasies of childhood to fully internalize and become emotionally invested in religious rituals and symbols. To some extent, I agree. Many respondents in this study repeatedly expressed difficulties understanding and accepting Buddhist rituals and symbols. But repeated exposure and increased familiarity, while it did not work for everyone, did help some respondents gain greater acceptance and emotional connection to the new rituals they encountered at the centers.

Ritualizing involves learning in all three of Bloom's domains. Physical skills are received, repeated, refined and adapted. If the activities are regarded as elevated, special, set aside, transcendent, and so on, their performance can result in affective changes, that is, new attitudes, emotional responses, and new values. The addition of conceptual and factual data on the cognitive end also assists the reception-acceptance-application flow of affective learning. This learning process can be illustrated as repeated loops of a pattern of learning, moving from one domain to the next and returning (see figure 5.1). The process may begin with any one of the domains, but Gerald's experience suggests that beginning with the psychomotor (observing, imitating, and refining the physical performance of the rite) made the learning more intimate and personal. Those who started at the cognitive end, questioning the meanings before becoming involved, were those who less readily accepted the centers' more ritualized activities. Gerald had experienced increased emotional involvement when he unquestioningly took on the water offerings. Although Carol also performed water offerings at Chandrakirti Centre, she was still questioning their meanings and purposes, and did not indicate the same kind of emotional connection to them. At the other end of the spectrum from Gerald was Diane, who wanted to know all about the various rites before performing them, and was not yet motivated to participate.

Grimes points out that that ritualizing is nondiscursive, that intellectual analysis, particularly during emergent rituals, can impede the development of those rituals.[19] Too much cognition in advance may, therefore, be an obstacle to the kind of experiential learning Gerald described. As Catherine Rathbun said, there is something to be said for the "just do it" approach.

There's a certain point where that's exactly what I'll say to a student. And, partway through Vajrasattva,[20] it comes from every single student: I can't stand this practice, why do I have to do it? Why do I have to keep doing it? And I'll say: You know what? Just do it. Sorry, you've made this intention, you've made this determination to do your foundation practice and this is very good and it's very good that you're having such trouble. It's very good that nothing is happening and you're not getting anything resolved and it's hard. Just do it. Because, on the other side comes the illumination.

Catherine suggests that enacting the practice first and thinking about it later may result in more profound responses to the formal practices. Hence, gaining information about the rituals and evaluating or analyzing their meanings in advance may have the effect of preempting the experiential and intimate means of learning through and with the body that comes with ritualizing.

Bloom and colleagues and several other commentators on Bloom's taxonomy[21] point out that cognitive and affective learning do overlap. The need for cognitive learning in order to participate in ritual activity does not necessarily preclude affective learning processes like receiving and accepting new attitudes and values. For some practitioners, it is clear that gaining and analyzing information about a ritual is a necessary starting point. Cognitive learning can, therefore, open the door to other domains of learning about and through ritual. But, as many respondents indicated, intellectual understanding is merely the first step. Many felt that the full experience of learning through practice involves receiving and accepting new attitudes and values and embodying new activities and skills.

RITUALIZING AND MEDITATION

Most Friends of the Heart respondents believed that meditation was the primary means by which they gained new knowledge, attitudes, skills, and perhaps insights. Meditation as a whole certainly involves formal gestures and postures, such as stylized breathing or the prescribed postures of the legs, spine, head, hands, and so forth. But meditative concentration exercises—the practices that take place in or with the mind of the meditator—also constitute ritualizing. Like postures and gestures, meditative concentration techniques are deliberately cultivated behaviors whose sources are—or are believed to be—traditional. They can be rearranged, experimented with, and can develop into regular, stable ritual.

Practices referred to here as meditative concentration techniques include but are not limited to those taught at Friends of the Heart and Chandrakirti Centre: concentrating on or counting the breaths; silent repetition of a short phrase such as a mantra or prayer; metta or loving-kindness meditation; paying attention to physical sensations in the body; paying attention to images or emotions; reflecting on a teaching; or complex visualizations of Buddhas or Bodhisattvas. The last is a practice not usually performed by introductory students, but by participants in higher-level courses, empowerments, or pūjās.

Grimes has discussed meditative breathing, in the context of the Zen tradition, as ritualizing.[22] Normally, breathing falls under ritualization: It is, for the most part, a preconscious activity. But the way we breathe is influenced—Grimes calls it stylized—by culture and society. Once we begin to focus on the breath, to take it as an object of awareness or concentration, breathing becomes ritualizing.

> Strictly speaking, breath attended to is ritualizing rather than ritualization. To consider breathing a ritualization process is not to deny its obvious biological function but to recognize that any action, no matter how practical or survival-oriented, can become symbolic once it becomes the focus of attention and bearer of meaning.... Until one begins breath-following, the stylization of our breathing is likely preconscious. We were not aware of it, though with effort we could have been. Respiration feels so simple—in and out, that is all. Yet the rhythm, depth, and rate are culturally and personally distinctive, sometimes intentionally so, particularly in traditions that maintain strong meditative traditions. In zazen one becomes aware of the stylization of the breath but refrains from stylizing it any further. Zen breathing does not occur under a "breathe naturally" dictum. Trying to breathe naturally is self-contradictory.[23]

Now, one could argue that breathing entails movement, and is therefore gestural. But what qualifies breathing as ritualizing is the concentration or attentiveness that takes place in Zen meditation (*zazen*): the awareness of the stylization of the breath. This focus of the attention is an entirely mental "doing" or mind event. This and other concentration techniques performed in meditation are not normal thought processes. Quite the contrary: they are designed to interrupt ordinary thought processes. It is more like a physical posture or gesture of the mind than a thought. Dennis described an example of such a ritualized mental technique when I asked if he could teach me something he learned at Meg's Calm and Clear class.

> Well, the things I found most useful, anyway, were when Meg was talking about the idea of bringing your mind back. When you focus on something and your mind wanders, recognizing first of all that your mind is wandering, and then just acknowledging it, and then bringing it back to your focus. And also the idea of, instead of trying to block everything out—block out distractions—acknowledge distractions. In the early going, I would hear cars going outside and I wouldn't quite know how to handle it, so you calmly acknowledge the distractions and then come back to what you're trying to focus on.

The technique Dennis described involves consciously enacted behavior rather than the normal preconscious activities of the mind. It is a way of using the mind that is not cognitive or analytical: It is much more like an activity or a skill. Recognizing and calmly acknowledging distractions and bringing the mind back to the object of concentration, like focusing on the breath in zazen, is ritualizing.

John claimed that meditative concentration exercises were more like physical activities than ordinary thought processes. "It's like an activity. It might be mental, but it's definitely a mental activity, not like: memorize this list of ten words type thing." Learning meditation, in John's point of view, was akin to developing physical techniques for the mind, a kind of training. "I guess the theory is that you're going to build up your skills, much as you would build up your physical fitness. So, when you need it, it's there. In times of calm, you're going to build up these concentration and focus skills and in times of stress, you will be able to do this." The mental skills that practitioners are meant to develop through meditation are concentration, awareness, and patience: the ability to stay with the practice and not become frustrated by distractions. In her Calm and Clear class, Meg also made several references to training the mind, often referring to "building the awareness muscles." Several respondents, therefore, expressed the idea that concentration techniques were more like physical skills than cognitive thought processes.

Concentration practices like these demonstrate an important conceptual distinction between the mind and the brain. The mind that performs the practices is a kind of gestural entity, one which we imagine to be founded in the static organ, the brain. Meditative concentration techniques engage the mind in ways that ritualizing usually engages other parts of the body: through repeated practices that are formal, deliberate, and often predetermined. Moreover, they are embodied just as meditation postures and gestures are. They are, in fact, postures (concentration) and gestures (directing the attention) of the mind. In the following discussion, therefore, I refer to meditation as a ritual activity with respect to all of its elements: lighting candles or incense, for instance, or ringing a bell, performing meditation postures and mudras, as well as any of the various concentration techniques. All are embodied postures or gestures. In essence, I treat the mind as another limb, one with uniquely cognitive characteristics, to be sure, but it is another part of our bodies that can be directed and experimented with; in short, the mind can be made to act in ritualized ways.

MEDITATION AND EMBODIED KNOWING

Learning through meditation, like learning through all ritual activity, is learning through experience. It is not merely hearing or reading about new information, attitudes, skills, or insights; it is a means of experientially developing them. Alan Rogers writes: "Just as we all breathe but much of the time we are not conscious of it, so we all learn, even though at times we are not conscious of doing so. Learning, then, is the way we relate to our experiences—the way such experiences change us and the way we try to change our experiences and make sense of them."[24] If Rogers is right, then ritualizing, as experience—as embodied enactment—cannot but be a means of learning. Rather than inquiring whether ritualizing is a means of learning, it is more constructive to ask: In what ways do we learn through ritualizing?

If ritualizing serves a noetic function,[25] if it creates new knowledge about ourselves and our ways of being in the world, much of the knowledge it imparts is gained by and located in the body, in the muscles and bones rather than solely in the brain. The body becomes socially informed, it *knows* how to act in the ritual and in the world. As Jennings puts it, "my hand 'discovers' the fitting gesture (or my feet the fitting step) which I may then 'cerebrally' re-cognize as appropriate or right."[26] In meditation, respondents have told me, the mind may discover the "fitting" ways of concentrating and directing the attention. Later, meditators can "cerebrally" understand which of these techniques are most appropriate. Thus, it is more accurate to refer to the socially or ritually informed body-mind: The mind gains ritual knowledge through concentration techniques, while the legs, hands, knees, and spine learn through physical postures and gestures.

There was a strong emphasis on body awareness at all of the Friends of the Heart classes. Friends of the Heart teachers often claimed that one of their objectives was to overcome students' tendencies to separate mind and body and to overlook the significance of the latter. Meg said that the focus on exercise and movement in the center's classes helped her realize, as she put it, "how physical meditation experiences were." Tanit said she appreciated the way Joyce gave instructions, particularly with reference to the body, its postures, and gestures. "I liked the way she describes things, too, [such as] letting your body settle into the pose....I'm enjoying that aspect and I'm becoming a lot more aware of where my spine is in relationship to where I'm standing." The time and attention Joyce put into her instructions on posture and movement helped students become more aware of their bodies. In Catherine Rathbun's view, "traditional Buddhism, at least the way it's come down to us, has often left the body out of the equation. And in the West that's created what I call "neck up" Buddhists....If you leave out the body, you leave out one of your greatest teachers."

Several interview questions encouraged respondents to reflect on how and what they learned through meditation, particularly with respect to the body. What did they learn through meditation postures? Was there any new learning, knowledge, or understanding gained through meditation? I also asked a few respondents: What does the body know? In response to the latter question, Tanit said:

> I'm finding, once my eyes are closed, and I'm trying to find points inside my body, it's not so easy....So, I'm beginning to think that my body knows a lot, based on

what I have seen. And, of course, I'm a designer so I'm inclined visually, but so much of the information that I'm getting about my body is through what I see. Once my eyes are closed, it's a very different experience. So, I'm not sure what my body knows and I don't think I listen to my body. And I'm starting to try to listen to it, to try to understand it without my visual understanding locating everything for me....I think what I'm trying to do is learn to hear my body. I just assumed so many things about it, or I've just not even thought about it. But yeah, the body is there. You are in your body.

What does the body know? Apparently, more than we know it knows. The meditation techniques that Tanit was learning were teaching her new ways of experiencing and listening to her body. They drew her attention to embodied knowing, which is not normally accessible to conscious thought. But in ritualizing, some of this embodied knowing becomes a little more conscious as we deliberately perform or attend to it. As Tanit notes, we may not necessarily learn *what* that embodied knowing entails, but we can become more aware of its presence. This awareness appears to have given her a better sense of embodiment and an increased awareness of the body as a site of knowing. She has recognized that her body, in Csordas's words, is "socially informed." Note that the language that both Tanit and I use references the body as an object, something separate from the self. Where Csordas argues that the socially informed body is pre-objective—that our experience of ourselves does not naturally objectify the body—our language and our cultural conditioning do perpetuate that sense that self and body are separate. Tanit suggests, however, that the practice of meditating on the body has made her more aware of that gap.

Tanit spoke quite a bit about the meditation techniques she learned at Friends of the Heart, as well as the new understandings that she gained through them. She described, for example, what she had learned through one of the insight practices that Joyce had taught.

I liked the way she describes it, too, in terms of active areas being associated with touch and [other] areas at rest. Those two areas. And it was interesting because I know when we were first meditating, I was associating active as bad and rest as good. And you just begin to recognize that you have this language set up. And then I realized that she was deliberately not referencing it that way. It was being specifically referenced as "touch" which isn't necessarily a negative or positive thing.

The new perspectives Tanit gained as a result of meditation extended beyond the practice itself. The technique of applying neutral labels to sensations in the body made Tanit aware that she normally judged most of her experiences as either positive or negative. Developing neutral responses to body sensations thus taught her that she might be less judgmental at other times as well. Joyce did not explain this idea directly: She never said "do not regard tension in the body as bad and a lack of tension as good." Neither did she say that the objective was to change our usual ways of judging other experiences. But through the meditation practice of assigning neutral labels to sensations in the body, Tanit learned both of these things. She said

> I'm finding I have this structure set up as: this is good, this is bad.... Preconceptions, essentially. And Joyce, just by the nature of who she is and how the meditation goes, is starting to alert me to some of those preconceived ideas that I am carrying.... To be relaxed and at peace is good but the awareness isn't about that, it's about just being aware. And that's fascinating, it really is, that awareness. It's quite amazing.

Here, Tanit describes a technique that developed through practice into a skill that, in turn, led to changes in her attitudes. In time, this new perspective may also result in consistent changes to her behavior in other areas of her life. Tanit thus experienced an affective type of learning, since the practice had influenced her values, attitudes, and emotional responses. She believed she was inquiring into and discovering new ways of being and behaving.

When I asked Gerald if he thought that learning or training took place through practice, he replied:

> Definitely, with meditation, you have to have some sort of discipline in order to even begin to want to sit there. And then, to sit there, and try to sit there longer and try to concentrate on the breath: that simple exercise, you gain strength in muscle and that in turn gives rise to focus, because there is less ache.... The thing that I noticed is that in order to want to be focused on something positive, you have to direct your body in that way, too. And it turns out, I think, that every thought has a corresponding bodily posture: whether it be the most subtle or the most overt. And thoughts aim towards something virtuous or positive, it also helps the thought if you're more aware of your body being in that way, too. You try to recollect anything you can from the meditation process.

Jennings argues that what we learn in the performance of a ritual does not stay within the context of the ritual. It teaches us about our being in the world.[27] Both Tanit and Gerald had learned something new about themselves and the world around them through their meditation practice.

Schilbrack argues that ritual knowledge, the peculiar type of knowledge gained through ritual, is uniquely metaphysical. Schilbrack defines metaphysics, not as the world beyond human experience, but as "the character of experienced things in general."[28] In this view, metaphysical thinking arises through ritual when participants either experience the aspects of a ritual as aspects of the human condition or the ritual itself as a microcosm for human experience in general. For example: Meditating in the cremation grounds teaches the meditator that his or her body is impermanent and so, too, is everything else.[29] Through ritual, we develop a kind of understanding that connects our bodily activities to the world around us.[30] Rituals, therefore, are "embodied ways of knowing."[31] Schilbrack thus offers a way of understanding ritual as an experience through which we learn not only the right ritual gestures, but also how to authentically be in the world.[32] Ritual knowledge is, therefore, an embodied or psychomotor learning that is also affective, since it entails changes in values and attitudes.

Several respondents indicated that there was a strong connection between the physical aspects of learning meditation and certain affective changes that they experienced. "Adults act their way into a new way of thinking," Meg told me, "they don't think their way into a new way of acting." In Meg's view, the best approach to teaching meditation was to begin with the body. She said she sought moments in which she could use students' experiences of change in their bodies as teaching opportunities. Physiological changes were what Meg called a "feedback loop" for understanding the whole of the meditative experience.

> You will just notice yourself feeling differently, physically. And that is your first clue. You can't put words to it yet. Words are the back end of the learning curve. If you are able to articulate it, it means you are way down the exploration path. But one of the first things that comes is some kind of a physical feeling....Who knows where [the changes] start. But they become initially visible in the body.

Thus the changes that occur in meditation, Meg believed, are first noticed in the body. Moreover, students are more readily able to articulate their physical experiences. Meg described a progression of change, from "a lack of tension, a feeling of flow, a feeling of spaciousness, [to] a feeling of joy," thus indicating that physical changes assist the development of particular emotional responses. She also noted that learning through meditation necessitated developing effective habits, as she put it, "physically, emotionally, mentally, and spiritually." "[It is] about the discipline required to build new patterns. It is an active intention to make things concrete. There was a lovely sentiment I came across, I don't know where, about ritual being an enactment of an experience which is made concrete. So, if something you want to experience is spiritual unfoldment, you enact it in this ritual form."

The process Meg describes is a way of "thinking through and with the body."[33] As Meg had put it: one acts oneself into a new way of thinking, not the other way around. In this view, one begins with psychomotor learning processes, which may then result in affective change.

Rituals shape behavior by training the body and developing physical habits or skills which may, in turn, affect our emotions, attitudes, and values.[34] When asked what the body knows, Dennis replied:

> The body definitely adapts, there's no question about that. Again, through repetition it can train itself....I guess that's what working out and people who do exercises, they're really adapting to greater amounts of exertion. That's one way you might want to define exercise. But the way I would look at it is that your mind thinks through your body. So your mind might think of ways to adapt through the body.

The mind "thinks through the body," Dennis said, expressing the idea that the body also engages in inquiry and interprets experience.[35] Gwen expressed this perspective as well: "I learn to take concepts and see how they sit in my body," she said. I asked if her meditation practice influenced her beliefs, and she replied:

> I would like to answer that question in a physical way, because I think that one can have beliefs that are of a cerebral nature, right?...What I know seems more physical, seems more holistic than just knowing it in the brain. There is something about experience that is connected to Buddhism, to me, very, very deeply. So, there isn't that sense of separation like my mind knows this, but my body doesn't....What is it to be one being? What is it to be whole? What is it to have heart-mind?...So the practice helps to unify that.

Gwen's observations indicate a strong sense of the body and mind as one. She believed that meditation practice created that sense of unity of body and mind. She distinguished between knowledge of a cerebral type and knowing through the body, as I have done by positing different domains of learning. But in Gwen's view and in mine, there are distinct types of learning experienced by the body-mind: one is intellectual, that which we regard as involving processes in the brain. The other is physical: it is the way in which muscles and bones are trained to experience and to "know" about the world. Gwen is suggesting what I have alluded to: that the mind, as part of the body, also develops the second type of knowing.

Because of its physical nature, learning through ritualizing often involves a changing awareness of the body. But when I asked Diane if we learn through the body in meditation, she said that she did not experience a strong sense of her body when she meditated. "Sometimes I just feel my heart beating, that's all. So, yes I'm embodied, but I don't have a sense of: I'm sitting here and my feet are on the floor. That's gone. I like that." Because she meditated seated in a chair, Diane experienced little discomfort while meditating. She said that, unless she had a pain, she often felt disconnected from her body and felt few areas of "touch" sought in the insight practice Joyce had taught. "I haven't even tried to sit on the floor," Diane said. "In some places I have read that you should force yourself to try to do it, because the pain is part of it." Meditators often assume cross-legged postures that are accompanied by varying levels of tension, discomfort, or even pain in the legs. But without pain or discomfort, Diane lost her sense of her body. The sense of the body disappearing may have appealed to what Diane often described as her intellectual nature or her tendency to live from the "neck up." All the same, Diane said that she would like to become more aware of her body.

> I'm just so disconnected from my body, so for me a part of wanting to do the insight *vipassanā* practice is to try and get that kind of connection....I need to develop that relationship, that's part of the way I meditate, that's part of making some connection....Am I learning it? I feel like it is possible. But when, for example, we try and see body sensations, I don't have any. So it's like: okay, there's nothing there, go back up to the head.

Diane's experience highlights an important point: If ritual activity is to teach us something about or through the body, it is perhaps necessary to have an awareness of the body during the practice. Catherine and Joyce both pointed out that the insight techniques taught at Friends of the Heart were intended to get practitioners out of their heads and into the rest of their bodies. But concentration techniques alone may not be sufficient. The connection between posture, discomfort, and body awareness may explain why some meditation teachers insist on traditional meditation postures, even when practitioners find them difficult or painful.

I asked Carol if she thought the body was important in the practices: Does the body learn, too? She said that assuming the same posture each time, "making the body a ritual and being aware of that, encompassing it in the meditation," was important. Like Diane, she had read that it was important to maintain a particular meditation posture and to "go through the experience of being uncomfortable." Carol said, "I try to be ritualistic about it but it is not always comfortable, and sometimes I cheat." She did not feel badly about her so-called "cheating," however. If there is too much discomfort, she said, it becomes a barrier to practice. Even so, Carol expressed an understanding that standard or traditional meditation postures were important.

In an article exploring meditative experience, Janet Gyatso points to the significance that Tibetan Buddhist teachings place on physical experience for the
development of spiritual realization. "Produced by and in the body, experience is
cultivated in meditation…so as to make the practitioner more aware of the body,
to render the body subject, as it were, to the realizations of Buddhist doctrine,
indeed to expand the domain of the subject not only to the body as such but to all
the activities in which it engages."[36] Skilled meditators are said to experience the
truths of impermanence, suffering, and no-self first in the body and then as conditions inherent in all other phenomena. Higher insight, Gyatso notes, requires
a unified experience of the body and mind.[37] The indication is, therefore, that
higher insights into Buddhist principles require more than a cognitive understanding: they must also be felt in the body. Gyatso notes that, particularly in
the Mahāmudrā stream of Tibetan Buddhism, spiritual realization necessitates
freedom from body-mind dualism. The meditator becomes one with his or her
body and with the object of concentration. Having a sense of the body during
meditative practice, in this view, is necessary for spiritual realization to take
place. Traditional postures may be a means of ensuring the necessary body
awareness.

The significance of posture as a ritualized means of learning, however, is not
limited to producing body awareness through body sensation. There is something
about the ritualized nature of meditation posture that is significant as well, even
postures assumed when seated in a chair; especially if a posture is specifically
reserved for meditation. When I asked respondents to reflect on how or what they
might learn through meditation posture, several of them said they had noticed
strong associations between physical postures and gestures and what was going on
in their minds. That is to say, formal, repetitive physical postures and gestures
were associated with, and had an influence on, the mind states that usually accompanied them.

The most common association of this sort was between the straight, upright
meditation posture and alertness or concentration. Diane, for example, said:
"Well, the sitting up for me means concentration. It means finding a place
where my body is centered. I also see, if my spine is upright, that there is a
better connection between brain and the body. So it means something physical
about the transmission of energy." Diane described a direct association between body-state and mind-state. "If I were like this," Diane said, assuming a
slouched posture leaning on her elbow, "I don't even think of meditating like
that. It's a really alert thing for me, so I automatically sit in a way that feels
right to me now." Diane had discovered a connection between her body posture and her ability to maintain alertness and concentration. I asked her if she

made similar associations with the mudra she used in meditation, and she said the hand posture was not significant. Even so, she did have a sense of which mudra "felt right."

> In terms of the hand movement, you know holding your hands; I don't think it has a particular significance. It just becomes part of the posture, the way of sitting. Although, I did switch [from hands on the knees to the cosmic mudra], because after I tried it a couple of times, it felt right to me. It felt like it was part of sitting upright. So, it is more of a posture, a body thing, to help me stay alert. That's it: the alertness.

Thus on reflection, Diane indicated that the "right" mudra was part of the habitual posture that she associated with meditation and thus with concentration. Gerald made a similar association between posture and meditation. "Meditation, I think, is physical training on a certain level. You are asked to sit as still as you can and breathe quite calmly. Mentally, it's training too. But . . . if you want your mind to be still your body has to be."

Nicolette, who also said that the physical aspects of meditation helped her focus, asserted that this was the case because "the mind and body are one." In fact, it becomes very easy, when arguing for associations between body and mind states, to slip once again into body-mind dualism. If body and mind are one, then the premise that the body influences the mind is mere tautology. But these associations between posture and concentration are not mechanical: If we still the body, we do not necessarily or automatically calm the mind.

On some level, meditative body states act as metaphors or symbols of the concentrated mind-state. Diane made habitual associations between posture and concentration, but she also regarded the straight, unmoving posture as a symbol of an alert, concentrated mind. "I view it as a way of staying alert and being able to concentrate. And if I get slumped over, mind follows body, right? If I'm all slumped over I feel that my mind is slumped over." As another example, Margaret had learned a technique that made a metaphorical connection between the body and the mind in meditation. When I asked her if she could teach me something that she had learned, she said:

> Well, this is a tiny piece, but a piece I find very helpful when my mind is busy talking to me. And that is the trick Joyce taught us about letting our tongue relax. When I'm really busy, I realize my tongue is fairly firmly implanted on the roof of my mouth and by relaxing it, even if the rest of my body has taken on the right posture, I am amazed at how that . . . It's hard to have that mind-chatter going on if your tongue isn't engaged.

By practicing the technique Joyce had taught, Margaret understood that there were direct associations between the tongue and speech, and learned that she made figurative connections between physical and mental "chatter." Having made these connections, Margaret learned that relaxing the tongue helped her "relax" the mind. For these respondents, a relaxed tongue or upright posture, therefore, were symbols of concentration and alertness.

Habit formation is also an effective means of linking meditation posture and concentration techniques. Repeatedly assuming the posture while simultaneously concentrating the mind, meditators forge habitual associations between the two activities. Dennis said: "Your body is in the position, and maybe it gets familiar with it, so maybe subconsciously it will know it's time to settle down." With time and familiarity, then, meditation posture facilitates meditative concentration. Speaking about meditation postures and gestures, Carol said, "It can be helpful to have something that you're familiar with to put you in a place that you identify with calmness or focusing on a certain thing. I guess it's...kind of a comfort level with those things [i.e., the meditation postures and gestures]." Repetition and habit formation thus forged a direct connection between body posture and mind states.

Schechner also explores connections between mind and body states. To demonstrate how physical postures and gestures can affect mood or emotion, Schechner describes two experiments conducted by psychologist Paul Ekman, working with professional actors.[38] In the first, Ekman asked his subjects to generate six different target emotions (surprise, disgust, sadness, anger, fear, and happiness) by reliving past experiences. In the second experiment, another group of actors was instructed, step by step, to contract specific facial muscles to produce prototypical facial expressions of the same six emotions. The instructions directed subjects on how to produce the expressions muscle by muscle but did not reveal to the subjects which emotions were associated with the expressions. For Schechner, the surprising outcome of Ekman's experiments was that the second group experienced changes in the autonomic nervous system (ANS), such as heart rate and skin temperature, that were of a larger magnitude and more recognizable than those of the first group. In other words, ANS responses indicated that the subjects were more profoundly affected by the mechanical production of specific facial expressions than by producing the same emotions by reliving memories.[39]

Schechner is interested in Ekman's experiments because of their implications for theatrical performers. Most western actors follow a technique called "the method," in which they relive experiences in order to produce desired emotions in performance. Mechanical reproduction of prototypical expressions, Schechner notes, is despised by most western actors. In light of Ekman's findings, however,

Schechner concludes that mechanical methods may be more effective at producing intensity of emotion. For purposes of this argument, Ekman's findings provide evidence of strong physiological responses to body posture and gesture, which may, in part, account for respondents' experiences of associating the physical and mental aspects of meditation.

When John spoke about how and what the body learns, he initially speculated on the physiological responses that might occur in meditation. "I could see if meditation perhaps lowered your heart rate or through a general sort of calming, lowered your blood pressure or things like that. The body might associate that with sitting down to meditate." But John also raised another possibility. "Even at the sight of something, if there is some sort of visual thing or incense, or anything like that, the body might sort of instantly begin calming down." John suggested, therefore, that the sight or smell of objects such as a shrine or incense may initiate some of the physiological states associated with practices normally performed in the presence of such objects. Sensing such objects, therefore, helps prepare the participant for the practice. John describes this process as a kind of reflexive conditioning. Such a response, however, is not necessarily a result of learning. As Harrow points out, reflexes are not learned. Learning is change: it is not merely change in patterns of acting (as is conditioning), it is change in patterns of acting *resulting from* changes in knowledge, understanding, skills, and attitudes.[40] Where John describes a physiological process of conditioning taking place, most other respondents noted that meditation postures and gestures supported concentration skills, led to a sense of decorum or commitment to practice, and so on. These responses are more conscious and more affective than simple reflex.

Diane, for example, suggested that an opening prayer acts to establish a ground for her meditation practice. Before meditating at home, she often spoke a refuge prayer she had learned from her readings on Buddhism. Saying the prayer, she said, "feels like it's delineating this time to do this. So, I wonder if this [the prayer] is me setting myself up: this is what I'm doing now. And doing that refuge reminds me that that is what I am doing now: mindfulness, what I am paying attention to." Alan also suggested that certain things helped "set up" meditation. For a time, he lit candles before meditating at home. He said that doing so "sets up the idea that this is what you're going to do. I think it gets your mind focused to say: okay, I'm ready to get into this position." These reflections by John, Diane, and Alan refer to ritual's function as a framing device.

If I might be permitted an example from personal experience: When I sit down to meditate, I don't "just sit," despite the idiom of the Zen tradition in which I was originally taught. First, I go to a special place, either a Buddhist center or a corner set aside in the spare bedroom of my home. These are special places because they are designated for meditation. If I am meditating at home, I often light a candle and a stick of incense. Sometimes I will perform three prostrations before I sit. At the very least, I will place my hands together in the prayer mudra and bow. Then I sit on my mat and cushion, in a posture usually called half-lotus; legs crossed with one foot on the opposite leg, the other foot on its side on the mat. I regard this posture as special, since it is only used for meditation. It also has practical functions: it automatically keeps my spine straight and is slightly painful, thereby keeping me alert. After settling into the posture I ring a bell three times and place my hands first in the prayer mudra and then the cosmic mudra in my lap. After all of these things are done, I begin meditation practice proper, concentrating on my breath and a chosen concentration technique.

The preparations are an important part of my formal meditation practice. They have various meanings. Some of the meanings, at the time I perform them, are unexamined, even vague. But the purpose they serve is clear: They express, if only to myself, that this is a special time, a time out of my regular routine, a time that I will dedicate specifically to meditation. In other words, they create the frame, temporally and spatially, in which I will meditate. If, after having performed the framing rituals, the phone rings or I feel hungry or the dog barks, I will not interrupt my sitting. Such things might disrupt me if I had simply taken a seat without such preparations. The ritualized activities tell me, when I finally do sit on the cushion, that I am not *just* sitting. I am not relaxing, taking a break, or ruminating about the things I have to do next. If I have, for example, ten minutes before I need to leave the house, and I decide to meditate in a chair without my usual preparations, I find it very difficult to concentrate on my practice. In such circumstances, it is difficult to regard myself as performing meditation, and I am much more likely to become distracted and stop meditating all together.

I make deliberate references to performance here: I am both the performer and the observer of the ritual. The framing activities set up the enactment as surely as a stage or a curtain. The lighting of incense and candle, the bow or prostration, the mudras, the cross-legged posture, and the concentration practice—all of these indicate to my body-mind that I am now meditating, doing something special or set aside from my ordinary activities. These rites, each a part of the whole ritual of meditation itself, motivate me to undertake and maintain meditation practice for a certain period of time without interruption.

Framing, in fact, is one of the key functions of ritual. Framing creates a center and periphery relative to a ritual, and is "meta-communicative": It enables and encourages participants to interpret the events and activities that take place within the frame.[41] Framing rituals thus delineate a time and space in which ritual activity can not only be performed but also explored and interpreted. Repeated each time a ritual is performed, framing activities become habitual performances, what Crossley terms body techniques.[42] They are enactments of biological and culturally influenced ways of being and knowing. But they are not simply rote, unconscious repetition. Crossley argues that habituation arising from ritual is not merely mechanical, a simple linking of stimulus and response.[43] Ideally, it is a learning experience. A specific kind of understanding, felt in the body, develops as habits are cultivated and new meanings absorbed.[44] Through such performances, we learn about ourselves and the various uses we make of our bodies.[45] Hence the body is not merely an object through which we experience our world. It is the body that receives new knowledge or understanding. In this view, ritual performance leads to a particular type of knowledge, one that consists of the body's familiarity with its own activities. It is the body's knowledge of how to move and behave. While it develops through habit formation, it is not habituation in the sense of redundancy wherein meaning may be lost. This type of knowing is significant for our understanding of ourselves and our experiences of the world. As noted earlier, however, it is usually inarticulate and inaccessible to our discursive minds.[46] It is tacit. We use this kind of knowledge without thinking about it.

Janet Gyatso, discussing the cultivation of physical techniques as prerequisite to ultimate realization in Tibetan Buddhism, employs the same example Rogers does when discussing tacit, experiential learning, namely learning to ride a bicycle. Comparing that example to the way meditative training leads to "ultimate nondualistic realization," she writes: "An awkward set of techniques are [sic] practiced with difficulty until certain break-throughs occur and the skills are mastered, leading finally to a feeling that riding a bike comes naturally."[47] The type of knowing that Crossley and Gyatso are describing here, however, is primarily physical: it is acquired through repetitive movements and postures assumed by hands, legs, feet, spine, and the like. The mind is not separate in this view, but it is generally regarded as a cognitive entity which is incapable of reflecting on this type of knowing without distorting it.[48] What respondents indicated to me was that meditation imparts the same type of tacit, habitual, nondiscursive knowing to the mind. In an exemplary response, Nicolette described Tibetan visualization practice as follows:

It's like learning any skill like riding a bike or making an omelet or throwing a baseball. You do it enough times that, once you get to the point where you have a body memory of it, or in this case, a memory of the images and the words and everything just sinks into your pores, once you get to the stage where you've got that deep memory, then you can get the full benefit of that skill that you have built up. So, if it's riding a bike, know you don't have to think about trying to balance, and you can go places.

Nicolette uses a number of physical images in this speech, but she is speaking about the images and words that are the focus of meditative concentration. To clarify, I asked if the same thing happens with the visualization practice, and she replied: "Yeah, or any kind of meditation." She thus connected visualization and other meditation practices, which are mental processes, with body memory, a physical one. Thus, the habituation of concentration practices also serves to cultivate Crossley's embodied practical reason, Jennings's ritual knowledge, or my embodied knowing. Like the rest of the body, the mind develops a familiarity with technique that becomes an embodied, tacit knowing that may, in turn, inform one's understanding of oneself and the world.

Gyatso does point to strong body-mind connections in the practices she describes. Through the formation of physical habits, initial theoretical conceptions are transformed into full realization, according to Mahāmudrā meditation practices. "Cultivating a bodily habit," Gyatso writes, "is in fact eminently appropriate, as the body seems to have a lot to do not only with the dawning of meditative experience in Mahāmudrā but also its conception of realization." The practitioner begins with an intellectual conception that the practice will lead, as Gyatso puts it, to "an unfolding of felt experience" and, in the end, to higher insight.[49] The significance of the body in Buddhist realization is further indicated by the fact that Tibetan literature often describes meditative realization using somatic metaphors. Realization is full and complete, for example, when it is "brought in to the 'belly of the mind.' "[50]

Concentration techniques are practices through which meditators develop new understandings and inquire about themselves and their worlds. Moreover, the ways in which they contribute to learning are similar to the ways that body postures and other ritualized body techniques do: through repetition, training, refinement, and so on. That is to say, meditative ritualizing is not wholly an affective process of gaining new understanding. The concentration techniques are not themselves attitudes, emotions, or values. They are, instead, skills that develop through psychomotor processes.

Nevertheless, many respondents said that concentration techniques influenced their emotions and attitudes. Diane, for instance, suggested that the special or elevated quality of meditation techniques was what influenced their affective results. At Friends of the Heart and Atisha Centre, she had learned practices in which she concentrated on what she called "virtuous" objects like metta or images of the Buddha. "I just like that concept of holding on, holding my attention on this virtuous object.... You can then begin to meditate on virtuous concepts like compassion, like loving kindness, like patience...." The techniques Diane described included certain positively valued concepts that she believed produced related affective changes. "There's a certain point at which meditation can become transformational. And that's really what I'm interested in. I can get to a level of feeling peaceful." Concentrating on virtuous objects, she believed, increased her ability to be compassionate, kind, patient, and peaceful. Evidently, affective changes—changes in emotions, attitudes, and values—may result from the special or elevated characteristics of the practice. Powers notes that objects that have soteriological value are often the focus of śamatha meditation.[51] But Buddhists also meditate on neutral and even negative objects as well—cremation ground meditation is an example—and these techniques are also believed to produce positive affective changes or desired insights into Buddhist truths.

Some respondents indicated that positively valued meditation techniques also affected physical changes. Tanit, for example, said that she had become strongly aware of changes in her body on one occasion during metta meditation.

> I realized that my whole body had changed during this metta. I had totally stilled, I know my heart beat had dropped, my breathing had deepened.... Now, it's happened on other occasions, but I've never been conscious that way. I find that partly it's time that goes into that stilling. This happened rapidly. There were probably two or three minutes and my body had completely changed in a meditation that had been very restless and erratic. So, that was really interesting, and a real acknowledgement that there are triggers that you can learn about yourself that you can use.

Tanit attributed the physical changes she experienced to the virtuous quality of the particular concentration technique, loving-kindness meditation. Similarly, Nicolette said that a meditation in which she visualized herself being cleansed with light translated into positive body sensations, and helped release tension in her body. "Your actual body clues into that sensation of being cleansed and letting all the detritus go that is clenched up inside it." Like Diane, then, Tanit and Nicolette believed that the positive or virtuous quality of the practices led to the particular changes they experienced. Alan also claimed that concentrating on virtues such as compassion or selflessness led to positive results. "If you dwell on and actually think about: cherish others, not yourself..., your mind, as you walk away from the meditation, it's been wired to believe that."

John, however, did not feel that meditating on compassion and kindness helped him attain particularly virtuous mind states. "I don't know, from the beginning I [thought] that meditation was focusing on your breath and not letting your mind intrude. When it got to be meditating on kindness or things like that, it was just not as successful. To me, it seemed artificial somehow. I didn't seem like the activity I should be doing." For John, then, metta meditation was an intellectual intrusion on meditative concentration because it involved thinking about words, phrases, and concepts. Thus the positively valued nature of the practice did not lead to affective changes in John's experience. John regarded what he learned as meditation training, a way of developing new skills. He reflected on how those skills might develop over time, comparing meditation to learning how to type:

> I don't know if you have plateaus in it or not. The classical learning curve for things like that is a plateau. Like, your typing speed. I remember they would say it was always the classic example of plateau learning, where you go along and you might type at this speed and all of a sudden, for some reason, after *n* weeks, you'll leap up to this speed. And I don't know if it [meditation] works that way or not. It may well work that way.

While he consistently made comparisons between meditation techniques and developing new physical skills, John did not regard meditative training as strictly physical. "It's sort of neutral physically, the actual meditation part," he said. "I seem to be noticing more of a connection between meditation and mood, possibly, but not between meditation and anything physical." In John's view, the concentration exercises were skills learned in the same way that physical skills are learned, namely through repetition and refinement. The affective changes John experienced were emotional: He said he felt more calm or mellow. He said he did not notice any changes in beliefs or values as a result of the practice. Neither did he connect positively valued practices like metta with positive moods. The outcomes John experienced were commensurate with his expectations: he did not regard meditation as a spiritual practice, but as a means of achieving practical benefits such as stress relief.

By contrast, Chandrakirti students described several different kinds of affective changes that resulted from meditation, primarily from meditating on the subjects of the lectures. Carol said that the meditation helped her develop compassion and kindness and a sense of personal responsibility, all of which were principles and values repeatedly emphasized in General Program talks. Gerald said that the guided meditation in the classes helped him quiet his mind and experience feelings of compassion and gratitude. Bronwen believed that she was beginning to reduce her attachment to things like personal possessions as a result of meditation practice. Priscilla, a student in Chandrakirti's Foundation Program, described how meditation on a teaching such as emptiness might lead to a deeper, embodied understanding of the concept:

> Something happens in meditation. I can't describe it really. Somehow it seems to settle in and click. Not all of the time, but sometimes you just go "oh," and then

it makes sense, whereas before it was kind of out there, it was words on paper. But then it becomes incorporated into you. When you're meditating, you're allowing the winds to flow through the central channel and part of what you're thinking about goes into that. And so it incorporates into your actual being.

Priscilla's description of winds and the central channel are references to tantric concepts in which energy streams move through the body, centered on focal points or chakras positioned along the spine and head. It is believed that these energy flows can be harnessed and used in meditation to affect physical and psychological changes in the meditator. Priscilla had incorporated this teaching into her meditation practice, and employed it as a method for internalizing and embodying the teachings she read in Foundation Program classes.

Alan had indicated that his primary practice was enacting teachings on compassion, selflessness, and generosity in his daily life, but he also said that he meditated on such principles. He noted that this kind of meditation produced changes in his attitudes and behaviors by refreshing the General Program class teachings. I asked him if meditating on a teaching produced a different kind of understanding of the teaching, and he said that yes, it did. He said that, when he dwelt on and repeated the idea of cherishing others, for example, the practice trained his mind and changed his responses and values. He believed that it was necessary to initiate the changes in meditation because it was not easy to do so in the midst of ordinary activities: "When you're working and doing things, you can't think like that." Alan, like other respondents, associated a psychomotor activity with a mental process; the training of the mind through repetitive mental acts. And, as Alan noted, changing the mind changed his behavior. Once again, this was an affective outcome, but it involved a psychomotor type of process. Alan described the practice as follows:

You think about cherishing or whatever the lesson might be: compassion. Bringing the mind back to that is the process. Unconsciously the idea is that contemplation on that helps it seep in, rather than consciously planning to be more patient. Meditating unconsciously gets into your psyche.... The more you do this the clearer the path will be for you. You do get too busy in the outside world. You don't spend enough time reflecting.

Alan regarded meditation as a discipline that develops unconscious understanding: a description similar to what Crossley and Gyatso describe as the tacit nature of knowledge generated through ritualizing.

While not physical, meditative concentration techniques do require the development of certain skills such as the ability to concentrate, to refine one's awareness of thoughts and body sensations, or to objectively observe oneself and the practice without becoming attached or judgmental. The development of such skills involves psychomotor processes, particularly repetition, refinement, and adjustment. But many respondents indicated that there were further changes that took place as a result of developing meditative concentration skills, changes corresponding to affective learning processes. Thus learning through meditation takes place in both domains. Bridging these two types of learning was the fact that learning took place through practices that were formalized, repetitive, elevated, formative, and so forth. The ritual qualities of meditation postures, framing activities, and concentration techniques thus initiated affective change alongside psychomotor development.

Buddhist teachings and practices, however, hold that there is another type of change intended to develop through meditation, which I have proposed as a fourth domain of learning, namely, insights. The Dīgha Nikāya sūtra and other Buddhist texts claim that meditation produces a deeper insight or a higher quality of wisdom than just hearing teachings or thinking about them. The deeply felt, nondiscursive realization of impermanence, suffering and no-self, believed to result from the combination of stabilizing and analytical meditation, is an exceptionally high level of achievement, something that may take years or, some believe, even lifetimes to achieve. Newcomers at meditation classes were not overtly taught traditional practices intended to develop insights into impermanence, suffering or no-self. The techniques taught were intended to indirectly open up the possibility of such insights. Experienced members, those who had taken higher level classes and had learned more about the Tibetan and, especially, the tantric stream of Buddhist practice, were aware of such insights as goals of meditation. But a few newcomers indicated a belief that they had experienced certain realizations beyond psycho-motor, affective, or cognitive types of learning. Others indicated that such insights were a hoped-for outcome of meditation.

Describing the kinds of insights meant to arise in meditation, Marlon said:

Meditation actually deepens the understanding. It actually helps our minds to realize the subtle things. Most of Buddha's teaching, what he talks about is subtle. He talks about the nature of our mind, and often we don't really understand what the nature and the function is or the various types of minds. But through meditation we can actually come to observe that for ourselves, so that we can identify the types of minds there are and the type of situation that arises, and when it arises how we can actually change our mind. Through meditation we learn all that. So, I would say meditation is the core of our practice.

Marlon's comments bring to mind a debate over the significance in traditional Buddhism of unmediated meditative experience. Robert Sharf has argued that the oft-touted centrality of meditative experience in Buddhism is a recent construction, propagated primarily by popular writers like D.T. Suzuki, and is not to be found in older, more traditional expressions of Buddhism in Asia.[52] In her study of Tibetan meditative systems, however, Janet Gyatso re-examines Sharf's position. She points out that the Tibetan terms usually translated as "experience" refer to different degrees of perception, from the mundane all the way up to the direct perception of Buddhist truths. In other words, what Tibetan teachings refer to as experience is akin to different and ever deepening degrees of insight. While Gyatso notes that Tibetan authors display considerable ambivalence with respect to experience, meditative experience does play an important role in achieving the kind of self-reflexive consciousness that is believed to accompany higher insight.[53] Gyatso also points out that meditation is a practice that not only involves both the body and the mind, it is intended to result in a fully integrated, non-dualistic experience of body and mind.[54] As such, psychomotor learning—with respect to both physical and mental processes—is vital for developing Buddhist insights.

The path begins with cognitive learning, an intellectual understanding of the teachings. Along the way, the meditator develops an increasing acceptance of Buddhist values and worldviews, while cultivating the necessary meditation skills. Ideally, the meditator achieves higher insights as a result of this path. Meditative ritualizing, therefore, repetitively cycles through the three main learning domains, with the goal of arriving at the fourth.

CONCLUSION

Learning meditation begins with the how: first cognitive and then experiential knowledge of how to sit and how to concentrate. Factual and conceptual (that is, cognitive) knowledge about the reasons for and benefits of meditation may make the practice more attractive or accessible to newcomers. Next, students' attitudes about what meditation is, whether or not they can perform it, and whether or not it will be beneficial, begin to shift. Finally, students learn the physical and mental techniques on a psychomotor level: receiving, imitating, developing, practicing, and adapting the practices. Many respondents indicated that, with the cultivation of meditation skills there developed additional affective changes. At this point, respondents indicated that the changes were not just attitudes, feelings, or values *about* meditation, but changes that happen *through* meditation. Examples given were: letting go of stress or attachments, feeling peaceful, being better able to concentrate, or developing feelings of equanimity, gratitude, or compassion toward others.

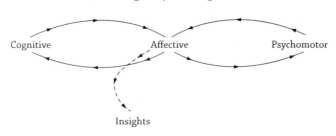

FIGURE 5.1 Ritualized learning pattern

Finally, many respondents indicated that they then interpreted and analyzed the new attitudes developed in meditation, thereby engaging in further cognitive learning. New cognitive understandings affected the way respondents valued meditation practice and its results, so many of them continued practicing and refining the skill. Moreover, because meditation is formalized, repetitive, structured, held in enough esteem to be repeated and to elicit a degree of commitment from most respondents, the cycle was repeated. The pattern of learning thus moved from cognitive to affective through the psychomotor and back again. Some respondents indicated that they had either experienced a kind of insight, or that they believed that insights were the ultimate goal of the practice. At some point, therefore, the process is meant to break out, either once and for all, or every now and again, into the fourth domain. The pattern of learning, therefore, might be depicted as in figure 5.1.

For some respondents, affective change was only incidental. Some more strongly stressed the psychomotor end of the cycle, others the cognitive. Based on the emphasis most respondents placed on affective learning, however, I place the affective domain at the nexus of the pattern. The changes through which practitioners began to accept new attitudes and values, for many, inspired a commitment to the practice. Students were also inspired to institute voluntary behavioral changes. Examples were: continued or increased meditation practice, changes in behavior toward others in accordance with feelings of equanimity or compassion, efforts to change habitual responses in the face of anger or irritation, and the like. Some respondents suggested that such behavioral changes were internalized over time, becoming increasingly instinctive.

At his first interview, Gerald used a metaphor to describe his learning that nicely corresponds to the pattern demonstrated here. "Some of the principles are like a Mobius strip, I find. You can start and then go a long way and then come back to the simplicity of it. It's really intriguing. It's like a little adventure in your mind."

6

Learning is Change

"SOMEWHERE ALONG THE way," David tells me in his interview, "things start changing. You react differently to things. After you take a step back, after a year or two years, then all of a sudden you [realize], wow, I'm kind of different. What's going on?"

A practitioner of Chinese medicine and thirty-four years old at the time of his interview, David had been a member of Friends of the Heart for about four years. By the conclusion of my fieldwork in 2007, he was teaching some of the center's introductory meditation classes. There had certainly been some important changes with respect to his involvement at the center. But in his interview, he spoke about the changes that resulted from his personal practice, the meditation, mantras and prayers that he undertook daily. "I'm not the same. I'm not overreacting. You know, being able to sit presently with people. What happened? Obviously, it's the practice. But it's somehow percolating, somehow it's coming from down under and slowly percolating up and infusing you.... That's my experience with the Tibetan work. It's really slow, but it's deep and comes up nice and easy." If learning means change, then we might track students' learning by asking what changes resulted from their participation at Friends of the Heart or Chandrakirti Centre. One way I measured change through the interview data was to compare the experiences of long-term members with those of newcomers, since experienced members were where some newcomers might be a few months or years down the road.

The most notable difference between long-term members and introductory students were their attitudes toward strongly ritualized practices. Consider the following reflections on Chenrezig visualization and mantra recitation, for instance. Diane, a Friends of the Heart newcomer, said: "I'm just not sure about some of the practices. So if we were going to, for example, do the same meditation every Monday, I'm not sure that I will continue to come. You know, the Chenrezig, that meditation. I mean, I like it very much, but it would be then too ritualistic to me." The following is David's description of the same practice:

> The sādhana starts with taking refuge, the Bodhisattva vow, there are parts where you dissolve into emptiness and then from that, all of a sudden, you're doing something where you come back into formation. And then there's a lot in the sādhana about [energy] in the heart, going out and then you're drawing [energy] back in. So there's a lot of this radiating, drawing back in. Poof, something comes up, poof, it dissolves back down into nothing.... We have the Lotus in our heart, and then the Chenrezig is above our heads, so that Chenrezig dissolves, goes into light, and comes into us and then we dissolve into the Lotus.... You focus on one syllable of the mantra: light radiating out to the god-realm, light radiating out to the hungry ghost realm, focusing on one little area, and then just focusing on that for a while, getting the feeling for it.

As an experienced member who had participated many times in the Chenrezig pūjā, David had a much more detailed understanding of the different parts of the practice, and of its meanings and symbols. While it is not surprising that, as a newcomer, Diane did not have this detailed knowledge, it is informative that even though she said she liked the practice, it did not interest her for the simple reason that it was strongly ritualized. David quite easily accepted the ritualistic elements of the meditation, and regarded them as significant, transformative elements of his overall practice.

Members who had more experience with the centers and were involved in higher level classes had learned more and participated more often in practices like visualization meditation, chanting mantras, and performing chanted prayers. All four experienced members whom I interviewed had not only accepted such practices and their symbolic meanings, they found them to be valuable learning experiences. Their acceptance of and commitment to strongly ritualized practices may be due to the fact that they have had more opportunity to learn about them, but it may also be a sign of their own preferences from the start. Long-term members may simply be those who were not put off by the rituals in the first place.

When he first started participating at Friends of the Heart, David said, he "jumped right in" to the more advanced practices at Friends of the Heart after attending a workshop on the Chenrezig mantra with Catherine Rathbun. He had not attended any of the Friends of the Heart introductory classes. David more readily accepted formal Buddhist ritual from the outset than had many Friends of the Heart newcomers who participated in this study. When we spoke in March 2007, David was working his way through foundation practice. He described his daily practice as follows:

> Six days a week, in the morning...I usually do an hour of practice....I'm doing the Vajrasattva, trying to get through that, so I'll be working through that sādhana. And I usually do it for about an hour. And then I get ready for my day and then usually throughout the day, what I've been doing is Chenrezig mantra. And then in the afternoon, it kind of varies, but maybe around three to five, I'll do my two hundred prostrations.

Working through the Vajrasattva sādhana, in this case, means performing the preparatory practices for purifying and clearing the mind, then chanting a series of prayers and mantras to the deity Vajrasattva and performing meditative visualizations of that deity. David performed this detailed ritual nearly every day. In addition to this, he repeated the Chenrezig mantra (*om mani padme hung*) daily and performed two hundred full-body prostrations, despite the fact that he found them physically difficult and "mentally oppressive." I asked if he had considered Catherine's adapted prostrations, and he said he thought they were the easy way out. He felt there must be a reason for the full-body prostrations, and believed that they were having a "strong effect" that he wanted to work through. He said he was developing the stamina to perform prostrations—initially he had only been able to do twenty at a time but had worked up to two hundred each day. I asked if prostrations were getting any better mentally, and he replied: "Yeah. The aversion is less. It still pops up, usually in the beginning. But it's kind of like: just go through it, just do it. Often times it's like my mind is thinking: okay, I've done two. I have one hundred and ninety-eight to go. So, sometimes it's just a matter of being present and going one step at a time. Stop thinking ahead into the future, just do the one, do the one. That makes it easier." Like meditation, prostration practice was teaching David about focusing the mind and helping train him to maintain that focus. He had learned that concentrating on one prostration at a time was the best way to get through the arduous practice. He said he was still learning to develop that meditative mindset through the practice. "I'm not there yet. I've heard, I've read that it's good. You do enter some state. But I'm not there yet." I then asked if he regarded the practice as a means of generating spiritual merit, but he said "I find it's more about purification." David regarded the practice as more than simply a physical or mental training exercise; he stressed instead its ritualistic aspects. He saw it as efficacious and transformative, in that it generated spiritual purity. David's initial attraction to the ritualized practices at Friends of the Heart had evidently continued unabated. Four years on, he maintained a strong commitment to performing his daily rites.

Marconi, a management consultant who was forty-eight, and also an experienced member at Friends of the Heart, attended Catherine's Tibetan Meditation and Richard's Intermediate Meditation courses every week. Like David, he had accepted many of the formal practices like pūjās and had made them part of his ongoing personal practice. "I do White Tara two or three times a week on my own. I meditate at least once a day, I spend about an hour in the mornings with my own practice. That feels right." Marconi also said that he was reading books on guru yoga and the Tibetan deity Tara. He said his studies and his practices were providing him with a sense of "awareness and presence." Marconi had recently gone through some difficult times in his life, and he believed that the White Tara practice helped him face such difficulties. "I follow White Tara as a sādhana. And that is an important tool for me in terms of settling because I have gone through a massive amount of change." Even so, Marconi admitted that his practices and what he was learning through them were not always easy.

> There's stuff that I struggle with. I absolutely hate it. And I just go: this is just horrific. But I'm in it, and I just go: okay, so here I am, it's gross and it's awful and I hate it, but I'm in it and often that particular experience will last for four or five minutes or half an hour. So, where is my breathing, where am I, what's this? And then, okay. . . . Afterwards, I went, Oh, that feels so good . . . to let go of that.

The difficult "practices" that Marconi spoke of were experiences and encounters that arose in his life, not necessarily the formal practices he performed. He spoke in particular about strained relations with certain family members. The practice he described, the practice he found most difficult, was relating to such people with respect and equanimity while at the same time not giving in to habitual behaviors that perpetuated the painful relationships. He felt that an important means of supporting that practice was performing the prayers to White Tara. Marconi thus felt that performing the formal practices gave him the resources for coping with difficult circumstances in his life.

The two experienced members from Chandrakirti Centre also indicated that they more readily accepted some of the more religious and ritualistic elements that they followed at Foundation Program classes and Chandrakirti's chanted prayer services. But acceptance was not always there from the start. Priscilla, who had been taking Foundation Program classes for three years at the time of her interview, said: "My bugaboo is I always want to understand everything because I figure I don't get anything out of it [otherwise]. But I keep being told by different people: it doesn't matter. Doing it is going to be changing you anyway."

Priscilla, at fifty-eight, had retired from her career as a teacher. I spoke to her primarily about her participation in the Foundation Program. She had been a member at Chandrakirti Centre for four years. She had taken General Program classes for one summer, then decided to try the Foundation Program. At her first Foundation Program class, however, she discovered that it included the performance of a pūjā, and she said she could not wait to leave. "Pūjās seemed too weird to me. What is all this weird chanting and stuff? I don't think I got into pūjās until I was in FP, and even then I still had trouble. It took me several months before I understood what all of the preparatory prayers were. Not that I understand them completely, but I felt it just was a waste of time." Despite her unease, Priscilla persisted with the class and gradually became more familiar with the chanted prayers. "I slowly started to get more comfortable with them and started to like them. And now, I can't imagine not having them at the beginning of the meditation. We do them with meditation at home too." At the time she was interviewed, Priscilla was regularly attending Foundation Program classes, had completed some of the commentary texts, and had written examinations on them. She described what she saw as the significance of the prayers for meditation practice and for studying the commentary texts in Foundation Program class:

> If you look at the prayer, the stages of the path, I think you're asking for blessings twelve or thirteen times. . . . You need the blessings so that you can really take in what's going on in the teaching. You have to set your mind, you have to set the stage, you have to get everything in order, and you have to ask for blessings so that you understand the teaching better. . . . Usually, we will do some of the prayers before we start the exam, too.

Priscilla had therefore not only accepted the chanted prayers, she had also internalized the religious meanings behind them, such as the significance of blessings from gurus and deities.

Marlon, a writer and teacher who was forty-seven years of age, began taking General Program classes in 1993, when Chandrakirti Centre was just starting up. Eventually, Marlon began to take the Foundation Program classes as well. Like Priscilla, he noted that Foundation Program classes involved more ritual: Chanted prayers were sung from prayer books, and students received an oral transmission of Kelsang Gyatso's commentary texts from the teacher at each class.[1]

Marlon frequently participated in the Heart Jewel pūjā at the center, and performed it on his own as part of his personal practice. Describing the purposes of Heart Jewel, Marlon said:

There are actually three things that help us to meditate: first of all, we need to get the blessings from the Buddhas. So this [Heart Jewel] helps us to achieve that. And also, in order to meditate, we need to clear our mind which is called purification. You know, like if our mind is cluttered up or it is distracted, we can't really concentrate, so this practice actually helps us to clear our mind. And the other thing that it helps us is to generate what is called merit. That's something like a positive energy, it helps us to gather some positive energy so that we can actually focus. So, these are the three main functions of this practice.

When I asked Marlon how his involvement with Buddhist practices or teachings would be different if he did not attend Heart Jewel at Chandrakirti Centre, he replied:

If I don't practice that, my involvement with Buddhism wouldn't be as deep, it would be more superficial and it would be more like just reading about it and forgetting about it. It wouldn't be a practice, it would be more like mere reading, intellectual thinking. But with this practice it actually goes deeper. It actually has a more subtle effect on our mind. I'm slowly learning about that, actually. I guess the purpose of our practice is to develop the inner potential of our mind.

In Marlon's view, learning through practice—in this case, performing chanted prayers asking for blessings from buddhas—was experienced differently to learning through reading or intellectualizing. Marlon had thus accepted many of the formal Tibetan practices and faith-based teachings.

From these reflections on their practices, we can see that the four experienced members indicated a much greater acceptance of the centers' rites and rituals and their religious meanings. For some, like David, acceptance of the more ritualized elements was ready-made. He was interested in the prayers and other rites from the start. Priscilla, however, said that she had initially had the same discomfort with such rites as did the newcomers who were interviewed. But with time and familiarity, Priscilla began first to accept the rites and their religious meanings, then to regard them as essential to her ongoing practice. She did note, however, that she was willing to set aside her doubts when she began attending Foundation Program classes, and this is what eventually led to her acceptance. It is perhaps worth noting here that Carol, a long-term member who had not moved on to Foundation Program classes, still expressed some uneasiness when it came to

Chandrakirti rituals. The reason may be her lack of attendance at the class, or her lack of attendance at the class may have to do with its rituals. This indicates that newcomers who are unwilling to overcome their aversion to religion and ritual may be less likely to take up long-term membership.

NEWCOMERS, LEARNING, AND CHANGE

"What meditation is really demonstrating to me," Tanit told me at her second interview in May of 2007, "is that you can change. Not that it's easy, and not that it happens like: 'I have meditated. There, it's all done.' But it is an ongoing process and you can change anything about who you are." To bring to a close the stories of the six participants whose discovery stories appeared in chapter 2, this section explores the changes that took place between their first- and second-round interviews. What role did learning through ritualizing have to do with those changes and to what degree did their motivations for joining the meditation classes affect the outcomes?

Tanit's journey to Friends of the Heart began with an interest in Daoism. She was particularly intrigued by Daoist teachings that life is an illusion and that there was a practice, namely meditation, for seeing past that illusion to achieve enlightenment. Unable to find Daoist meditation classes in Toronto, she decided to go to a Buddhist center. Her main motivation for participating at Friends of the Heart, therefore, was a desire to learn how to meditate as a means to a spiritual goal.

When we first met in December 2006, Tanit spoke a great deal about the practicalities of meditation postures, gestures, and concentration techniques. She mentioned the techniques she was learning and how she adjusted them in order to develop an effective and personally relevant practice. She regarded meditation as a long-term journey: She had read in her book on Daoism that it took twelve years or more to achieve enlightenment, and she was keen to work toward that goal. By May of 2007, however, Tanit's reflections on the goal had changed. "Well, I'm now beginning to think that, in fact, enlightenment is the goal, but it's actually not important. It's the journey, it's what's happening to you as you travel towards this state."

This change in perspective came about as Tanit began to experience certain results from her meditation practice. One result she attributed to the practice was an increased awareness of her body in the midst of her ordinary activities. She had discovered that she was holding a lot of tension in her body when sitting at the computer, riding her bicycle, and so on. With this awareness, she found she could release the tension. Tanit also believed that meditation had helped her learn not just about her physical habits, but something about her psychology and spiritu- ality as well. She said, for example, that she had begun to explore feelings of fear in her meditation: "One of the things I've been trying to let go of, or even acknowl- edge it exists, is fear. At first, it's just fear as in this general category. And then, I began to start getting a little more specific. . . . And I finally accepted that I'm afraid of dying alone. And, yeah, that's pretty obvious, but it isn't until you really face it [that] you have acknowledged this. Why are you afraid of that? What is this fear based on?" The questions Tanit was exploring related to aspects of her self and her life that were psychological, but also spiritual: of ultimate concern to herself as a person. Tanit felt that meditation had led to some profound new understandings.

Did the changes Tanit described come about because the means of learning, meditation, was ritualized? Repetition certainly aids learning, but there were other influential ritual qualities: the fact that Tanit regarded the practice as something special, elevated, and associated with spirituality and tradition—these factors shaped the nature of her learning. Her motivation—to find a practice that would help her develop spiritually—was a clear influence on the outcome, her belief that she had made spiritual progress.

Another significant change that Tanit noted was inspired not by meditation but through reading. After her first interview, she had begun reading several books on Buddhism by and for westerners: She mentioned Jack Kornfield, Pema Chödrön, and Sharon Salzberg. From these readings, Tanit began to gain a new perspective.

> The thing that I'm beginning to understand is the whole idea of being able to help other people: it is a privilege, which hadn't been something I had understood that way. It's something I'm going through right now with my mom, who has broken her hip. She doesn't like the food at the hospital. So, I said: I have the time, I'm in a unique situation right now, so I will make stuff for you and bring stuff in. . . . And I dropped her lunch off just before I came here, and it's a fantastic day, and I thought: yeah, it's a privilege. It's an honor to have the opportunity to do this. That is definitely coming out of the reading that I'm doing, [and] being involved with the center, understanding sharing with people is great. It's an amazing thing about being a human being and being able to do those kinds of things.

Tanit felt that her readings were also a means of gaining new spiritual perspec- tives. The changes she described, therefore, were not only attributed to meditation practice or to her involvement at the center, although she believed that all of these elements had contributed to what she regarded as her spiritual progress. In the months that had passed since our first interview, she believed that her self-aware- ness had increased through self-reflection, a type of learning she described as intellectual. "I do keep a diary, and it's really interesting looking back, even just a few months, seeing how you are progressing and changing. . . . I realize that it has changed dramatically from when I saw you in December to now. The intellectual aspect wasn't part of my practice at that time at all. The self reflection and examination wasn't part of it." Tanit had begun to practice a kind of analytical or insight meditation, an analysis into her own nature. While she described it as intellectual, the results she described were changes in attitudes, outlooks and values, changes that were more affective than cognitive. The new information she had gained from her readings had led to affective changes as well, primarily because she regarded the readings as spiritual teachings rather than technical or academic information.

After the ten-week introductory course with Joyce ended, Tanit took out a full membership at Friends of the Heart rather than enrolling in a second ten-week temporary membership. I asked Tanit what she thought her future involvement at Friends of the Heart might be. She said that she wanted to become more involved, perhaps by volunteering to help with the center's administration. But she was very busy. She knew that when her sabbatical ended the following September it would be more difficult to continue the level of practice that she had developed to that point. But she did intend to continue at the weekly classes at Friends of the Heart, perhaps even joining the individual mentoring program later on. As a teacher, she had also considered the possibility of teaching meditation down the road.

Tanit felt she had learned the meditation techniques, postures, and practices she had hoped to learn. She had made some discoveries about herself and her relationships with others that she regarded as steps along a long spiritual path to enlightenment. She had also become a longer term member of Friends of the Heart, with plans, at that time, to continue.

Like Tanit, Diane regarded meditation as a means of exploring spirituality. Reflecting on her motives for taking a meditation class, Diane said, "I knew what I was interested in had something to do with religions and philosophy, but I didn't know what exactly. But it was more along the lines of: Who am I? What am I doing here? What is the meaning of life?" Having discovered that academic courses did not provide the kinds of answers she was looking for, Diane began exploring Buddhist practices and teachings. "It feels like there are more answers about meaning in Buddhism than I have had in any other place," she said. Diane enrolled at Friends of the Heart in order to receive some instruction on how to meditate, but she also said she wanted "a serious teaching," which she felt she received at the General Program classes at Atisha Centre.

Diane's first interview was in February 2007. By September, she was no longer attending Friends of the Heart, having left at the end of her second ten-week membership, around the time that Catherine Rathbun went into semi-retirement. Diane had continued at Atisha Centre, but she said she was still reluctant to become involved in an organized religion. While she insisted that she did not regard Buddhism as a religion, she had encountered what she believed were religious elements at both centers, elements with which she was uncomfortable. Even so, she decided to continue with the Atisha Centre General Program classes because she liked the teacher and the teachings. At the time of her second interview, in September of 2007, Atisha Centre had been closed over the summer, and Diane had not attended a Buddhist center for a few months.

Even so, Diane continued her personal meditation practice. "I'm still practicing almost every day at home." She had gradually increased the length of her sittings and had reached fifty-five minutes. Describing the results of nearly an hour of meditation, Diane said: "Mostly, I feel energy. . . . I feel awake and alert, and I like it. But it's carrying out over into the day, trying to just pay attention. I'm just trying to be mindful during the day." But with more intensive practice, Diane also began to have some negative experiences. "I started to be very disturbed in my meditation practice. I had originally thought meditation was about peace. . . . Well, I was not feeling very peaceful. I was beginning to feel a lot of fears and being disturbed in my meditation practice." Looking for solutions to this problem, Diane began reading books on meditation by western writers like Jack Kornfield, Pema Chödrön, and Ayya Kema. She learned from their writings that meditation can give rise to negative emotions, an experience that, paradoxically, is said to happen among more experienced meditators. Diane was comforted to learn that what she had experienced was not unusual. She began to integrate what she had learned from her readings with the meditation practices taught at Friends of the Heart.

> I would focus on "active" and it would be a turning in my stomach, so I'm sitting there centered on that churning, and it gets fear and anxiety. Then I would try to go some place to "rest," but mostly I didn't go to rest. I would stay with that churning and see what would happen to it. And sometimes I would stay churned up, and that's the part I didn't like. But I decided after reading, I'm just going to stay with it. So, I'm churned up, and just accept the fact that I'm churned up and see what happens.

Diane believed that sitting through the negative experiences made her more aware of her responses to such situations. "That led me to see that I'm a negative person!" she said with a laugh. "I just see so much of that: how judgmental and how many of my thoughts go right to judgment. I find that interesting." Diane's discoveries about herself derived from a meditation practice she had learned at Friends of the Heart, but she might not have kept up the practice were it not for the encouragement she gained from her readings.

Diane's readings also introduced her to another way of envisioning Buddhism, and of applying it in her life: "It's almost like Buddhism as psychology as opposed to Buddhism as a religion.... Because I never really thought about Buddhism as a kind of theory, a psychological theory. But it is." Diane had thus accepted a common perspective by which Buddhism has often been presented in the West: as compatible, not only with modern science, but also as a form of psychology or psychotherapy. There are numerous works currently available on the topic of the intersection between Buddhist practices and western psychology.[2] While some commentators believe that applying Buddhist-style practices in psychotherapy can be fruitful, others have argued that this is a reductive appropriation of Buddhist teachings and practices.

Speaking about insight meditation, Diane said: "I'm seeing it more from a theory of development, a theory of the development of the mind. And I'm fascinated by that, which is more comfortable for me, maybe, because it's in my head and I can wrap myself around that." Several months on, Diane's preference for intellectual learning about Buddhist teachings and practices remained. Her investigations into Buddhism and psychology introduced an analytical approach that she could apply through insight or analytical meditation. This approach appealed to Diane's interest in cognitive learning.

There were forces of push and pull in Diane's experience at Friends of the Heart and Atisha Centre: She had an attraction to Buddhist teachings and practices, but continued to be uncomfortable with religious symbols and rituals and was unwilling to participate in devotional practices. Her reluctance to become involved in ritual may have precluded the kind of intimate, experiential learning about religious symbols and practices that Gerald claimed to have had, for example. Still, she believed she had made significant changes in her attitudes and outlooks as a result of the practices and teachings she learned at Friends of the Heart and Atisha Centre. For instance, her daughter had recently moved home for the summer, and the situation was difficult for both of them. But Diane believed that she was able to be patient and considerate as a result of her practice and the Buddhist principles she had learned.

Diane did not rule out the possibility of learning about the more religious aspects of Buddhism. Speaking of her discomfort with the doctrine of karmic rebirth, she said: "Maybe if I continue with meditation and at some point have an insight that reaches into subtler levels of consciousness in a way that I get insight into some of those concepts; but with my current mind in its current state of development, I cannot grasp it."

With respect to her future involvement, Diane said she intended to return to Atisha's General Program classes when they resumed. But she was looking for more as well. "I would like to meditate longer in a group, but also to have access to an individual teacher." She said she was not fond of the guided meditation at Friends of the Heart and Atisha Centre, and wanted to find a group with which to meditate in silence. She was also planning on an intensive week-long retreat with another organization in southern Ontario. Having left Friends of the Heart, she was keeping up her meditation practice, and was still interested in participating at other Buddhist centers in the future.

When John enrolled in the Friends of the Heart meditation class, he was purely interested in learning about meditation techniques and how to develop the skills involved. While he acknowledged that there might be a spiritual side to meditation, he was neither seeking spiritual practice nor a religious or spiritual community. In February of 2007, when John and I first met for an interview, it was near the end of Joyce's Introduction to Insight class. I asked John if he still had any questions about meditation, and he said: "No. It's just time on the cushion now." John felt that all he needed was the time and commitment to refine and practice his meditation techniques. In many ways, John regarded meditation as strictly a psychomotor type of learning. Although it was not entirely physical, he regarded meditation as a skill to be developed, through practice, like other physical skills. While he said it altered his mood, making him feel more calm or mellow, he did not think that any other kinds of affective changes resulted from the practice. He did not associate such changes in mood with any change in belief, attitude, values, or behaviors.

At his first interview, John said that meditating with others was helpful. Without the group, he believed, it would be much easier to fall out of the habit. His prediction turned out to be true. When we met for a second interview in June of 2007, John had left Friends of the Heart and the Toronto General Hospital meditation group and had not meditated for a few months. After the two courses he had been taking had ended, he had suffered a period of depression during which he found it impossible to meditate. Describing the effects of depression, John said: "The simplest things become insurmountable, and the insidious thing about it is that everything you want to do is exactly the opposite of what you should be doing. You should be going out, exercising and socializing and that's the last thing you want to do." The depression had not only interrupted John's home practice, it had made him unwilling to continue attending meditation sessions with others. By the time of our second interview, however, he was ready to start looking for a group with which to meditate again. He said that he might return to the Toronto General Hospital to participate in a continuing meditation program offered there. He did not intend to go back to Friends of the Heart, partly due to its Buddhist—that is, religious—orientation. But there was a more practical reason, as well; the course at the hospital was simply closer to home.

John said he did not think he learned anything in particular through other formal practices like prayers, bows, or mudras. But he did believe that meditation had taught him something about himself and about how his mind worked as he observed its processes. Even so, he described what he learned in terms of the factual information he had gained rather than referring to changes in his attitudes or insights. "Everyone's mind wanders," he said. "That will go on as long as you have a mind. That's definitely a good thing to learn." He said that he had not gone as far with meditation practice as he would have liked, and felt that there was more that he could gain should he return to it.

Like most other participants, the outcome of John's learning at the meditation classes he took corresponded to, and was perhaps influenced by, his initial motivations for taking the courses. He had not been looking for answers to deeply spiritual questions, nor insights into Buddhist principles. He learned how to meditate, and that was what he had enrolled in the classes to do.

Reflecting on his reasons for attending the Chandrakirti General Program classes, Alan said he had been looking for ways of being happier in his life. He said: "I'm sixty-five, so I figure I've got x amount of years left, and I'd like to change that to being in a better place, mind-wise, than where I've been: attached to the business where, if you have a bad day, you take it home with you. Now, if I have a bad day it's a different point of view." The General Program classes introduced Alan to the idea that being happy meant changing some fundamental assumptions and beliefs by which he had lived his life. Inspired by the values and ethics taught at the class, he decided to make changes in his outlook and behavior. At his first interview in May of 2007, he said that his practice had improved his relationships with others, especially his family. He also believed he had become more thoughtful, caring, patient, and generous. "The basic thing that I keep thinking about is not to think about yourself," Alan said. "And that seems to be the hardest lesson.... So that, to me, is important." An important element of his learning, therefore, was not a practice but a personal ethic.

Through his learning process, Alan assessed and began to accept new attitudes and values, which he then consciously applied. Alan's "practice" was a kind of informal training, a means of acquiring skills over time by noting and reacting to what is going on.[3] For Alan, it meant learning new ways of behaving with his family, his social groups, and his clients. It was a kind of play: experimenting with behaviors he had not tried before—an example he gave was consciously welcoming people who came in to his store to socialize rather than to shop—and seeing how he reacted to his new behaviors, and what changes they made in his attitudes. Successful informal training results in inherent changes in behavior, as learners begin to practice on their own.[4] Alan believed that, with time and with the help of his meditation practice, the new behaviors and attitudes would become innate rather than something that required effort to enact.

Alan also believed that meditation was an important part of the practice. He said it helped him "refresh" or "sharpen" the changes he was trying to make in his life. At his first interview, Alan said he had been meditating once or twice every day for fifteen to twenty minutes each time. He regarded Buddhist meditation as a means of change. "It works for me if I can contemplate on changing things. And you do that, as I understand it with this meditation, the Buddhist. It's work, it isn't just sitting there and just trying to block out all thought. It seems to be more about working on moving forward, or merit as they call it. I like that idea." Initially, then, Alan spoke of meditation as a means of becoming more naturally familiar with the values he wanted to enact: generosity, compassion, and selflessness, for example. He believed that this familiarity was achieved by training the mind in seated meditation, and by the merit the practice generated. By the time of his second interview in October 2007, Alan's perspectives on his daily practice and on meditation had changed: they had merged, in a sense. Alan said, "You can meditate anywhere. I do it now with my eyes open, and I'm not so self conscious about it." He said he sometimes meditated on the subway, or in the line at the grocery store. When he went for a walk in the morning, he would perform a metta recitation for building merit, wishing suffering to end for all living beings. He said that the energy he put into that particular practice felt more positive than "just thinking about cherishing other people." He thus discovered that a ritualized repetition of a loving-kindness mantra felt like a more effective practice than simply resolving to be compassionate or selfless. In the five months since we had first spoken, then, Alan had begun incorporating more of the ritualized practices taught at Chandrakirti Centre into his daily activities.

I asked Alan about taking the same class over again: Was it still fresh? He said that he was still learning. "It's the same message, really. You evolve each time you're practicing these things. Suddenly I notice I've moved a little bit forward from what they said a year ago. I hear it again and think about a different way now." He said that initially he heard the teachings in an academic way, but he was now able to enact what he had learned. The practice, he said, was "cherishing, getting the information from them [the General Program teachers]. You will never get it if you cherish yourself, the point is to forget yourself." He said he had noticed a difference in himself. He believed he was able to be less judgmental and was now operating on "insights rather than automatic drive."

Alan had learned something that both experienced members from Chandrakirti Centre, Marlon and Priscilla, had also expressed: that meditation is not the only form of practice, and that General Program teachings were also intended to encourage students to change their outlooks and their lives. Alan came to Chandrakirti Centre looking for ways of being happier. He believed he had found just that. He had also become a long-term, regular participant at the center, finding it to be what teacher Thekchen had hoped: a safe, welcoming environment where people can explore and discuss the ideas coming out of Buddhist doctrine. After Chandrakirti Centre closed for renovations, Alan and his daughter Bronwen continued to attend General Program classes at a public library. By October of 2007, Alan's wife was attending the classes, too. What was next for Alan? He had not yet heard about the higher level classes at Chandrakirti Centre, but he intended to keep attending the General Program. "It just becomes part of your life," he said, "something you do."

Originally, Carol began participating at Chandrakirti Centre out of an interest in meditation and a desire to receive some detailed instruction on the practice. What she encountered at the General Program classes were talks on Buddhist teachings and principles that she found appealing. But she was unsure about the strongly ritualized elements at the center. Although she had been attending General Program classes and volunteering at the center for seven years, she said she continued to evaluate the rituals and her responses to them.

As a long-term member, Carol's participation at Chandrakirti Centre had leveled off before she and I first spoke in April of 2007. She had been participating at its introductory class and, by the time of her second interview in October of 2007, had not yet participated in Foundation Program classes. She was content to remain at the General Program classes, and said that she was always learning something new as the same topics were repeated. She was, she said, a slow learner, and was content to take her time with what she was learning. When we spoke a second time, Carol reiterated some of what she had told me at her first interview.

> I think that I re-visit and reconnect with the responsibility that I require in my life towards myself and the world around me. That is a key word, responsibility: to learn how to operate in the world and to be open and caring about everybody. That gets revisited in the class as opposed to sitting on my own. There are a lot of deeper lessons to be learned. Emptiness, truth, specific aspects. But generally how to be in the world—I'm resisting the word positive—rather, honest in what I feel is important in regard to the teachings: compassion and selfless love.

Like Alan, Carol believed that the General Program lectures served to refresh and deepen her understanding of the teachings. She primarily spoke about her learning in terms of an increased understanding of Buddhist values surrounding compassion and selflessness. She said she participated at the center for her own benefit, but also so that she might pass on some of those benefits through her relationships with others.

Also at our second interview, Carol said that she continued to re-evaluate the ritual elements, even after all of her time at the center. Like Gerald, she had been changing the water offerings on the center's shrines once a week. While she was willing to participate in the ritual, she still wanted to keep an open mind about it. "I don't want to be stuck in a routine. Rituals are accessories, like jewelry—sometimes it is nice to be pretty. I'm not attached to that at all. Rituals are a helping gesture, they have a nice, reflective quality that helps you stop things in your life for a while." When I asked experienced members Priscilla and Marlon about the offerings on the shrines, they spoke about their symbols and meanings. Priscilla described almost exactly the same meanings of the offerings as had Catherine Rathbun at Friends of the Heart: water for washing, drinking, light representing enlightenment, and so on. Marlon spoke about the purposes of making offerings: They are made to the Buddhas in order to gain their blessings, which are regarded as necessary to the Buddhist path. Carol, however, did not speak about the water offerings' meanings or purposes, preferring to discuss her responses to the ritual. While I am certain that Carol *could* have told me about the offerings' symbols and their meanings, it is significant that she did not. Because she was still evaluating them, I believe she had not wholly accepted the received meanings and symbols of the ritual as had fellow members who had, incidentally, participated in the advanced classes.

Carol more readily accepted the ritualized aspects of her meditation practice. At her second interview, she said she was finding ways of refreshing her earliest experiences with meditation, especially the simplicity of the Zen approach. She also said she was trying to be ritualistic about her meditation posture, but not so much that discomfort became a barrier. Books she had read by a Zen writer, Brad Warner (*Sit Down and Shut Up* and *Hardcore Zen* were the books she mentioned), emphasized the importance of posture and staying with the discomfort. But, she said, she sometimes "cheated," and that that was all right if discomfort was enough to get in the way of meditating at all. Carol was, in a sense, returning to the beginning. Her earlier experiences with Zen meditation, her earliest motivations for finding a Buddhist center at which to study, were coming to the fore again. After seven years participating at Chandrakirti Centre, she had accepted the rituals to some degree, but not fully. She felt she had gotten away from her original intentions and was, in small ways, consciously returning to them.

Attending General Program classes was still an important part of what Carol considered her practice, however. Following the closure of Chandrakirti Centre in June 2007, Carol was volunteering weekly at General Program classes at a local library. She said that helping out at the classes gave her the opportunity to receive a teaching and to have a role in the center's operations. She intended to continue her involvement at the center and at the General Program classes. Whether she had accepted the rituals or not, she was a fully involved member of the Chandrakirti community.

Gerald began attending classes at Chandrakirti Centre primarily to do something positive with his time and engage in an activity that was intellectually, emotionally, and socially stimulating. At his first interview in October of 2006, he did not indicate that there were any particularly spiritual reasons for attending, although he did say he was assessing the teachings to decide whether or not they corresponded with his perspectives on life in general. He believed that they did: "My initial feeling about the center is that I have verified for myself that it's for real, and the teachings are for real, and it's worth continuing." In May of 2007, reflecting back on his early experiences at Chandrakirti Centre, Gerald said: "When I joined I had a sense of spirituality at the beginning. I didn't have it within the element of Christianity. So, I was very protective of [i.e., against] any belief system that didn't correspond to that emotional, spiritual feeling or connection. And it has. It is very spiritual. It's a drip at a time. Spirituality, for me, has always been a drought. So, if you get a drip of something, it's very good." What made the greatest change for Gerald was his participation in the water offerings at Chandrakirti Centre. Although he had been skeptical about the ritualistic side of the center, Gerald said that he learned a great deal about himself and the center, including its ritualistic and religious elements, once he agreed to go in and change the water offerings once a week. His experience suggests that the learning that took place as a result of performing the water offering was qualitatively different than that which he gained in meditation or through attending the classes and enacting their lessons. He told me that performing the water offerings gave him a learning experience that was direct, intimate, and tactile and in some ways deeper and more personal than the learning he gained through other forms of participation at the center. Performing the water offerings also had the effect of drawing Gerald more fully into the Chandrakirti community. It was when he started doing the water offerings that he began to feel more like a full member at the center.

Of all of the six principal participants, Gerald experienced the most significant changes between his two interviews. As well as increasing his level of participation at the center, Gerald said at his second interview that he was now more willing to dedicate time to meditation. His knowledge about different meditation practices and their goals had also grown. At his second interview, Gerald spoke about analytical and placement meditation, and described how they were taught in the General Program class. "You would try to analyze a certain feeling that you feel when people have helped you, and you try to remember it as much as you can and then try to hold that feeling single pointedly, and then feel it out. And I think later, in daily life, if you can remember that feeling, you will generate a feeling of bodh- icitta." Gerald's knowledge of certain Buddhist practices and the terms used to describe them had obviously grown in the time since we first met. While several common Buddhist terms such as Theravada were new to him at the time of his first interview, by the second he was comfortably using specialized Buddhist terms such as bodhicitta. Moreover, he felt he had gained some capacity to generate bodhicitta through his meditation practice.

Another significant change for Gerald had to do with his sense of Buddhist iden- tity. At our first interview, when I asked Gerald if he would say that he was a Buddhist, he said:

> No, no I wouldn't. Only because I don't want to have that label yet. I could easily say that I'm a Buddhist and believe it. I could say that I'm a Christian and believe it too. At the moment, though, if someone said: are you studying Buddhism? I would say yeah I was. Do you find a lot of benefits from it? I would say certainly. But I've almost said it a few times or thought it anyway, that I'm a Buddhist, and I don't like it.

At that time, Gerald regarded himself as a student rather than a member of Chandrakirti Centre. He said he was "more of a tourist," primarily because he was still assessing the center, trying to decide how well its teachings applied to his personal circumstances and whether or not he felt they were, as he put it, "accu- rate." In May when I asked again if he was a Buddhist, he replied "Yeah, I was waiting for that question. Yeah I do." I asked Gerald what had changed over the months since we had first spoken, and he said: "Seeing the similarities between what I believed in before, seeing no contradiction towards my concept of God, appreciating and grafting onto the Buddha from all of my other beliefs and seeing whether it fits. And his teachings complemented and embellished those beliefs, so it's a chance to grow more." For Gerald, then, identifying as a Buddhist meant accepting and reconciling the teachings with his preexisting beliefs. Even so, Gerald equivocated about what it meant to be a Buddhist. "I guess I would consider myself a Buddhist. I had trouble with that question. I thought maybe I'm not still. But, in a good sense: I don't feel like Buddha is a god. It doesn't feel wrong to think about him as a friendly person, which is quite neat. He's a good teacher and a decent person. There isn't much more you could ask for. It's pretty nurturing." It is interesting that the caveat Gerald put upon his Buddhist identity was the fact that he did not regard the Buddha as a god. He was more comfortable with the idea that the Buddha was a good teacher and a friend. Neither did he indicate any belief in the presence of the enshrined deities to which he had been making weekly offer- ings. Even so, he still felt that the term "Buddhist" more accurately applied to someone with a more theistic conception of the tradition. He is suggesting, therefore, that he regards theistic belief as an important part of religious identity. Despite this, Gerald had begun to consider himself a Buddhist not as a result of changing religious beliefs, but due to his involvement in the offering rites—through performing a special ritual service to the center.

From these and other respondents' reflections, it is evident that the ways in which they regarded their involvement at the centers shaped how and what they learned in meditation classes. Furthermore, motivations for joining the classes corresponded to what they identified as the most important outcomes. There was more emphasis placed on learning, practicing, and refining meditation skills among Friends of the Heart participants, who more often identified meditation as their main practice. For those who attended strictly to learn how to meditate—which was the case for Friends of the Heart students Erin, Dennis, and John—the learning processes focused on psychomotor learning, with the addition of some cognitive information. But most interview respondents indicated that the more significant elements of their learning consisted of affective changes: receiving, accepting, valuing, and internalizing new attitudes and values. For Chandrakirti students Brenda and Catherine H. as well as Alan and Carol, affective change came from hearing teachings on Buddhist ethics in the classes, then experimenting with behaviors inspired by those ethics in their lives. Participants who were seeking spiritual changes—that is, changes that affect the person on the level of their whole experience—tended to emphasize affective change when describing what they had learned. Carol was perhaps the one principal participant who noted that her goals had changed after she began attending General Program classes. She originally went to Chandrakirti Centre seeking meditation instruction, but the class also involved detailed teachings on Buddhist ethics. While she was returning to her earlier style of meditation practice by the time of her second interview, she still regarded her attendance at General Program classes as her main practice.

TEACHERS' OBJECTIVES

While the introductory meditation classes were, to some extent, a form of outreach through which the centers attracted new members, none of the teachers to whom I spoke believed that increasing membership numbers or inspiring conversion to Buddhism were significant goals of the classes they taught. Richard noted, in fact, that the retention rate among Friends of the Heart introductory students was fairly low. The short-term structure of the Friends of the Heart courses may have contributed to this low retention rate. Joyce noted that many students felt they had what they came for after the ten-week course and decided to move on.

> We recognize that there are students that come and they learn some of the basics of meditation. Certainly a fair percentage of those simply say: okay, I've learned about meditation. And off they go. Whether they practice going into the future, it's hard to say. Certainly at least it's a seed. They may turn up at some other center five years from now or ten years from now and say: I originally learned to meditate way back at Friends of the Heart. And then some of the students who come will really decide to take up the path and continue to practice with us.

Of the Friends of the Heart participants I interviewed, John, Diane, and Dennis indicated that they would be interested in continuing with a meditation group, although all three had left Friends of the Heart by the time of their second-round interviews. Still, it would seem that, for these participants, a "seed," as Joyce had put it, had been planted.

Retention rates for the Chandrakirti General Program classes were difficult to determine, for the very reason that the course had a drop-in structure and there were no enrollment records. I can only speculate from my research that the percentage of students who continued at Chandrakirti Centre in the long term was higher than at Friends of the Heart. Of the nine Friends of the Heart introductory students I interviewed, two were still participating at Friends of the Heart at the time of their second interview, an average of five months later. A third, whom I was unable to contact, may have continued as member. Of the six Chandrakirti newcomers, four were still participating at General Program classes by the time of their second interview; this despite the fact that the center had closed by that time and classes were being offered in other spaces. The potentially higher retention rate at Chandrakirti Centre may have been due to the structure of its General Program: There was no official ending to the course, and students could continue to come as long as they liked without having to officially become members or change their level of participation.

On the topic of membership retention, Rodney Stark and Roger Finke have argued that the more exclusive a religious community, the more committed its membership.[5] They argue that the higher the degree of tension—the distinctiveness, separation, or even antagonism—between a religious group and the rest of society, the more likely it is to inspire dedicated, exclusive commitment among its members.[6] Friends of the Heart is an eclectic and open group where new members are coming and going all the time and the retention rate of new members appears to be low. By contrast, the NKT appears to be a consciously exclusive, insular organization. All of the Chandrakirti courses I attended were strictly self-referential. In the General Program and higher level classes, students are introduced to the teachings and commentaries of the organization's founder, Kelsang Gyatso. No references to other teachers, apart from the lineage founder Je Tsongkhapa, are made. Gyatso's commentaries and translations are the only books sold at Chandrakirti and Atisha Centre. In informal conversations with some Chandrakirti teachers, I quickly learned that mention of other Buddhist centers or teachers was unwelcome. Two of the people I interviewed noted this as well. This attitude seemed a strange contrast to the openness of the General Program and the strongly inclusive ethics taught at its classes. The exclusive focus on the organization's own teachings may be the reason for Chandrakirti Centre's apparent success at retaining new members. Members are introduced to a comprehensive and organized system of Buddhist teachings that relies on no outside sources, and a few of the students I interviewed felt that, at least for the time being, they need not explore other approaches. In this sense, then, exclusiveness does contribute to members' commitment.

Stark and Finke's analysis, however, refers to groups whose influence over all aspects of their participants' lives is much stronger than that of Chandrakirti Centre over its adoptive Buddhist students. Tension of the sort Stark and Finke describe refers to a kind of "subcultural deviance," wherein the religious group defines members' social groups, dress, leisure time, and so on.[7] Chandrakirti members are encouraged to see all aspects of their lives from the perspective of Buddhist ethics, but this does not result in behavior that departs from cultural norms, nor does it separate them from society. I had a strong sense that the NKT's inward focus was a response to the negative attention it has had since the Shugden dispute in the mid-1990s. Organizers with the NKT have stepped back from the controversy and chosen to go their own way. But for a westernized Buddhist organization especially, this kind of exclusiveness can be problematic. One Chandrakirti student I interviewed, for instance, said:

> I think that there are some very good energies in the place, and there are some very good people. . . . [but] I have my exit papers, and I think we all have exit papers for all kinds of things. And mine are: if ever there was a conversation that would [indicate] that the Kadampas feel that they are better than anybody else. That would be sufficient to have me tell them that I appreciate everything, and my relationship with them, but that I'm leaving. That would drive me out the door. And I get whiffs of it every so often. I don't like it . . . And I think: it's not the only thing that's been written. It is not the last word.

One of the very reasons that adoptive practitioners and sympathizers become interested in Buddhism is because it has been received as a doctrinally open, nonexclusive tradition. Many sympathizers to whom I have spoken have said they like the fact that one can be Buddhist *and* Christian, for example, or that Buddhist teachings do not claim to be absolute. Whether this has been true for all of Buddhist history or not, this perception of the tradition is an important part of its attractiveness among adoptive practitioners and sympathizers. The exclusive style of Chandrakirti Centre and its parent organization is in contrast to what some of its members and visitors expect when they seek out Buddhist teachings. While exclusiveness may lead to greater commitment among some members, it may discourage others from participating.

Like the balance between tradition and transformation, and the degree of religiousness present at westernized Buddhist groups, there is also a fine line to be walked between exclusiveness and openness if such groups aim to develop committed, long-term memberships. Having said that, however, none of the teachers I interviewed expressed concerns about membership retention. They regarded the introductory courses as a means of introducing Buddhist principles and practices to a steady stream of interested newcomers. All of the teachers I interviewed were more concerned with disseminating the dharma than with creating new Buddhists.

Given this attitude, I wondered to what degree teachers encouraged introductory students to move on to higher level programs. Friends of the Heart offered the Intermediate and Tibetan Meditation classes, but it also offered a mentoring program and a foundation practice similar to traditional Tibetan foundation practice in which dedicated practitioners performed hundreds of thousands of mantras, prayers, and prostrations. When I asked Catherine Rathbun if one of her goals was to see students complete the foundation program, she laughed and said, "Oh, well they'd better!" But then she said: "Those are the small, human agendas. If you do this so many times, it you will have this and this and this. . . . Small goals are there to help us humans have a sense of linear accomplishment. The true changes are deep and long-lasting. Those are more important to me than the continuation of a center or the fealty of a student or anything else." When I asked Thekchen if he hoped students would move on from the General Program to the Foundation Program, he also said that the numbers were not important. He said that he had gone through periods where he assessed himself as a good or bad teacher based on "external things" like how many people go to Foundation Program, but that was not his overall goal. He said, rather, that his objective was to provide a welcoming place for learning about meditation and listen to and discuss "new perspectives." Thekchen also spoke about teaching objectives in terms of establishing Buddhism in the West. It was an interesting experiment, he said, to train western teachers who can then teach other westerners. The difficulty was trying to find a way to adapt a traditionally monastic system to make it relevant for householders. In his view, the NKT was still working on this goal. With tongue in cheek, he said: "A lot of people are just sitting back and watching to see if people like me [i.e., western monastic dharma teachers] explode or go on some weird rampage or are happy."

Introductory classes, therefore, were regarded as an opportunity to open a door for interested westerners and to introduce them to something new. What students did with what they learned was entirely up to them. Joyce and Meg likened the introductory classes to planting or scattering seeds. Thekchen said: "What seems to work is just letting people relax and take it at whatever level they want." Most of the teachers indicated a hope that students would be inspired to continue some involvement with the teachings or practices they learned. Although each worded it differently, it is interesting to note that all of the teachers identified their main goal as disseminating the dharma or the teachings of Buddhism. Joyce said that in the ten-week class students would begin to experience benefits of meditation and of "bringing the dharma to life." Richard reiterated this goal. Meg spoke about specific benefits of meditation: the ability to change one's perceptions and awareness. But these were the effects of teaching, not the main objective. Meg saw herself as using a time-tested tool, the dharma, to teach students certain beneficial techniques. Some benefits, Meg said, may be experienced immediately, but with time the techniques will yield deeper and deeper results.

Catherine Rathbun also spoke about deep and long-lasting changes that were, in her view, the more significant goal. I asked: What kind of changes? She responded with a story.

> I met with an old student a couple of days ago. She brought me news of some other old students that I haven't seen in a number of years. And one of them described having her baby and how meditation played a huge part in her delivery, and what part it had played. She also said she had now started the job that I had suggested to her when she was here studying early on. And she was saying: "you know, I wish I'd listened to Catherine however many years ago." Her life is blooming. I haven't seen her for a long time. It doesn't matter. When I first met her, she was suicidal and in a terrible state with her education, with her family, with her life. That's what it's about: the dharma.

Catherine believed that her overall objective was to help students realize certain effects of the dharma and the practice in their lives. She regarded deep, long-lasting changes as the ones that are lived, that come out in the life experiences of the person who has been changed. When I asked Catherine what constituted success in her teachings, she simply said: "The lady who had her baby." I then asked her what she considered to be failure. She replied:

Ego formation. People who learn a little and think they have learned a lot. Those who use the teaching to reinforce the ego instead of letting it go. I have been surprised on occasion when it first started arising, because it was with the more intensive program that I see ego formation. I was surprised at first, because I don't teach on that basis. It really took me aback. I wasn't prepared for it. But, the fact of the matter is, you can use knowledge and you can use some levels of attainment...for building the ego. And when you do that...it destroys the work in ways that the person doesn't realize.

Here again is an indication that, ideally, the objectives of the meditation classes were to inspire profound and long-lasting changes in the ways students regarded themselves and their world, in the values they held, and in the way they lived their lives. Such changes did not happen for all students, and sometimes the outcomes were not the positive ideals at which teachers aimed. It is clear from the interview responses cited throughout this book, however, that the majority of respondents reflected positively on their experiences. Very few interview participants had much that was negative to say about their experiences at Friends of the Heart or Chandrakirti Centre. Complaints I heard had to do with participants' concerns about the centers as religious organizations, and about ritual in general and prostrations in particular. When it came to the teachings about meditation and Buddhist ethics, all respondents were positive and enthusiastic. Newcomers especially were very interested in and intrigued by what they were learning. I believe that this had to do with the fact that respondents had chosen to participate in a tradition that is not part of the cultural mainstream. To some degree, they were justifying that choice, indicating that the worldviews expressed in the meditation classes corresponded to their own. Respondents' positive attitudes may also be a testament to the teachers' abilities to share their enthusiasm for teaching meditation and their skill at adapting those teachings to the attitudes and expectations of their students.

The positive reflections on learning outcomes, more significantly, indicate something else: Respondents were elevating and positively valuing their learning experiences along with the specific teachings and practices that they had learned. This indicates that what they learned and the ways they learned it had affective outcomes: Students assessed and positively valued their experiences, and made a commitment to the new practices and principles. Some said that they had experienced lasting positive changes in their lives, suggesting that affective learning had gone beyond a change of mood to changes in attitudes, values, and behaviors. Students and teachers alike expressed the hope that what was learned in the introductory meditation classes would make lasting change in students' attitudes and emotional responses, changes inspired by Buddhist values and reinforced through Buddhist practice.

The outcomes that respondents spoke about were not final outcomes, of course, but only descriptions of where they were at the time of their interviews. Experienced members may eventually leave, moving on to other centers or giving up involvement with Buddhist practice altogether. Newcomers may in time become experienced members, or may choose not to continue. For the most part, westernized Buddhist centers tend to have a high attrition rate: Those who arrive at their doors are, by definition, seekers. Some will continue to seek.

CONCLUSION

ONE OF THE initial objectives of this study was to uncover what newcomers at Buddhist meditation classes learned about Buddhism. If this question refers to the history, doctrine, and various cultural manifestations of the tradition—that is, detailed information about Buddhism as a historical world religion—then the answer is that newcomers learned very little. Nor was that the objective of the introductory courses. The classes were not, as one respondent put it, intended as "Buddhism 101." What was unique about the courses, and I believe unique about the learning processes as a result, was the fact that they were strongly ritualized settings intended to teach or transmit practices that were formal, traditional, transformative, and, for some, highly valued or spiritual. While some learning at the intellectual or cognitive level did take place, ritualizing in meditation classes primarily initiated changes in physical and concentration skills as well as attitudinal, emotional, and behavioral change.

The pattern of learning I have proposed suggests that learning through ritualizing links and cycles through the three (and possibly four) learning domains established in chapter 4. The pattern goes something like this: Gaining knowledge about Buddhism or meditation before ever visiting a Buddhist center—through reading, especially—constituted respondents' first cognitive learning. Books, articles, and websites on Buddhism introduced them to meditation and its potential benefits for stress relief, concentration, and the like. Respondents may have read that Buddhism was an open, nontheistic philosophy and way of life rather than a religion, a view that appealed to many who participated in this study. Some respondents had learned about certain Buddhist principles, such as impermanence and no-self, and were curious about them. All of this refers to cognitive learning, the acquisition of factual or intellectual knowledge. Having learned a little about Buddhism and its practices, respondents decided to seek out a Buddhist center and enroll in meditation classes. The ritualized settings and activities they encountered there instigated certain affective changes, initiated by observing the decorum in the shrine rooms, which, for some participants, prompted a sense of respect for the teachers and for what was being taught.

At the classes, students then began engaging in various rites. These were primarily meditation techniques, but they also included other formal practices, as well as the ritualizing of everyday activities. Ritualizing, in its physical and mental aspects, involves learning activities in the psychomotor domain: receiving or observing pre-established behaviors or activities, imitating them, repeating and practicing them, and adapting them to create new forms. Psychomotor learning is a process by which we gain the tacit type of learning I call embodied knowing. When gained through strongly ritualized actions, it may be described as ritual knowledge. But the ritualized qualities of what is learned and how it is learned—the fact that it takes place in special settings, is set aside or elevated, formalized, regarded as traditional and possibly spiritual—connects the physical aspects of learning to the attitudes, emotions and values of the learner. Ritualized learning, therefore, links psychomotor and affective learning processes.

The development of psychomotor skills, for many respondents, thus led to new affective changes as they began to learn about new attitudes, experience new emotional responses, and to positively value the practices and outlooks they were taught. Students could then reflect on and analyze those experiences, adding more cognitive learning over time. Intellectual reflection on the practices and values they learned encouraged some respondents to keep up with the practice. Thus, although it was downplayed somewhat, cognitive learning also fed into the pattern of learning through ritualizing. The pattern cycled from affective through psychomotor and back again to cognitive learning. With continued practice, the cycle repeated. At some point, according to Buddhist belief, practitioners may break out of the cognitive-affective-psychomotor cycle to a qualitatively different experience of spiritual insight, described in Buddhist teachings as direct, experiential awareness of emptiness, impermanence, or no-self.

How much of this pattern relies on ritualizing? Learning may have occurred because the activities I observed were educational, not because they constituted ritualizing. After all, nearly all learning involves repetition, much of it formalized.

Do we not highly value other things that we learn? In his discussion of ritual knowledge, Jennings makes a distinction between "mere" pedagogical repetition and the knowledge-generating function of ritual. In his view, strict repetition merely reproduces what is known: It teaches us how to perform the ritual and no more.[1] Ritual knowledge is gained not through detached imitation but through engagement, which necessarily changes our understandings. While these are important observations, engagement, imitation, and response still apply to other educational forms. What makes ritual knowledge distinct from other learning outcomes is the depth and breadth to which that learning is applied. Ritual becomes a means of discovery, Jennings argues, because it proposes a pattern of action that evokes imitation or response not only in the ritual but in all of our activities. So, Jennings says, we recite the "Our Father," and thus learn to act as God's children.[2] Similarly, McLaren identifies ritual knowledge as the "deep codes" that become the blueprint for all of our reactions.[3] It develops through the legitimation and sanctification of the settings in which we learn and the ritualized nature of what we learn. Schilbrack claims that ritual knowledge is deeply metaphysical: What we learn in the ritual is a microcosm for the whole of human experience.[4] As the discussion about learning meditation versus subjects at school showed, the majority of respondents regarded what they were learning at meditation classes as qualitatively different from more conventional types of learning.

The depth and breadth to which new learning is applied depends to a large extent on how we regard what we are learning. For instance, of the two examples cited earlier from Jennings—chopping wood and taking the chalice—one is typically regarded as more ritualized than the other. Do we consciously understand more about holding the chalice than we do about swinging the axe? I believe so, because of the nature of the circumstances in which we handle each. My analysis of learning through ritualizing suggests that the learning that takes place via more strongly ritualized activities is more reflexive and potentially more accessible to our conscious understanding. In addition to that, there is a stronger sense of prescription in the strongly ritualized act, a sense of how one *ought* to move and act in a ritualized setting. It has to do with an understanding of proper decorum, but also with the sense that the act itself is received from the outside: an object given to the performer, passed down through, and honored by, tradition. While these actions can and do change over time, they maintain a sense of rightness, a sense that goes beyond practicality, comfort, or expediency like the right way of chopping wood. The lotus position, for example, is a meditation posture that has a very long history,[5] and is practiced in its traditional form among meditators all over the world. It has changed, however. Different meditation postures have been introduced. But the core of seated meditation remains: the straight spine, the stable base, the stillness. These are the elements that become the received, respected objects, and are taken with a sense that they are the "right" way to sit in meditation. Because of this, the newer postures are also respected, preserved, and repeated, eventually becoming tradition. The ritualized nature of practices such as these underscores them in a way that other actions are not. Ritualizing thus links physical techniques and skills with our emotions, attitudes, and values. Remember that this is a matter of degree. Any act can be regarded as more or less ritualized. Brenda turned sweeping up seed pods into a ritual. Alan regarded giving change to panhandlers as a special, elevated activity inspired by Buddhist values. Learning the right movements for chopping wood may produce a strong affective response, or even influence one's spiritual values, if the activity is understood and performed ritually. I may take a chalice merely to put it away, a movement that teaches me less about my attitudes and values than receiving the Eucharist.

Whether or not affective change took place had much to do with students' initial motivations for enrolling in the meditation classes. If they were seeking a means of changing their outlooks and ways of living at the outset, they tended to see, in their experiences at Friends of the Heart or Chandrakirti Centre, the potential for that kind of change. Those who came seeking a spiritual practice or answers to ultimate concerns tended to speak about finding such things. This suggests that when they regarded what they were learning as more ritualized—in this case, more elevated, special or spiritual—there was a greater connection to the things they valued and were willing to commit to; the things that gave them a felt connection to their whole experience, to others, and to the world around them. For those who did not see what they were learning as qualitatively different from other kinds of training or education, the outcomes of their learning were more immediate, practical, and had less to do with generating the ultimate outcome of Bloom's affective domain, namely "characterizing values." For John, Erin, and Dennis, learning meditation was a formal, repetitive, embodied activity, but it was not particularly elevated or spiritual. For some respondents, then, learning meditation was strictly educational and not especially ritualized.

With its focus on performance and embodiment, this study did not explore links between myth and ritual in any depth. The interview and field data do suggest, however, that some myths or narratives were present in the meditation classes. Diane, for example, said that she appreciated Catherine Rathbun's explanation of the meanings of the water offerings on the shrines. Learning the story behind the offerings consisted of cognitive learning that helped Diane overcome some of her discomfort with the centers' rituals. The fact that meditation students sought out, learned, and transmitted such meanings shows that some myths and narratives do surround the ritual activities at Friends of the Heart and Chandrakirti Centre.

Grounding my study in performance theory may, in fact, account for its reduced focus on cognitive learning. I do believe, however, that there was sufficient indication, from students and from my observations at the classes, that cognitive learning was often downplayed by teachers and students. The reduced emphasis on cognitive learning, therefore, was not solely a result of the performative approach taken here. Furthermore, the discussion of the Dīgha Nikāya sūtra in chapter 4 indicates that long-standing Buddhist doctrine also downplays intellectual learning.

Performance theory has been a useful model for investigating learning through ritualizing because it allows for the possibility of change, which Jennings claims is essential for discovery. Ritual as performance is not limited to formality and rote repetition; it is potentially adaptive, flowing, innovative. Each time ritual activities are re-performed, each time they are passed on to a new set of practitioners, they are re-assessed, and their complexes of meaning re-evaluated. Something new is learned. This process was happening among meditation students as they learned meditation postures, gestures, and concentration techniques and experimented with them, shaping them into new practices. Performance theory also highlights the body through its emphasis on the physical enactment of ritual. As a subset of embodied knowing, ritual knowledge is generated through ritual's physicality. Ritual's postures and gestures create what Csordas calls the socially informed body, in ways, according to my argument above, that are more encompassing than other, more ordinary social actions.

But this study takes the notions of performance and ritual knowledge one step further. Because meditation was the one of the key practices through which respondents learned, I needed to expand the analysis to include techniques that take place in the mind. Performance studies have paid due attention to the physical postures and gestures of ritual, an approach that takes us past theory and text to the actual performances of actual rites. But its focus on physical enactment tends to leave out less overtly performative elements like meditative concentration practices. Although not witnessed by anyone besides the practitioner, these techniques are still embodied ritualized enactments. They are rites. Respondents' reflections on the ways they learned through meditation demonstrate that the mind can perform and develop skills in the same way as the rest of the body. This is not to say that the mind gains cognitive knowledge—knowledge of a Buddhist sūtra, for example—in a bodily way. It learns *practice* in a bodily way. The mind learns to focus its concentration or to direct its movements just as the hand learns to hold the chalice, the arms to swing the axe. While the mind, as we normally expect, learns in the cognitive and affective domains, it also *performs* and *ritualizes*, and thus learns (changes) through psychomotor processes as well. I hope, therefore, that this study has contributed a new perspective on what is meant by performance and embodiment, in addition to different ideas about the ways the body and mind together learn, know, and act.

Ritual and embodiment theories suggest that there exists a distinctive, tacit kind of knowledge that develops through repetition and refinement. I call it embodied knowing. It takes place through ritualization in our everyday activities. In more strongly ritualized settings, this process can become more deliberate, conscious, even experimental. The knowledge that is inscribed in such settings is what I have called ritual knowledge. Through different techniques but similar processes, the knowing body and the moving mind both participate in these types of learning.

This study also proposes a fresh perspective on learning in general. Learning through ritualizing links the changes that take place in all three of Bloom's domains, each dependent upon the others. The discovery that ritualizing links psychomotor and affective learning may be applicable to other studies of ritual, or to other disciplines as well. This notion that internal or mental rites produce psychomotor learning outcomes would be applicable to a wide range of internal practices. Silent prayer or mantra recitation, especially where they involve repetitious performance that goes beyond the discursive meaning of their words or syllables, could be another form of mental rehearsing or ritualizing. To what extent are such practices cognitive? Do they, in fact, involve psychomotor types of change? Do they link to affective change by virtue of the fact that they possess various qualities of ritual? There are many intriguing avenues for investigating other types of formal practice. There may also be other, less ritualized, mental activities that develop psychomotor changes in the mind. Reading, for example, is a technique of concentration and absorption, something that involves gesturing the mind—that is, moving the focus of attention across the page—a skill that develops with practice. As a skill, it is distinct from the content of what is read and from the cognitive understanding of that content. I do hope others will find these observations worth testing and exploring further.

This book also touches on the ways in which ritualization, as preconscious, culturally stylized behaviors, changes when a tradition founded in one culture is adopted by members of another. We learn to enact our world through our bodies, through the culturally and biologically conditioned activities we perform. How, for example, do the movements of a traditional Tibetan Buddhist ritual change, in their performance and their meanings, when adopted by Canadians taking on Tibetan Buddhist practices? I have only begun to scratch the surface of this issue with the discussion of prostration practices in chapter 5. There is much more to explore. I hope that this research might serve as a starting point for further investigations into the ways in which we learn through and with our bodies.

As a scholar of ritual, I found it somewhat disappointing, although not at all surprising, that so many of my interview participants had strongly negative attitudes toward ritual. As teachers Catherine and Thekchen noted, such attitudes have to do with the ways in which ritual has been regarded in the West, a culture strongly influenced by Protestant thought. And yet, for those participants who were willing to suspend their aversion and participate in the rituals at Friends of the Heart and Chandrakirti Centre, the experience prompted what they believed were deeper, more personal connections to the Buddhist principles and practices they were taught. For those readers who regard ritual as dull, rote, meaningless repetition, I hope that this book will open up the possibility that ritual has the potential to be innovative, meaningful, and personally transformative.

All living religions have the capacity for change, a capacity that is necessary for a tradition to survive and remain relevant for subsequent generations. And, as Catherine Rathbun pointed out, change is at the heart of Buddhist teachings, the declaration that all things are impermanent. Even so, a tradition's followers must find ways to balance adaptation with the stable, tried-and-true forms of the past. This is the question that Buddhist teachers throughout the history of the tradition have faced: What is the essence of Buddhist tradition? What adaptations are necessary to transmit Buddhist teachings and practices to new geographical and cultural locales, and what needs to be maintained in order to preserve the tradition? Among participants learning about a new tradition, ritualizing, as formative, experimental behavior that contributes to new learning, is an important means of discovering what changes may be necessary, how those changes are to be made, and how to make traditional rituals resonate with new generations of practitioners. With its experimentation, play, adaptation, and reconstruction of behaviors, ritualizing is a "way in" to new rituals and ritualized practices. Ritualizing, however, is not the end. If it does not aim at becoming ritual, ritualizing may lack form and purpose.[6] For some respondents, this was the case: They tried meditation for a while, but when their classes ended, so did their practice. Several respondents indicated that participating with others was beneficial for maintaining a commitment to their practice. Hence, one factor that may assist the formation of stable ritual is ongoing involvement with a community of like-minded practitioners.

This book explores ritualizing as conscious experimentation with received behaviors that may become stable ritual over time. Since the mind is itself embodied, practices that take place in a meditator's mind are as embodied as the postures or gestures we perform with our hands and feet. Further, as the imagined center of our consciousness, the mind can literally move: Meditation techniques often take the focus of the mind into different areas of the body, or even outside the body. The mind is, therefore, another part of the body with which we can ritualize. And finally, the embodied mind, through ritualizing, comes to know in much the same way a muscle "knows"; through repetition, familiarity, training, the development of skills, and of skills into a pattern of behavior. With this view of ritualizing comes the understanding that not everything we do is with our muscles, and not everything we know is in our heads. Ritualizing can generate a kind of knowing that is located in blood, bone, and muscle, and in an embodied, gestural entity that we call the mind.

Appendix

STUDENT INTERVIEW PARTICIPANTS BY NAME

Alan: Chandrakirti Centre introductory meditation student. Attended General Program classes. Menswear retailer, age 65.

"Anna"[1]: Friends of the Heart introductory meditation student. Attended Tibetan Meditation and Energy Training classes. Volunteer, age 50.

Brenda: Chandrakirti Centre introductory meditation student. Attended General Program classes. Retired English teacher, age 65.

Bronwen: Chandrakirti Centre introductory meditation student. Attended General Program classes. Chef, age 25.

David, Friends of the Heart experienced member. Attended Tibetan Meditation classes. Chinese medicine practitioner, age 34.

Carol: Chandrakirti Centre long-term member and introductory meditation student. Attended General Program classes. Administrative volunteer, age 56.

Catherine H.: Chandrakirti Centre introductory meditation student. Attended General Program classes. Salon owner and hairstylist, age 41.

"Dennis": Friends of the Heart introductory meditation student. Attended Calm and Clear meditation classes. Financial analyst, age 33.

Diane: Friends of the Heart introductory meditation student. Attended Introduction to Insight meditation classes. Semi-retired civil servant, age 59.

Erin: Friends of the Heart introductory meditation student. Attended Calm and Clear meditation classes. Clothing company sales representative, age 30.

Gerald: Chandrakirti Centre introductory meditation student. Attended General Program classes. House painter and artist, age 46.

Gwen: Friends of the Heart newcomer intermediate meditation student, teacher of T'ai Chi classes. Attended Intermediate Meditation classes. Community support counselor, age 53.

John: Friends of the Heart introductory meditation student. Attended Introduction to Insight meditation classes. Retired teacher and systems analyst, age 60.

"Marconi": Friends of the Heart experienced member. Attended Tibetan Meditation and Intermediate Meditation classes. Management consultant, age 48.

"Margaret": Friends of the Heart introductory meditation student. Attended Calm and Clear introductory meditation class. Administrator, age 60.

Marlon: Chandrakirti Centre experienced member and occasional General Program teacher. Attended General Program and Foundation Program classes. Writer and teacher, age 47.

Nicolette: Friends of the Heart introductory meditation student. Attended Introduction to Insight and Tibetan Meditation classes. Librarian, age 45.

"Priscilla": Chandrakirti Centre experienced member. Attended General Program and Foundation Program classes. Retired teacher, age 58.

Tanit: Friends of the Heart introductory meditation student. Attended Healing Body, Healing Mind meditation class. Professor and theater production designer, age 48.

NOTES

INTRODUCTION

1. Janet McLellan, *Many Petals of the Lotus* (Toronto: University of Toronto Press, 1999), 81.

2. Ibid., 74.

3. Janet McLellan,"Buddhism in the Greater Toronto Area: The Politics of Recognition," in *Buddhism in Canada*, ed. Bruce Matthews, Routledge Critical Studies in Buddhism, Charles S. Prebish and Damien Keown, general editors (London: Routledge, 2006), 89.

4. For a discussion of parallel congregations in Buddhist centers in the United States, see Paul David Numrich, *Old Wisdom in the New World* (Knoxville: University of Tennessee Press, 1996), 63–74.

5. McLellan, "Buddhism in the Greater Toronto Area," 102n.1.

6. Victor Hori and Janet McLellan discuss the factionalism in Canadian Buddhism in more detail in: Victor Sōgen Hori and Janet McLellan, "Suwanda H.J. Sugunasiri: Buddhist," in *Wild Geese: Buddhism in Canada*, ed. Victor Sōgen Hori, John S. Harding, and Alexander Soucy (Montreal: McGill-Queen's University Press, 2010), 377–399.

7. Victor Sōgen Hori, "Buddhism: The Religion of Dispersion," Keynote address at the Buddhism and Diaspora Conference, University of Toronto–Scarborough, 2010b; Victor Sōgen Hori, "How Do We Study Buddhism in Canada?" in *Wild Geese: Buddhism in Canada*, ed. Victor Sōgen Hori, John S. Harding, and Alexander Soucy (Montreal: McGill-Queens University Press, 2010), 14–38; Natalie E. Quili, "Western Self, Asian Other: Modernity, Authenticity, and Nostalgia for 'Tradition' in Buddhist Studies," *Journal of Buddhist Ethics* 16 (2009), 1–38; David L. McMahan, *The Making of Buddhist Modernism* (Oxford: Oxford University Press, 2008); Wakoh Shannon Hickey, "Two Buddhisms, Three Buddhisms, and Racism," *Journal of Global Buddhism* 11 (2010), 1–25.

8. See especially Hori, "How Do We Study Buddhism in Canada?"

9. McMahan, *Making of Buddhist Modernism*, 6–8.

10. Thomas Tweed suggests the term "sympathizers" to refer to people with an interest in, but not full affiliation with, Buddhism. See Thomas A. Tweed, "Who Is a Buddhist? Night Stand Buddhists and Other Creatures," in *Westward Dharma: Buddhism Beyond Asia*, ed. Charles S. Prebish and Martin Baumann (Berkeley and Los Angeles: University of California Press, 2002), 17–33.

11. McMahan, *Making of Buddhist Modernism*.

12. This is an important point that has been raised recently by several scholars: for example, see Hori, "Buddhism: The Religion of Dispersion"; McMahan, *Making of Buddhist Modernism*; and Alexander Soucy, "Asian Reformers, Global Organizations: An Exploration of the Possibility of a 'Canadian Buddhism,'" in *Wild Geese: Buddhism in Canada*, ed. Victor Sōgen Hori, John S. Harding, and Alexander Soucy (Montreal: McGill-Queen's University Press, 2010), 39–60.

13. It is worth pointing out that there are some convincing arguments that North American and other western cultures have themselves been transformed by religious and cultural influences from Asia. See, for example, Colin Campbell, *The Easternization of the West* (Boulder: Paradigm Publishers, 2007).

14. In an article on Theravada Buddhism in Britain, Sandra Bell investigates ways in which tradition is used to justify change. See Sandra Bell, "Being Creative with Tradition: Rooting Theravada Buddhism in Britain," *Journal of Global Buddhism* 1 (2000), 1–23.

15. See Quili, "Western Self, Asian Other."

16. Notable works are Wendy Cadge's study of westernized Theravada centers in the United States, Paul Numrich's text on two heritage Theravada centers, which also explores experience of its "American Buddhist" members, and an informative article on Buddhist identity by Angie Danyluk. Cadge, *Heartwood* (Chicago: University of Chicago Press, 2005); Numrich, *Old Wisdom in the New World*; Danyluk, "To Be or Not to Be: Buddhist Selves in Toronto," *Contemporary Buddhism* 4, no. 2 (2003), 128–141. See also Campbell," Transforming Ordinary Life: Turning to Zen Buddhism in Toronto," in *Wild Geese: Buddhism in Canada*, Victor S. Hori, Alexander Soucy and John Harding, eds. (Montreal: McGill-Queens University Press, 2010), 187–209.

17. Ronald L. Grimes, *Rite out of Place: Ritual, Media and the Arts* (Oxford: Oxford University Press, 2006), 55.

18. Jan A.M. Snoek, "Defining 'Rituals,'" in *Theorizing Rituals: Issues, Topics, Approaches, Concepts*, ed. Jan Snoek, Jens Kreinath, and Michael Strausberg (Leiden: Brill, 2008), 4.

19. Don Handelman argues that the meta-category "ritual" precludes any meaningful comparison of events because it makes presumptions about events before comparison can begin. See Don Handelman, "Conceptual Alternatives to Ritual," in *Theorizing Rituals: Issues, Topics, Approaches, Concepts*, ed. Jan Snoek, Jens Kreinath, and Michael Strausberg (Leiden: Brill, 2008), 37–49. I respectfully disagree: As long as we recognize that the meta-category is problematic, and acknowledge that the term refers to a nonmonothetic grouping with open boundaries, then I believe that the term can be usefully applied in this way.

20. See especially Ronald Grimes's chart of ritual characteristics: Ronald L. Grimes, *Ritual Criticism: Case Studies in Its Practice, Essays on Its Theory* (Columbia: University of South Carolina Press, 1990), 14.

21. Ronald Grimes, "Performance," in *Theorizing Rituals: Classical Topics, Theoretical Approaches, Analytical Concepts, Annotated Bibliography*, ed. Jan Snoek, Jens Kreinath, and Michael Strausberg (Leiden: Brill, 2004), 392.

22. Snoek, "Defining 'Rituals,'" 9.

23. For this distinction, I draw upon Jan Snoek's definitions of rites and ceremonies. See ibid., 9.

24. Ronald L. Grimes, *Beginnings in Ritual Studies*, 2nd ed. (Columbia: University of South Carolina Press, 1995), 61.

25. Theodore W. Jennings, "On Ritual Knowledge," in *Readings in Ritual Studies*, ed. Ronald L. Grimes (Upper Saddle River, N.J.: Prentice Hall, 1996), 326.

26. See, for example, Ronald L. Grimes, "Performance Theory and the Study of Ritual," in *New Approaches to the Study of Religion* 2 (2004); Grimes, *Rite out of Place*; and Grimes, "Performance," in *Theorizing Rituals*.

27. Richard Schechner, *Performance Theory* (New York: Routledge, 1988), 7.

28. Ritual studies dating from the mid-nineteenth to mid-twentieth centuries, for example, were primarily concerned with ritual's origins in textual sources or myths (or, conversely, myth's origins in ritual) or with a proposed ancient, primeval ritual that was regarded as the source of all subsequent ritual and theater. For a detailed discussion of the development of methods in ritual studies, see Catherine Bell, *Ritual: Perspectives and Dimensions* (New York: Oxford University Press, 1997).

29. Jennings, "On Ritual Knowledge," 326.

30. Ibid., 325–327.

31. Ibid., 327.

32. In Kevin Schilbrack, ed., *Thinking through Rituals: Philosophical Perspectives* (New York: Routledge, 2004).

33. Kevin Schilbrack, "Introduction: On the Use of Philosophy in the Study of Rituals," in *Thinking through Rituals: Philosophical Perspectives*, ed. Kevin Schilbrack (New York: Routledge, 2004), 2.

34. Nick Crossley, "Ritual, Body Technique and (Inter)Subjectivity," in *Thinking through Rituals: Philosophical Perspectives*, ed. Kevin Schilbrack (New York: Routledge, 2004), 31.

35. Ibid., 35.

36. Michael L. Raposa, "Ritual Inquiry: The Pragmatic Logic of Religious Practice," in *Thinking through Rituals: Philosophical Perspectives*, ed. Kevin Schilbrack (New York: Routledge, 2004), 125.

37. Crossley, "Ritual, Body Technique and (Inter)Subjectivity," 35.

38. Cited in Rosalind C. Morris, "Gender," in *Theorizing Rituals*, 369.

39. Thomas J. Csordas, "Embodiment as a Paradigm for Anthropology," *Ethos* 18, no. 1 (1990), 6.

40. Ibid.

41. Steven Van Wolputte, "Hang on to Your Self: Of Bodies, Embodiment and Selves," *Annual Review of Anthropology* 33 (2004), 258.

42. Csordas, "Embodiment as a Paradigm for Anthropology," 36.

43. Crossley, "Ritual, Body Technique and (Inter)Subjectivity," 34.

44. Ronald L. Grimes, *Deeply into the Bone: Re-Inventing Rites of Passage* (Berkeley and Los Angeles: University of California Press, 2000), 7.

45. Csordas, "Embodiment as a Paradigm for Anthropology," 8.

46. John M. Koller, "Human Embodiment: Indian Perspectives," in *Self as Body in Asian Theory and Practice*, ed. Roger T. Ames, Thomas P. Kasulis, and Wimal Dissanayake (Albany: State University of New York Press, 1993), 57.

47. B. S. Bloom, *Taxonomy of Educational Objectives, Handbook I: The Cognitive Domain* (New York: David McKay Co. Inc., 1956).

48. Paul Tillich most famously coined the term "ultimate concern," but where he uses it to define religion, I apply it to spirituality as well. Paul Tillich, ed., *Theology of Culture* (New York: Oxford University Press, 1964), 8.

49. See Ronald L. Grimes, "Forum: American Spirituality," *Religion and American Culture* 9, no. 2 (1999), 151–152.

CHAPTER 1

1. At both of the centers discussed here, becoming a full member involved paying a monthly (Chandrakirti) or yearly (Friends of the Heart) membership fee. Members were allowed access to regularly scheduled events and courses.

2. "History Friends of the Heart," (2007), http://www.friendsoftheheart.com/Toronto_ meditation_centre/history.php.

3. Joyce Allen and Richard Johnson, personal communication, January 2007.

4. "History Friends of the Heart."

5. Joyce Allen and Richard Johnson, personal communication, January 2007.

6. Anonymous, "Friends of the Heart Home Page," Friends of the Heart.http://www. friendsoftheheart.com/

7. See Patricia Q. Campbell, *Buddhist Values and Ordinary Life among Members of the Toronto Zen Buddhist Temple*." (MA Thesis, Wilfrid Laurier University, 2004), chap. 4.

8. Joyce Allen, personal communication, January 2007.

9. Chenrezig is the Tibetan name for Avalokiteśvara, the Bodhisattva of Great Compassion.

10. For a full description of Tibetan preliminary practice, see John Powers, *Introduction to Tibetan Buddhism*, rev.ed. (Ithaca, N.Y.: Snow Lion Publications, 2007), 294–311.

11. Mahāmudrā is a philosophy and teaching found primarily in the Kagyu but also in the Géluk schools of Tibetan Buddhism. It combines sūtra study for the comprehension of the truth of ultimate reality, which is believed to be bliss and emptiness, and tantra, in which the practitioner works toward realizing that truth through spiritual practice. "Mahāmudrā," in *The Oxford Dictionary of World Religions*, ed. John Bowker (Oxford: Oxford University Press, 1997), 600.

12. Kadampa Buddhism, Meditation Centres, http://kadampa.org/en/reference/about-dharma-centers/, accessed June 2010.

13. Anonymous, "The Dharma Protector," The New Kadampa Tradition, International Kadampa Buddhist Union, http://kadampa.org/en/buddhism/the-dharma-protector/.

14. For more details on the Shugden issue, see David Kay, "The New Kadampa Tradition and the Continuity of Tibetan Buddhism in Transition," *Journal of Contemporary Religion* 12, no. 3 (1997); Stephen Batchelor, "Letting Daylight into Magic: The Life and Times of Dorje Shugden," *Tricycle Magazine* (1998); Donald S. Lopez, "Two Sides of the Same God," *Tricycle Magazine* (1998), and Anonymous, "Dorje Shugden Versus Pluralism and National Unity," in *The Worship of Shugden: Documents Related to a Tibetan Controversy* (Dharamsala: Department of Religion and Culture, Central Tibetan Administration, 1998).

15. Anonymous, "Chandrakirti Kadampa Meditation Centre Canada CKMCC," http://www. kadampa.ca/.

CHAPTER 2

1. Three other respondents had also been interviewed by this time, but the Zen-based center they attended was, in the end, not included in this study.

2. See Russell Bernard, *Research Methods in Anthropology* (Walnut Creek, Calif.: Altamira Press, 2002), 187.

3. Thomas A. Tweed, "Who Is a Buddhist? Night Stand Buddhists and Other Creatures," in *Westward Dharma: Buddhism Beyond Asia*, ed. Charles S. Prebish and Martin Baumann (Berkeley and Los Angeles: University of California Press, 2002), 18.

4. Charles S. Prebish, *American Buddhism* (North Scituate, Mass.: Duxbury Press, 1979), 188; and Tweed, "Who Is a Buddhist? Night Stand Buddhists and Other Creatures," 24.

5. See Danyluk, "To Be or Not to Be: Buddhist Selves in Toronto." *Contemporary Buddhism* 4, no. 2 (2003), 128–141.

6. James Coleman discusses various circles of involvement among western Buddhist sympathizers in the United States. See James William Coleman, *The New Buddhism: The Western Transformation of an Ancient Tradition* (Oxford: Oxford University Press, 2001), 186–191.

7. Tweed, "Who Is a Buddhist? Night Stand Buddhists and Other Creatures," 18–20.

8. With his admission that Buddhist classes were "available," Gerald highlights an interesting fact about Buddhism in the West. Over the last several decades, opportunities for westerners to come into contact with Buddhists and Buddhist groups have grown. Since immigration policies changed in the mid-1960s to allow more people from Asian nations to settle in North America, there has been much more contact between Buddhists and non-Buddhists here. Transportation and communication technologies have developed to the point where westerners can easily come into contact with Buddhist institutions and practitioners around the globe. Media coverage of well-known Buddhists east and west has also penetrated local communities.

9. Daoism in fact had a strong influence on the development of Buddhism in China, particularly on the Ch'an (Zen) school.

10. The Friends of the Heart Refuge Prayer reads, in part: "The Mind of Light is called Enlightenment/In this we take Refuge/The Body of Truth is called the Dharma/In this we find solace/. . . Our minds are not separate from the Mind of Enlightenment/Let us vow to sweep away its cobwebs/Our knowledge can grow to be an exhibition of Truth/Let us vow to burnish our awareness/ . . . The midpoint of balance is the place of union/Where Body, Speech and Mind join together/And the jump to Transcendent Wisdom becomes possible." Written by Catherine Rathbun. *Friends of the Heart Student Handbook* (Toronto, Ont.: Friends of the Heart, 2005), 12. Permission to quote the Refuge Prayer is given by Catherine Rathbun, 2010.

11. The section Tanit was referring to from the Friends of the Heart handbook reads: "The Buddha taught not a religion or a philosophy, but rather how to meditate." *Friends of the Heart Student Handbook* (Toronto, Ont.: Friends of the Heart, 2005), 10.

12. Ron G. Williams and James W. Boyd, *Ritual Art and Knowledge: Aesthetic Theory and Zoroastrian Ritual* (Columbia: University of South Carolina Press, 1993), 78–82.

13. Peter Harvey, *An Introduction to Buddhist Ethics* (Cambridge: Cambridge University Press, 2000), 18.

14. International Kadampa Buddhist Union, "Chandrakirti Kadampa Meditation Centre Canada," International Kadampa Buddhist Union, http://www.kadampa.ca/index.php?section=home.

15. See McMahan, *The Making of Buddhist Modernism*, (Oxford: Oxford University Press, 2008), 45–46.

16. Sangha, a word traditionally reserved for the Buddhist monastic community, is commonly used in western Buddhist groups to refer to their full memberships; lay people, teachers, and monastics included.

CHAPTER 3

1. See Alan Rogers, *What Is the Difference: A New Critique of Adult Learning and Teaching* (Leicester, UK: NIACE, 2003), 17–27.

2. Schechner discusses formal and informal training among theater performers and ritualists. See Richard Schechner, *Performance Studies: An Introduction* (London: Routledge, 2002), 193–195; and Richard Schechner, "Magnitudes of Performance," in *By Means of Performance*, ed. Richard Schechner and Willa Appel (Cambridge: Cambridge University Press, 1990).

3. Rogers, *What Is the Difference*, 16.

4. Ibid., 38.

5. Ibid., 28.

6. B. S. Bloom, *Taxonomy of Educational Objectives, Handbook I: The Cognitive Domain* (New York: David McKay Co. Inc., 1956), 7.

7. Jennings, "On Ritual Knowledge," in *Readings in Ritual Studies*, ed. Ronald L. Grimes (Upper Saddle River, N.J.: Prentice Hall, 1996), 327.

8. John Powers describes a variation of the prayer mudra, used in Tibetan Buddhism, called the "gem holding position" where only the base of the palms and the fingertips are touching. Powers, *Introduction to Tibetan Buddhism*, rev. ed. (Ithaca, N.Y.: Snow Lion Publications, 2007), 299.

9. Arnold Van Gennep, *The Rites of Passage*, ed. Monika B. Vezedom and Gabrielle Caffee (Chicago: University of Chicago Press, 1960), 15–25.

10. Ibid., 21.

11. Victor W. Turner, "Liminality and Communitas," in *Readings in Ritual Studies*, ed. Ronald L. Grimes (Upper Saddle River, N.J.: Prentice Hall, 1996), 513.

12. Feminist scholars have pointed out that Turner's purportedly universal qualities of liminality, including separation, anti-structure, and the removal of status, do not apply in the majority of women's rituals. See Caroline Walker Bynum, "Women's Stories, Women's Symbols: A Critique of Victor Turner's Theory of Liminality," in *Anthropology and the Study of Religion*, ed. Robert L. Moore and Frank E. Reynolds (Chicago: Center for the Scientific Study of Religion, 1984).

13. Communitas is indicated in respondents' discussions about shared experiences and the development of commitment through practicing with others. See chapter 2.

14. In the Mahayana branch of Buddhism, a Bodhisattva is a being who has vowed to become a Buddha or enlightened being for the sake of all others. There are numerous steps along the path to becoming a Bodhisattva, beginning with the six perfections.

15. For details on the characteristics and development of "modernist" Buddhism, see McMahan, *The Making of Buddhist Modernism* (Oxford: Oxford University Press, 2008).

16. Anonymous, *Friends of the Heart Student Handbook* (Toronto, Ont.: Friends of the Heart, 2005), 11.

17. Peter McLaren, *Schooling as a Ritual Performance* (London: Routledge&Kegan Paul, 1986), 197.

18. Ibid.

19. Caroline Humphrey, and James Laidlaw, *The Archetypal Actions of Ritual* (Oxford: Clarendon Press, 1994), 64.

20. Ibid., 5.

21. This is true for the majority of meditation practices taught to newcomers at Friends of the Heart and Chandrakirti Centre. Tantric visualizations and analytical meditation practices (described in chapter 4) do focus on the content of the mind. Even so, such practices also entail stylized concentration techniques that, I am arguing here, are ritualized.

22. Humphrey and Laidlaw, *Archetypal Actions of Ritual*, 5.

23. Roy A. Rappaport, *Ritual and Religion in the Making of Humanity* (Cambridge, U.K.: Cambridge University Press, 2005), 24.

24. Grimes, *Beginnings in Ritual Studies* 2nd ed. (Columbia: University of South Carolina Press, 1995), 43.

25. Ibid., 42.

26. Compare C sordas, "Embodiment as a Paradigm for Anthropology"*Ethos* 18, no. 1 (1990). and Dietrich Harth, "Ritual and Other Forms of Social Action," in *Theorizing Rituals: Issues, Topics, Approaches, Concepts*, ed. Jan Snoek, Jens Kreinath, and Michael Strausberg (Leiden: Brill, 2008).

27. Grimes, *Beginnings in Ritual Studies*, 41.

28. Ibid., 43.

29. Ibid., 61.

30. Ibid., 60.

31. Ibid., 62.

32. Schechner, *Performance Studies*, 22.

33. Richard Schechner, "Restoration of Behavior," in *Readings in Ritual Studies*, ed. Ronald L. Grimes (Upper Saddle River, New Jersey: Prentice Hall, 1996), 441.

34. Schechner, *Performance Studies*, 22.

35. Schechner, "Restoration of Behavior," 457.

36. Ibid., 441–442.

37. Schechner, "Magnitudes of Performance," 41.

38. Ibid.

39. Ibid., 40.

40. This list once again draws on Grimes's chart of qualities of ritual, found in Grimes, *Ritual Criticism: Case Studies in Its Practice, Essays on Its Theory* (Columbia: University of South Carolina Press, 1990), 14.

41. Jennings points out that "ritual is above all a pattern of action." Jennings, "On Ritual Knowledge," 325.

CHAPTER 4

1. McMahan, *The Making of Buddhist Modernism* (Oxford: Oxford University Press, 2008), 64–65.

2. Gordon A. Walter and Stephen E. Marks, *Experiential Learning and Change* (New York: John Wiley & Sons, 1981), 2.

3. Rogers, *What Is the Difference: A New Critique of Adult Learning and Teaching* (Leicester, UK: NIACE, 2003), 9.

4. Rogers's fourth term, "understanding," was substituted for "comprehension" under the cognitive domain by the team who revised Bloom's taxonomy in 2001. David R. Krathwohl, "A Revision of Bloom's Taxonomy: An Overview," *Theory into Practice* 41, no. 4 (2002), 215.

5. Bloom, *Taxonomy of Educational Objectives, Handbook I: The Cognitive Domain* (New York: David McKay Co. Inc., 1956), 7.

6. Ibid.; and D. R. Krathwohl, B. S. Bloom, and B. B. Masia, *Taxonomy of Educational Objectives, the Classification of Educational Goals, Handbook II: Affective Domain*. (New York: David McKay, 1973).

7. Bloom, *Taxonomy*, 7–8. Presumably they overlooked sports, music, and drama programs.

8. Krathwohl, "A Revision of Bloom's Taxonomy: An Overview," *Theory into Practice* 41, no. 4 (2002), 214.

9. Ibid., 215.

10. Bodhicitta refers to the commitment to achieve enlightenment for the sake of all sentient beings.

11. In Buddhist doctrine, the Eightfold Path is the fourth of the Four Noble Truths, which are among the earliest teachings and are common to most Buddhist schools. The Eightfold Path advises practitioners to practice right view, right thought, right speech, right action, right livelihood, right effort, right mindfulness, and right concentration.

12. The first four lay precepts advise practitioners against killing or causing harm, stealing, sexual misconduct, and speaking untruths. For a detailed discussion of Buddhist precepts and ethics, see Harvey, *An Introduction to Buddhist Ethics* (Cambridge, U.K.: Cambridge University Press, 2000).

13. Walpola Rahula, *What the Buddha Taught* (New York: Grove Press, 1974).

14. Étienne Lamotte, *Histoire du Bouddhisme Indien* (Louvain: Institut Orientaliste Bibliothèque de l'Université, Place Mgr Ladeuze, 1958), 48, my translation.

15. Krathwohl, *Taxonomy of Educational Objectives, the Classification of Educational Goals, Handbook II: Affective Domain.*, cited in Teaching and Learning with Technology, "Bloom's Taxonomy," Pennsylvania State University, http://tlt.psu.edu/suggestions/research/Blooms_Taxonomy.shtml.

16. See, for example, Chris Frakes, "Do the Compassionate Flourish? Overcoming Anguish and the Impulse Towards Violence," *Journal of Buddhist Ethics* 14 (2007).

17. McLaren, *Schooling as a Ritual Performance* (London: Routledge&Kegan Paul, 1986), 6.

18. Ibid., 202. McLaren takes a negative view of the hegemony of the instructional rituals at the school he studied. He is influenced by the relative powerlessness of a particular ethnically defined group of students compared to that of the teacher. His concerns are that students internalize (perhaps unwittingly) worldviews and codes of behavior that inculcate them into a particular social class and culture.

19. Krathwohl, *Taxonomy of Educational Objectives, the Classification of Educational Goals, Handbook II: Affective Domain.*, cited in Technology, "Bloom's Taxonomy."

20. McMahan, *Making of Buddhist Modernism*, 246–248. See also Bell, "Being Creative with Tradition: Rooting Theravada Buddhism in Britain" (*Journal of Global Buddhism* 1, 2000), 1–23.

21. Technology, "Bloom's Taxonomy."

22. Anita Harrow, *A Taxonomy of Psychomotor Domain: A Guide for Developing Behaviour Objectives* (New York: David McKay, 1972).

23. Bloom and his later commentators do acknowledge that there are overlaps between the three learning domains. See especially L. W. Anderson and D. R. Krathwohl, et al., ed., *A Taxonomy for Learning, Teaching and Assessing: A Revision of Bloom's Taxonomy of Educational Objectives* (New York: Longman, 2001).

24. Schechner, "Restoration of Behavior," in *Readings in Ritual Studies*, ed. Ronald L. Grimes (Upper Saddle River, N. J.: Prentice Hall, 1996), 442.

25. Ibid., 441.

26. Schechner, "Magnitudes of Performance," in *By Means of Performance*, ed. Richard Schechner and Willa Appel (Cambridge: Cambridge University Press, 1990), 36.

27. Crossley, "Ritual, Body Technique and (Inter)Subjectivity," in *Thinking through Rituals: Philosophical Perspectives*, ed. Kevin Schilbrack (New York: Routledge, 2004), 31.

28. Schechner, "Restoration of Behavior," 457.

29. Grimes, *Beginnings in Ritual Studies* (Columbia: University of South Carolina Press, 1995), 69.

30. Ibid.

31. Jennings, "On Ritual Knowledge," in *Readings in Ritual Studies*, ed. Ronald L. Grimes (Upper Saddle River, N.J.: Prentice Hall, 1996), 326.

32. Schechner, "Restoration of Behavior," 443–445.

33. Ibid.

34. Krathwohl, *Taxonomy of Educational Objectives, the Classification of Educational Goals, Handbook Ii: Affective Domain.* cited in Technology, "Bloom's Taxonomy."

35. See, for example, Schechner's discussion of Ekman's experiment in which muscle-by-muscle construction of facial expressions resulted in subjects experiencing the associated emotions. Schechner, "Magnitudes of Performance," 30.

36. Ibid., 40.

37. In addition to the *Dīgha Nikāya*, the three wisdoms can be found in the *Vibhaṅga* of the *Abhidhamma* of the Pali Canon, in Buddhaghosa's *Visuddhimagga*, and in Sanskrit sources such as Vasubandhu's *Abidharmakośa-bhāṣyam* and in *Bhāvanākrama* I and III of *Kāmalaśila.* H-Buddhism network, email communication, Brian Nichols, January 2008.

38. "Three Wisdoms," in *Digital Dictionary of Buddhism*, ed. Charles Muller (2007).

39. *Dīgha Nikāya* 3:219.

40. Maurice Walshe, *The Long Discourses of the Buddha: A Translation of the Dīgha Nikāya* (Boston: Wisdom Publications, 1995), 486. The passage is preceded by another three wisdoms: "of the learner, the non-learner and one who is neither," which are also listed as the three kinds of persons. H-Buddhism network, email communication, Brian Nichols, January 2008.

41. H-Buddhism network, email communication, Brian Nichols, January 2008.

42. Early Buddhist doctrine, particularly the Four Noble Truths, teaches that the root of all suffering is delusion or the desires that arise from delusion. In this perspective, the ordinary mind does not realize the true nature of the world, which is that everything, including the self or ego, is impermanent and nothing has inherent existence outside of its causes and conditions.

43. Powers, *Introduction to Tibetan Buddhism*, rev.ed. (Ithaca, N.Y.: Snow Lion Publications, 2007), 75.

44. Lamotte, *Histoire du Bouddhisme Indien*, 49.

45. Powers, *Introduction to Tibetan Buddhism*, 75.

46. Lamotte, *Histoire du Bouddhisme Indien*, 49.

47. Ibid.

48. Powers, *Introduction to Tibetan Buddhism*, 75.

49. Ibid., 86.

50. The Tibetan terms for śamatha and vipaśyanā, which Powers gives as *zhignas* and *lhag-mthong* respectively, are not generally known or used by western practitioners. Ibid.

51. "Vipassanā," in *The Oxford Dictionary of World Religions*, ed. John Bowker (Oxford: Oxford University Press, 1997), 1025.

52. Powers, *Introduction to Tibetan Buddhism*, 86.

53. Geshe Kelsang Gyatso, *The New Meditation Handbook* (Ulverston, U.K.: Tharpa Publications, 2004), 8.

54. Several Friends of the Heart respondents also noted that everyday activities could be performed as though they were meditations, meaning that the concentration and mindfulness generated in meditation might be carried into other activities.

CHAPTER 5

1. I found that this was especially the case among western Zen practitioners whom I had interviewed for an earlier study. See Patricia Q. Campbell, "Transforming Ordinary Life: Turning to Zen Buddhism in Toronto," in *Wild Geese: Buddhism in Canada*, ed. Victor Sōgen Hori, John S. Harding, and Alexander Soucy (Montreal: McGill-Queens University Press, 2010), 198–199.

2. Grimes, *Beginnings in Ritual Studies* 2nd ed. (Columbia: University of South Carolina Press, 1995), 40–56.

3. Ibid., 46.

4. Ibid.

5. I find Diane's references to different means of learning intriguing, here: She said she had learned that experiential learning through prostration practice was possible, but she had learned about that possibility through a book!

6. Powers, *Introduction to Tibetan Buddhism*, rev.ed.(Ithaca, N.Y.: Snow Lion Publications, 2007), 300.

7. Ibid., 299.

8. Vietnamese monk and founder of the international Order of Interbeing, Thich Nhat Hanh, for example, teaches a special prostration practice which he calls "touching the earth," a practice intended to overcome westerners' reluctance to performing prostrations. The practice, as NhatHanh teaches it, is a means of connecting with one's family and spiritual teachers, and has no association with deities. Patricia Hunt-Perry and Lyn Fine, "All Buddhism Is Engaged: Thich Nhat Hanh and the Order of Interbeing," in *Engaged Buddhism in the West*, ed. Christopher S. Queen (Boston: Wisdom Publications, 2000), 52.

9. Guru yoga involves visualizing one's teacher as a fully enlightened being, capable of helping one achieve full buddhahood. Guru yoga visualizations like the one Marconi described involve imagining a vast tree in which sit one's teacher and all the teachers of one's lineage. The visualization is intended to bestow the practitioner with a sense of a close connection to the teacher and all of the other gurus in the lineage. For a description of guru yoga, see Powers, *Introduction to Tibetan Buddhism*, 310–311.

10. Jennings, "On Ritual Knowledge," in *Readings in Ritual Studies*, ed. Ronald L. Grimes (Upper Saddle River, N.J.: Prentice Hall, 1996), 326.

11. Grimes, concerned that ritual is too often associated with habituated behavior, argues that habituation is, in fact, the bane of ritualization. Grimes, *Beginnings in Ritual Studies*, 43.

12. Williams, *Ritual Art and Knowledge: Aesthetic Theory and Zoroastrian Ritual* (Columbia: University of South Carolina Press, 1993), 72.

13. Ibid., 78.

14. Tom F. Driver, *Liberating Rites: Understanding the Transformative Power of Ritual* (Boulder, Colo.: Westview Press, 1998), 7.

15. Ibid., 30.

16. Jennings, "On Ritual Knowledge"; Kevin Schilbrack, "Ritual Metaphysics," in *Thinking through Rituals: Philosophical Perspectives*, ed. Kevin Schilbrack (New York: Routledge, 2004). See also Crossley, "Ritual, Body Technique and (Inter)Subjectivity," ed. Kevin Schilbrack

(New York: Routledge, 2004); and McLaren, *Schooling as a Ritual Performance* (London: Routledge&Kegan Paul, 1986), 200–204.

17. Michael Raposa notes that repetition and redundancy in ritual is a means of confirming religious beliefs by embodying them in practice. Ritual is thus a means of induction or strengthening "belief-habits" or of inculcating them in practitioners who are marginal, such as newcomers or the "spiritually lukewarm." Raposa, "Ritual Inquiry: The Pragmatic Logic of Religious Practice," ed. Kevin Schilbrack (New York: Routledge, 2004), 115–116.

18. Richard Hayes, *A Buddhist's Reflections on Religious Conversion* (Montréal, Québec: Elijah School Lectures for the fourth summer program, 2000), 44–45.

19. Grimes, *Beginnings in Ritual Studies*, 66.

20. By Vajrasattva, Catherine was referring to the foundation practice of reciting the hundred-syllable mantra of the deity Vajrasattva and performing one hundred thousand prostrations. David, in fact, had confessed to being one such student.

21. Anderson, ed., *A Taxonomy for Learning, Teaching, and Assessing: A Revision of Bloom's Taxonomy of Educational Objectives* (New York: Longman, 2001), 259–286.

22. Grimes, *Beginnings in Ritual Studies*, 107–109.

23. Ibid., 108.

24. Rogers, *What Is the Difference: A New Critique of Adult Learning and Teaching* (Leicester, U.K.: NIACE, 2003), 10.

25. Jennings, "On Ritual Knowledge."

26. Ibid., 327, emphasis in original.

27. Ibid., 329.

28. Schilbrack, "Ritual Metaphysics," 137–139.

29. Ibid., 138.

30. Ibid., 139.

31. Ibid., 136.

32. Ibid., 139.

33. Raposa, "Ritual Inquiry," 115.

34. Raposa explores body habits and their influence on beliefs in some detail. Ibid., 113–116.

35. Ibid., 124.

36. Janet Gyatso, "Healing Burns with Fire: The Facilitations of Experience in Tibetan Buddhism," *Journal of the American Academy of Religion* 67, no. 1 (1999), 140.

37. Ibid., 129.

38. Schechner, "Magnitudes of Performance," in *By Means of Performance*, ed. Richard Schechner and Willa Appel (Cambridge: Cambridge University Press, 1990), 30–31.

39. Ibid., 31.

40. Rogers, *What Is the Difference*, 9.

41. McLaren, *Schooling as a Ritual Performance*, 46.

42. Crossley, "Ritual, Body Technique and (Inter)Subjectivity," 35.

43. Ibid.

44. Ibid., 36.

45. Ibid., 35.

46. Ibid., 37.

47. Gyatso, "Healing Burns with Fire," 128–129.

48. So Bourdieu describes his habitus. Cited in Morris, "Gender," 369.

49. Gyatso, "Healing Burns with Fire," 129.

50. Ibid.

51. Powers, *Introduction to Tibetan Buddhism*, 87.

52. See, for example, Robert H. Sharf, "The Zen of Japanese Nationalism," in *Curators of the Buddha: The Study of Buddhism under Colonialism*, ed. Donald S. Lopez (Chicago: University of Chicago Press, 1995).

53. Gyatso, "Healing Burns with Fire," 128–130.

54. Ibid., 129.

CHAPTER 6

1. Texts studied in the NKT Foundation Program classes are Kelsang Gyatso's commentaries on traditional Buddhist scripture. As listed on the NKT website in the order that they are studied, these texts are: *Joyful Path of Good Fortune, Universal Compassion, Eight Steps To Happiness, Heart of Wisdom, Meaningful to Behold* and *Understanding the Mind*. The New Kadampa Tradition – International Kadampa Buddhist Union, "Books on Buddhism and Meditation," http://kadampa.org/en/books/, 2010.

2. See, for example, Harvey B. Aronson, *Buddhist Practice on Western Ground: Reconciling Eastern Ideals and Western Psychology* (Boston: Shambhala, 2004); and Franz Aubrey Metcalf, "The Encounter of Buddhism and Psychology," in *Westward Dharma*, ed. Charles S. Prebish and Martin Baumann (Berkeley and Los Angeles: University of California Press, 2002). Both Aronson and Metcalf point out significant differences between Buddhist doctrine and western psychology. Aronson's approach is to suggest ways of mediating those differences.

3. Schechner describes informal training in this way, with reference to performer workshops and restoration of behavior. Schechner, *Performance Studies: An Introduction* (London: Routledge, 2002).

4. Ibid., 194.

5. Rodney Stark and Roger Finke, *Acts of Faith: Explaining the Human Side of Religion* (Berkeley and Los Angeles: University of California Press, 2000), 141–146.

6. Ibid., 143–144.

7. Ibid., 144.

CONCLUSION

1. Jennings, "On Ritual Knowledge," in *Readings in Ritual Studies*, edited by Ronald L. Grimes (Upper Saddle River, N.J.: Prentice Hall, 1996), 326.

2. Ibid., 329.

3. McLaren, *Schooling as a Ritual Performance* (London: Routledge & Kegan Paul, 1986), 202.

4. Schilbrack, "Ritual Metaphysics," in *Thinking through Rituals: Philosophical Perspectives*, edited by Kevin Schilbrack (New York: Routledge, 2004), 138.

5. It is sometimes claimed, based on seals uncovered in the Indus Valley from the Harappā civilization (c. 2,500–1,500 BCE), that this meditation posture has been used for millennia.

6. Driver, *Liberating Rites: Understanding the Transformative Power of Ritual* (Boulder, Colo.: Westview Press, 1998), 30.

APPENDIX

1. Names appearing in quotation marks are pseudonyms.

Anderson, L. W., and D. R. Krathwohl, et al., ed. *A Taxonomy for Learning, Teaching, and Assessing: A Revision of Bloom's Taxonomy of Educational Objectives*. New York: Longman, 2001.

Anonymous. "Chandrakirti Kadampa Meditation Centre Canada CKMCC." http://www.kadampa. ca/ 2011.

———. "The Dharma Protector." The New Kadampa Tradition, International KadampaBuddhist Union.http://kadampa.org/en/buddhism/the-dharma-protector/, 2010.

———. "Dorje Shugden Versus Pluralism and National Unity." In *The Worship of Shugden: Documents Related to a Tibetan Controversy*, 3–15. Dharamsala: Department of Religion and Culture, Central Tibetan Administration, 1998.

———. "Friends of the Heart Home Page." Friends of the Heart http://www.friendsoftheheart. com/, n.d.

Aronson, Harvey B. *Buddhist Practice on Western Ground: Reconciling Eastern Ideals and Western Psychology*. Boston: Shambhala, 2004.

Batchelor, Stephen. "Letting Daylight into Magic: The Life and Times of Dorje Shugden." *Tricycle Magazine* (1998), 60–66.

Bell, Catherine. *Ritual: Perspectives and Dimensions*. New York: Oxford University Press, 1997.

Bell, Sandra. "Being Creative with Tradition: Rooting Theravada Buddhism in Britain." *Journal of Global Buddhism* 1 (2000), 1–23.

Bernard, Russell. *Research Methods in Anthropology*. Walnut Creek, Calif.: Altamira Press, 2002.

Bloom, B. S. *Taxonomy of Educational Objectives, Handbook I: The Cognitive Domain*. New York: David McKay Co. Inc., 1956.

Bynum, Caroline Walker. "Women's Stories, Women's Symbols: A Critique of Victor Turner's Theory of Liminality." In *Anthropology and the Study of Religion*, edited by Robert L. Moore and Frank E. Reynolds, 105–125. Chicago: Center for the Scientific Study of Religion, 1984.

Cadge, Wendy. *Heartwood*. Chicago: University of Chicago Press, 2005.

Campbell, Colin. *The Easternization of the West*. Boulder: Paradigm Publishers, 2007.

Campbell, Patricia Q. "Transforming Ordinary Life: Turning to Zen Buddhism in Toronto." In *Wild Geese: Buddhism in Canada*, edited by Victor Sōgen Hori, John S. Harding, and Alexander Soucy, 187–209. Montreal: McGill-Queens University Press, 2010.

———. "Buddhist Values and Ordinary Life among Members of the Toronto Zen Buddhist Temple." MA Thesis, Wilfrid Laurier University, 2004.

Coleman, James William. *The New Buddhism: The Western Transformation of an Ancient Tradition*. Oxford: Oxford University Press, 2001.

Crossley, Nick. "Ritual, Body Technique and (Inter)Subjectivity." In *Thinking through Rituals: Philosophical Perspectives*, edited by Kevin Schilbrack, 31–51. New York: Routledge, 2004.

Csordas, Thomas J. "Embodiment as a Paradigm for Anthropology." *Ethos* 18, no. 1 (1990), 5–47.

Danyluk, Angie. "To Be or Not to Be: Buddhist Selves in Toronto." *Contemporary Buddhism* 4, no. 2 (2003), 128–141.

Driver, Tom F. *Liberating Rites: Understanding the Transformative Power of Ritual*Boulder, Colo.: Westview Press, 1998.

Frakes, Chris. "Do the Compassionate Flourish? Overcoming Anguish and the Impulse Towards Violence." *Journal of Buddhist Ethics* 14 (2007), 99–128.

Friends of the Heart Student Handbook. Toronto, Ont.: Friends of the Heart, 2005.

Grimes, Ronald L. *Rite out of Place: Ritual, Media and the Arts*. Oxford: Oxford University Press, 2006.

———. "Performance." In *Theorizing Rituals: Classical Topics, Theoretical Approaches, Analytical Concepts, Annotated Bibliography*,edited by Jan Snoek, Jens Kreinath, and Michael Strausberg, 379–394. Leiden: Brill, 2004.

———. "Performance Theory and the Study of Ritual." *New Approaches to the Study of Religion* 2 (2004), 109–138.

———. *Deeply into the Bone: Re-Inventing Rites of Passage*. Berkeley and Los Angeles: University of California Press, 2000.

———. "Forum: American Spirituality." *Religion and American Culture* 9, no. 2 (1999), 131–157.

———. *Beginnings in Ritual Studies*, 2nd ed. Columbia: University of South Carolina Press, 1995.

———. *Ritual Criticism: Case Studies in Its Practice, Essays on Its Theory*. Columbia: University of South Carolina Press, 1990.

Gyatso, Geshe Kelsang. *The New Meditation Handbook*. Ulverston, U.K.: Tharpa Publications, 2004.

Gyatso, Janet. "Healing Burns with Fire: The Facilitations of Experience in Tibetan Buddhism." *Journal of the American Academy of Religion* 67, no. 1 (1999), 113–147.

Handelman, Don. "Conceptual Alternatives to Ritual." In *Theorizing Rituals: Issues, Topics, Approaches, Concepts*, edited by Jan Snoek, Jens Kreinath, and Michael Strausberg, 37–49. Leiden: Brill, 2008.

Harrow, Anita. *A Taxonomy of Psychomotor Domain: A Guide for Developing Behaviour Objectives*. New York: David McKay, 1972.

Harth, Dietrich. "Ritual and Other Forms of Social Action." In *Theorizing Rituals: Issues, Topics, Approaches, Concepts*, edited by Jan Snoek, Jens Kreinath, and Michael Strausberg, 15–36. Leiden: Brill, 2008.

Harvey, Peter. *An Introduction to Buddhist Ethics*. Cambridge, U.K.: Cambridge University Press, 2000.

Hayes, Richard. *A Buddhist's Reflections on Religious Conversion*. Montréal, Québec: Elijah School Lectures for the fourth summer program, 2000.

Hickey, Wakoh Shannon. "Two Buddhisms, Three Buddhisms, and Racism." *Journal of Global Buddhism* 11 (2010, forthcoming).

"History Friends of the Heart." (2007) http://www.friendsoftheheart.com/Toronto_meditation_centre/history.php.

Hori, Victor Sōgen. "Buddhism: The Religion of Dispersion." Paper presented at the Buddhism and Diaspora Conference, University of Toronto–Scarborough, 2010.

———. "How Do We Study Buddhism in Canada?" In *Wild Geese: Buddhism in Canada*, edited by Victor Sōgen Hori, John S. Harding, and Alexander Soucy, 14–38. Montreal: McGill-Queens University Press, 2010.

———, and Janet McLellan. "Suwanda H.J. Sugunasiri: Buddhist." In *Wild Geese: Buddhism in Canada*, edited by Victor Sōgen Hori, John S. Harding, and Alexander Soucy, 377–399. Montreal: McGill-Queen's University Press, 2010.

———, John S. Harding, and Alexander Soucy, eds. *Wild Geese: Buddhism in Canada*. Montreal: McGill-Queen's University Press, 2010.

Humphrey, Caroline, and James Laid law. *The Archetypal Actions of Ritual*. Oxford: Clarendon Press, 1994.

Hunt-Perry, Patricia, and Lyn Fine. "All Buddhism Is Engaged: Thich Nhat Hanh and the Order of Interbeing." In *Engaged Buddhism in the West*, edited by Christopher S. Queen. Boston: Wisdom Publications, 2000.

Jennings, Theodore W. "On Ritual Knowledge." In *Readings in Ritual Studies*, edited by Ronald L. Grimes, 324–334. Upper Saddle River, N.J.: Prentice Hall, 1996.

Kay, David. "The New Kadampa Tradition and the Continuity of Tibetan Buddhism in Transition." *Journal of Contemporary Religion* 12, no. 3 (1997), 277–293.

Koller, John M. "Human Embodiment: Indian Perspectives." In *Self as Body in Asian Theory and Practice*, edited by Roger T. Ames, Thomas P. Kasulis, and Wimal Dissanayake, 45–58. Albany: State University of New York Press, 1993.

Krathwohl, David R. "A Revision of Bloom's Taxonomy: An Overview." *Theory into Practice* 41, no. 4 (2002), 212–218.

———, B. S. Bloom, and B. B. Masia. *Taxonomy of Educational Objectives, the Classification of Educational Goals, Handbook II: Affective Domain*. New York: David McKay, 1973.

Lamotte, Étienne. *Histoire du Bouddhisme Indien*. Louvain: Institut Orientaliste Bibliothèque de l'Université, Place MgrLadeuze, 1958.

Lopez, Donald S. "Two Sides of the Same God." *Tricycle Magazine* (1998), 67–82.

"Mahāmudrā." In *The Oxford Dictionary of World Religions*, edited by John Bowker. Oxford: Oxford University Press, 1997.

McLaren, Peter. *Schooling as a Ritual Performance*. London: Routledge&Kegan Paul, 1986.

McLellan, Janet. "Buddhism in the Greater Toronto Area: The Politics of Recognition." In *Buddhism in Canada*, edited by Bruce Matthews, 85–104. Routledge Critical Studies in Buddhism, Charles S. Prebish and Damien Keown, general editors. London: Routledge, 2006.

———. *Many Petals of the Lotus*. Toronto: University of Toronto Press, 1999.

McMahan, David L. *The Making of Buddhist Modernism*. Oxford: Oxford University Press, 2008.

Metcalf, Franz Aubrey. "The Encounter of Buddhism and Psychology." In *Westward Dharma*, edited by Charles S. Prebish and Martin Baumann, 348–364. Berkeley and Los Angeles: University of California Press, 2002.

Morris, Rosalind C. "Gender." In *Theorizing Rituals: Issues, Topics, Approaches, Concepts*, edited by Jan Snoek, Jens Kreinath, and Michael Strausberg, 361–378. Leiden: Brill, 2008.

Numrich, Paul David. *Old Wisdom in the New World*. Knoxville: University of Tennessee Press, 1996.

Powers, John. *Introduction to Tibetan Buddhism*. Rev.ed. Ithaca, N.Y.: Snow Lion Publications, 2007.

Prebish, Charles S. *American Buddhism*. North Scituate, Mass.: Duxbury Press, 1979.

Quili, Natalie E. "Western Self, Asian Other: Modernity, Authenticity, and Nostalgia for 'Tradition' in Buddhist Studies." *Journal of Buddhist Ethics* 16 (2009), 1–38.

Rahula, Walpola. *What the Buddha Taught*. New York: Grove Press, 1974.

Raposa, Michael L. "Ritual Inquiry: The Pragmatic Logic of Religious Practice." In *Thinking through Rituals: Philosophical Perspectives*, edited by Kevin Schilbrack, 113–127. New York: Routledge, 2004.

Rappaport, Roy A. *Ritual and Religion in the Making of Humanity*. Cambridge, U.K.: Cambridge University Press, 2005.

Rogers, Alan. *What Is the Difference: A New Critique of Adult Learning and Teaching*. Leicester, U.K.: NIACE, 2003.

Schechner, Richard. *Performance Studies: An Introduction*. London: Routledge, 2002.

———. "Magnitudes of Performance." In *By Means of Performance*, edited by Richard Schechner and Willa Appel, 19–49. Cambridge: Cambridge University Press, 1990.

———. "Restoration of Behavior." In *Readings in Ritual Studies*, edited by Ronald L. Grimes, 441–458. Upper Saddle River, N. J.: Prentice Hall, 1996.

———. *Performance Theory*. London: Routledge, 1988.

Schilbrack, Kevin. "Introduction: On the Use of Philosophy in the Study of Rituals." In *Thinking through Rituals: Philosophical Perspectives*, edited by Kevin Schilbrack, 1–30. New York: Routledge, 2004.

———. "Ritual Metaphysics." In *Thinking through Rituals: Philosophical Perspectives*, edited by Kevin Schilbrack, 128–147. New York: Routledge, 2004.

———, ed. *Thinking through Rituals: Philosophical Perspectives*. New York: Routledge, 2004.

Sharf, Robert H. "The Zen of Japanese Nationalism." In *Curators of the Buddha: The Study of Buddhism under Colonialism*, edited by Donald S. Lopez, 107–160. Chicago: University of Chicago Press, 1995.

Snoek, Jan A.M. "Defining 'Rituals'." In *Theorizing Rituals: Issues, Topics, Approaches, Concepts*, edited by Jan Snoek, Jens Kreinath, and Michael Strausberg, 3–14. Leiden: Brill, 2008.

Soucy, Alexander. "Asian Reformers, Global Organizations: An Exploration of the Possibility of a 'Canadian Buddhism.'" In *Wild Geese: Buddhism in Canada*, edited by Victor Sōgen Hori, John S. Harding, and Alexander Soucy, 39–60. Montreal: McGill-Queen's University Press, 2010.

Stark, Rodney, and Roger Finke. *Acts of Faith: Explaining the Human Side of Religion*. Berkeley and Los Angeles: University of California Press, 2000.

Technology, Teaching and Learning with. "Bloom's Taxonomy." Pennsylvania State University, http://tlt.psu.edu/suggestions/research/Blooms_Taxonomy.shtml.

"Three Wisdoms." In *Digital Dictionary of Buddhism*, edited by Charles Muller, 2007.

Tillich, Paul, ed. *Theology of Culture*. Edited by Robert C. Kimball. New York: Oxford University Press, 1964.

Turner, Victor W. "Liminality and Communitas." In *Readings in Ritual Studies*, edited by Ronald L. Grimes, 511–519. Upper Saddle River, N.J.: Prentice Hall, 1996.

Tweed, Thomas A. "Who Is a Buddhist? Night Stand Buddhists and Other Creatures." In *Westward Dharma: Buddhism beyond Asia*, edited by Charles S. Prebish and Martin Baumann, 17–33. Berkeley and Los Angeles: University of California Press, 2002.

Union, International Kadampa Buddhist. "Chandrakirti Kadampa Meditation Centre Canada." International Kadampa Buddhist Union, http://nkt-kmc-canada.org/, 2011.

———. New Kadampa Tradition. "Books on Buddhism and Meditation." http://kadampa.org/en/books/, 2010.

Van Gennep, Arnold. *The Rites of Passage*. Edited by Monika B. Vezedom and Gabrielle Caffee. Chicago: University of Chicago Press, 1960.

Van Wolputte, Steven. "Hang on to Your Self: Of Bodies, Embodiment, and Selves." *Annual Review of Anthropology* 33 (2004), 251–269.

"Vipassanā." In *The Oxford Dictionary of World Religions*, edited by John Bowker. Oxford: Oxford University Press, 1997.

Walshe, Maurice, trans. *The Long Discourses of the Buddha: A Translation of the Dīgha Nikāya*. Boston: Wisdom Publications, 1995.

Walter, Gordon A., and Stephen E. Marks. *Experiential Learning and Change*. New York: John Wiley & Sons, 1981.

Williams, Ron G., and James W. Boyd. *Ritual Art and Knowledge: Aesthetic Theory and Zoroastrian Ritual*. Columbia: University of South Carolina Press, 1993.

Page numbers in italics refer to tables and illustrations. Page numbers in bold indicate major treatment of a particular subject. The abbreviation 'n' refers to footnotes.